Applied Theatre: Facilitation

The **Applied Theatre** series is a major innovation in applied theatre scholarship, bringing together leading international scholars that engage with and advance the field of applied theatre. Each book presents new ways of seeing and critically reflecting on this dynamic and vibrant field. Volumes offer a theoretical framework and introductory survey of the field addressed, combined with a range of case studies illustrating and critically engaging with practice.

Series Editors

Michael Balfour (Griffith University, Australia)
Sheila Preston (University of East London, UK)

Applied Theatre: Development
Tim Prentki
ISBN 978-1-4725-0986-4

Applied Theatre: Resettlement
Drama, Refugees and Resilience
Michael Balfour, Bruce Burton, Penny Bundy,
Julie Dunn and Nina Woodrow
ISBN 978-1-4725-3379-1

Applied Theatre: Research
Radical Departures
Peter O'Connor and Michael Anderson
ISBN 978-1-4725-0961-1

Applied Theatre: Aesthetics
Gareth White
ISBN 978-1-4725-1355-7

Applied Theatre: Performing Health and Wellbeing
Veronica Baxter and Katharine E. Low
ISBN 978-1-4725-8457-1

Related titles from Bloomsbury Methuen Drama

Performance and Community: Commentary and Case Studies
Edited by Caoimhe McAvinchey
ISBN 978-1-4081-4642-2

Affective Performance and Cognitive Science: Body, Brain and Being
Edited by Nicola Shaughnessy
ISBN 978-1-4081-8577-3

Applied Theatre: Facilitation

Pedagogies, Practices, Resilience

Sheila Preston

Series Editors
Michael Balfour and Sheila Preston

Bloomsbury Methuen Drama
An imprint of Bloomsbury Publishing Plc
B L O O M S B U R Y
LONDON · OXFORD · NEW YORK · NEW DELHI · SYDNEY

Bloomsbury Methuen Drama

An imprint of Bloomsbury Publishing Plc

Imprint previously known as Methuen Drama

50 Bedford Square	1385 Broadway
London	New York
WC1B 3DP	NY 10018
UK	USA

www.bloomsbury.com

BLOOMSBURY, METHUEN DRAMA and the Diana logo are trademarks of Bloomsbury Publishing Plc

First published 2016

British Library Cataloguing-in-Publication Data
A catalogue record for this book is available from the British Library.

ISBN:	HB:	978-1-4725-7692-7
	PB:	978-1-4725-7693-4
	ePDF:	978-1-4725-7695-8
	ePub:	978-1-4725-7694-1

Series: Applied Theatre

Cover design: Louise Dugdale
Cover image © Shutterstock.

Library of Congress Cataloging-in-Publication Data
A catalog record for this book is available from the Library of Congress.

Typeset by Fakenham Prepress Solutions, Fakenham, Norfolk NR21 8NN

Contents

Contents

Acknowledgements

With much thanks and appreciation to Michael Balfour, Lynette Goddard, John Graves, Nick Moseley, Charlotte Preston and Oliver Preston. Thank you to those community members, students and artists who have contributed tremendously to furthering learning and understanding of the work that we do, and of ourselves.

Notes on Contributors

Michael Balfour is Chair and Professor of Applied Theatre at Griffith University, Brisbane, Australia. Michael's research explores theatre and multi-arts approaches in a range of community contexts. He has a particular interest in how theatre responds to war and conflict, including work with newly arrived refugees, and with returning veterans and their families. Recent publications include *Applied Theatre, Resettlement: Drama, Refugees and Resilience* (Bloomsbury Methuen Drama, 2015), co-written with Penny Bundy, Bruce Burton, Julie Dunn and Nina Woodrow.

Ananda Breed is Reader in Performing Arts and Co-director of the Centre for Performing Arts Development (CPAD) at the University of East London and former research fellow at the International Research Centre Interweaving Performance Cultures at Freie Universität (2013–14). Ananda is the author of *Performing the Nation: Genocide, Justice, Reconciliation* (Seagull Books, 2014) in addition to several publications that address transitional systems of governance and the arts. She has worked as a consultant for IREX and UNICEF in Kyrgyzstan on issues concerning conflict prevention and conducted applied arts workshops in the Democratic Republic of Congo (DRC), Indonesia, Japan, Kyrgyzstan, Nepal, Palestine, Rwanda and Turkey.

Cynthia Cohen is Director of the programme in Peacebuilding and the Arts at Brandeis University, where she leads action/reflection research projects, writes and teaches about work at the nexus of the arts, culture, justice and peace. She heads the Brandeis undergraduate minor in Creativity, the Arts, and Social Transformation (CAST). She directed the Brandeis/Theatre Without Borders collaboration Acting Together on the World Stage, co-edited the Acting Together anthologies and co-created the documentary and toolkit (www.actingtogether.org).

Dr Cohen has written extensively on the aesthetic and ethical dimensions of peacebuilding, including the chapters 'Creative Approaches to Reconciliation' and 'Engaging with the Arts to Promote Coexistence', and an online book, *Working With Integrity: A Guidebook for Peacebuilders Asking Ethical Questions*. Prior to her tenure at Brandeis, she founded and directed the Oral History Center, a community-based anti-racist organization based in the Boston area. In addition, Dr Cohen has worked as a dialogue facilitator with communities in the Middle East, Sri Lanka, Central America and the United States.

Kay Hepplewhite is a senior lecturer at Northumbria University, UK. Her teaching and research focuses on applied theatre and community collaborations with artists, in particular work with women and young people. Prior to lecturing, she was a performer, facilitator and theatre maker in Theatre in Education and community theatre. She is undertaking a PhD at the University of Manchester, UK, researching applied theatre practitioners. Kay has published in *Research in Drama Education: Journal of Applied Performance* and the *Theatre, Dance and Performance Training Journal*.

Paul Murray is director of Belgrade English Language Youth Theatre in Serbia, and guest professor at the University of Arts, Belgrade. A graduate of Bretton Hall College, Yorkshire, with an MA from Warwick University and a PhD from the University of Winchester, his academic interests include clowning, the figure of the fool and participatory theatre, particularly in the field of mental health. As a pedagogue, actor and director, Paul has been facilitating community-based theatre projects for over twenty-five years and has published numerous articles and book chapters.

Sheila Preston is Head of Performing Arts at the University of East London. She presently co-edits, with Michael Balfour, the book series *Applied Theatre*, published by Bloomsbury Methuen Drama, and is also currently directing Newham Speech Bubbles in association with

London Bubble Theatre Company. Sheila is a mediator and facilitator and her practice-based work previously involved work with Oval House Theatre Company and work with young people in Southwark and Lambeth. She has published in *Research and Drama Education*, including 'Back on whose track? Reframing ideologies of inclusion and misrecognition in a participatory theatre project with young people in London' (2011) and "Managed Hearts": Emotional Labour and the Applied Theatre Facilitator' (2013). Sheila has delivered key notes at Oxford University for the National Association of Teaching Drama conference and at Cambridge University entitled 'Applied Theatre Practices: Choosing the Centre or Margin?' Between 2008 and 2012 she was primary supervisor of an Arts and Humanities Research Council funded Collaborative Doctoral Award with Kids Company in London. She also co-edited with Tim Prentki *The Applied Theatre Reader* (Routledge, 2009).

Liselle Terret is a Senior Lecturer in Performing Arts at the University of East London and has twenty years experience of teaching, facilitating and managing applied theatre projects within and outside the UK. Liselle also makes and performs queer feminist 'low' performance art as Doris La Trine, and articulates practice within academic contexts. In 2014 she published a curatorial practice website that archives and articulates a series of 'low art' symposiums for the Royal Central School of Speech and Drama. Liselle co-founded the Diploma in Performance Making for adults with (perceived) learning disabilities as a partnership between Central and Access All Areas, and in 2015 the course won the Guardian University Award for Student Diversity and Widening Participation. She has recently co-published, with Sally Mackey, a conversation about the course in *Research in Drama Education*.

Sarah Woodland is a practitioner, educator and researcher in applied theatre, with a particular interest in prison theatre. Sarah spent four years from 2001 as a core ensemble member of the Geese Theatre

Company UK, and has since facilitated her own programmes in Brisbane Youth Detention Centre, Brisbane Women's Correctional Centre and Balund – a Residential Diversionary Program. Sarah has an interest in forms that draw on personal narrative, such as reminiscence, testimonial and verbatim theatre, and has drawn on these approaches in a range of community and correctional contexts. In 2008–9, she directed *Memoirs of the Forgotten Ones*, a testimonial performance by adult survivors of institutional childhood abuse and neglect, and in 2015, co-directed *Home Front*, based on the reminiscences of eight women who were children during World War II. In her latest project, *Daughters of the Floating Brothel*, Sarah is working with women prisoners to produce a contemporary radio drama that explores the history of institutional confinement for women in Australia. She completed a PhD in prison theatre at Griffith University in 2015, teaches undergraduate courses in applied theatre, Australian theatre and industry studies, and is the Director of Theatre Scope, Griffith's applied theatre outreach programme.

Introduction to Facilitation

From the Latin word *facilis* meaning 'easy' or 'easy to do' the English noun 'facilitation' meaning 'to make easy' has its origins in the late fifteenth century. For academics there is a tendency to look down on the idea of making something easy in case it might be seen as simplistic; the uncomplimentary English word 'facile', translated from the more positive French *facile* (meaning 'easy') presumes a potential superficiality about the term. Tim Prentki is cautious about the use of the term facilitation because of these etymological origins, which might imply a naïve approach to the complex process of theatre for change, and therefore be ideologically inconsistent (see Prentki, 2015). As indicated in this volume by many of the contributors, the activity of facilitation is, in reality, far from easy in practice or intent: it is rather difficult, messy and full of contradictions and, sometimes, uneasy compromises. Facilitation, like any other cultural practice such as schooling, can be seen as a site of both domination and liberation; it can function to empower as well as validate and sustain dominant class interests (McLaren, 2008).

When we look at the ideals of facilitation practice emerging out of participatory and community development, it is apparent that facilitation has become understood by those who work in these fields as a signifier for a particular *quality* of participatory working practices with people and groups. In this vein, facilitation is used to connote commitment to certain principles – of *enablement* and participant-centredness – and *processes* that involve equitable *negotiation* between those involved. These ideals of facilitation may aim to make easi*er* what is being experienced as *difficult*, whether this is helping a group dynamic, the move into drama, the exploration of an issue/topic, the articulation or the expression of an idea, self-advocacy, and so on; but the objective of making things easier sits in the context of a wider commitment to social justice and genuine co-intentionality across the board.

Neutrality

On the face of it, facilitation, *per se*, carries with it assumptions of neutrality, a practice free from agendas and not necessarily purporting any particular ideology or principles. However, we need to be cautious of such associations. Facilitation can be employed in various ways by literally anybody in any line of work, whatever one's political persuasions or intentions, and therefore we should not assume that any agenda is actually 'neutral'.

Within its broad continuum, facilitation as a technique or an approach might be consciously employed for diverse purposes: to create productive and creative interpersonal and social relationships in a social context; to help groups to have a difficult conversation or to enable a group discussion; to orchestrate the smooth running of a particular workshop, a consultation or sharing of ideas; to improve productivity in a business; or as an efficient method for conducting qualitative research such as market research for commercial purposes. In each of these contexts it might be appropriate and necessary for the facilitator to try to take on a neutral stance, but it needs to be acknowledged that such a decision represents a choice made by the facilitator taken in a particular moment or for a particular reason or purpose. Recognition that neutrality is a role that can be played provides us with a range of flexibilities to see its potential uses (and misuses) along with its potential fallibility in its attempt at such.

Instrumentalism

Facilitation is widely accepted as an effective and productive practice, utilized in various scenarios by organizations, for enabling groups' insight and awareness and helping through any change or growth process. For this reason, external facilitators are commonly brought in to service a range of industry, business or community settings to work with employees, communities and groups. It is broadly understood that skilful facilitation can be utilized as a technique to enable the right amount of participation and ownership to be felt by stakeholders and that this effectively eases processes of change. Consequently, there is an overwhelming array of books and manuals, often serving the area of working in organizations, business and community, offering tools, tips and techniques for the facilitator.

Facilitation is often assumed in instrumental terms to be a toolbox of techniques and 'good' delivery judgements, about whether things 'worked' or not. The action of the facilitator, or rather, what they 'do', is often reduced to or conflated with evaluations of technical capability, of effective 'delivery'; in reality the way of 'being' for the facilitator may be more multifaceted and harder to describe than this. Skill and application of practical techniques are certainly involved in facilitating; however, it is necessary to extend our understanding of this complex process beyond an individualized, instrumentalized notion of competency.

To develop a deeper notion of skilled facilitation we need to consider the values and intentions influencing practitioners who take on this role. We need to acknowledge the facilitator's persona that evolves in that moment, how they perform and how they negotiate their relationships with participants. We also need to consider the real constraints that are often involved in the moment of facilitating, not only with participants but by all parties concerned, including the facilitator.

Critical facilitation

What may often be unacknowledged behind a pretext of neutrality is the range of competing agendas, complex power relations and interests that are being served as a result of the work, which may or may not be present in the mind of facilitators as they practise. Although there may be a popular agreement of what might be broadly meant by facilitation, what we actually *do* when we facilitate and how we respond when working with diverse groups of people, within different contexts and with different objectives, will inevitably be performative, and pedagogically and politically diverse.

A *critical* facilitation practice will inevitably engage with this challenge by problem-posing its own practice, uncovering the complexity of the dynamics of facilitation and seeking to understand the power relations that exist within and beyond a workshop. Crucially, such a practice will engage in trying to understand what lies beyond people's responses in a moment (including those of the facilitator), considering at all times whose interests are being served by this intervention. The facilitator may not ever 'know' or be able to resolve all the contradictions that emerge in the process, but the process of being critically aware is key, as is the journey to understand what is happening in all of its contradictions.

Facilitator roles, constituencies, contexts

Those who seek to engage communities using the arts may refer to themselves as facilitators or find that other terms, such as artist, director, animateur, catalyst, joker, clown, actor-teacher, community worker, practitioner, more aptly describe their role, function and practice with participants. Some such practitioners may consider the term 'facilitator' too bland or 'neutral' to express their practice. These alternative 'character' descriptions also signify the nuances of the role being played in different contexts along with the kind of engagement that will be attempted, an indication of the emphasis of their interventionist 'style' or intent.

Those being facilitated may be members of diverse constituencies – children, adult learners, employees, community groups (of many kinds: inmates, young people, elders, etc.) – in formal or informal settings and attending voluntarily or compulsorily. The latter point is significant and will undoubtedly affect the 'agreement' to work (or play) negotiated with participants along with the subsequent role adopted by the facilitator. The different terms of reference used to describe the action or intentions of those who engage with participants in a range of creative processes will be explored in more depth as they relate to the context and the constituencies within which they operate.

Applied Theatre practices

Applied Theatre came to prominence in the 1990s amidst a changing social and economic climate. It describes an evolved set of drama/arts/theatre practices that had themselves emerged out of counter-cultural alternative theatre movements such as the British Workers Theatre movements of the 1920s and 1930s and community-based arts and educational theatre movements spanning the 1950s to the 1990s. Like its forerunners, Applied Theatre represented a broad diversity of community-based and socially engaged theatre and performance practices that often happened beyond the conventional boundaries of traditional theatre spaces.

Contemporary Applied Theatre projects, shaped often by a range of social and public agendas such as civic renewal, social justice, health promotion, welfare and social inclusion, are commonly targeted in communities in deprived areas or with participants who are marginalized socially, culturally and/or economically. The *raison d'être* of much of the work happening in applied and socially engaged theatre centres on the use of the arts in fostering a range of development outcomes such as community building, health promotion, self-reliance and well-being.

The pendulum swing from the more overtly politically motivated practices of the 1970s and 1980s to a less obviously activist agenda has reflected a political turn and cultural need which, in part, has been about legitimizing the growing proficiency and professionalization of arts provision in community settings, and importantly, accessing new funding streams and being seen as acceptable by *all* political persuasions. Significantly the increased use of the term 'facilitation' to describe the *doing* of practice, and the subsequent focus on Applied

Theatre's pro-social 'effects' as they impact on health and well-being, is also reflective of this historical and social shift. Likewise, in responding to changing priorities and agendas, the arts have moved away from cultural intervention towards a more instrumental intervention.

As a result of its diverse roots and the contemporary practice that has emerged in a range of contexts over the past forty years, an eclectic and specialized range of arts practices has sprung up, along with some aesthetic forms that have evolved almost into canonic structures for theatre facilitation. The roles played by practitioners facilitating these practices (animateur, artist, teacher-artist, practitioner and joker) grew out of the aesthetic practices that evolved from them, including Forum Theatre, Mantle of the Expert, process drama, forms of participatory, improvisatory/play-based theatre, games and role play, and can be traced back to the different contexts where they originated: schools, development work, prison and therapeutic group work. Arts-based and inquiry-led drama, in the form of practical games, exercises and creative processes, have in turn infiltrated into mainstream facilitation and group practices in organizations and business. Often unacknowledged as such, many of the practical and creative tasks that are employed in organizations, business, group work and development settings actually originated from Applied Theatre's origins in educational theatre, drama therapy, theatre for development and community theatre.

Perhaps unsurprisingly, given its uses, and despite the plethora of books and manuals on 'how' or 'what' to 'do' during facilitation along with a focus on theatrical technique, a critical perspective on the actual practice of facilitation itself has been underdocumented in the Applied Theatre field. By engaging with the politics of facilitation we can discover that it is not a neutral phenomenon but one practised against the backdrop of competing social and historical conditions, priorities, agendas and power relations. In addition, what a facilitator actually *does* emerges out of the complex relationships that are forged during that process. For any facilitator, wherever one is working and however one works, it is important to understand the politics of the work in its cultural context and to engage with the competing, perhaps contradictory, forces operating, while being constantly aware of how the pedagogical decisions made may renegotiate these realities. This is necessary even if one's practice as a facilitator means that one deliberately chooses *not* to engage directly or explicitly with the social and/or political context or world of the participants.

Facilitator perspectives

This book on facilitation offers an insight into the complexities of theatre facilitation in different social contexts, with a critical engagement with the politics and pedagogies of the facilitator's practice from the perspectives of practitioners. Part 1, made up of three chapters, is positioned from the perspective of the editor and acts as a theoretical framing of key issues indicated by the subtitle of the book – 'pedagogies, practices, resilience' – via the proposition of the notion of critical facilitation. Part 2 opens up the discussion on facilitation to encompass a range of perspectives and voices from academics/practitioners established in the field who offer case studies and postcards of practices. Some of these perspectives will enhance and perhaps mirror the issues and themes raised in Part 1; others may offer different viewpoints. Offering a plethora of voices via diverse contexts and analysis by established practitioners and academics is a crucial strategy for the *Applied Theatre* series generally (of which this book is a part), but is of particular importance in this volume with its task of furthering understanding of facilitation practice. A recognition of the plurality of approaches developed by facilitators as they respond with different intentions and practices in diverse contexts is essential to our understanding of practice and of the field of Applied Theatre in general.

Part 1 overview

Part 1 addresses the three sub-themes of the volume – pedagogies, practices and resilience – and offers a conceptual framework through which to understand the idea of critical facilitation. Critical facilitation sets out a proposition for a political practice that involves a critical (and self-critical) approach to pedagogies, practices and resilience.

Chapter 1, 'Pedagogies: Critical Facilitation', opens the discussion via introducing critical pedagogy as a key underpinning. In alignment with critical pedagogy, critical facilitation acknowledges that we are bound up in a complex relationship of pedagogy, politics and practices in which the facilitator's identity and even their feelings need to be acknowledged as part of this socially constructed dynamic.

Chapter 2, entitled 'Practices: Doing and Performing', moves to conceptualize a broader notion of what counts as facilitation beyond technique, to consider 'doing' and 'performing'. The discussion considers associated practices that seek, at their core, to enable participatory engagement either as 'end' or 'means' to an end (whether art/theatre related or not). The particular kinds of practices that have emerged from (applied) theatre practices, and the contexts where they happen, potentially extend understanding of the possibilities of facilitation practice in general.

Chapter 3, 'Resilience in Dilemmatic Spaces', explores conceptually the difficulty of facilitating in dilemmatic spaces and the need for the facilitator to embody a resilient practice. This discussion is framed against the material reality of neoliberal, dilemmatic spaces that are fraught with upheavals and conflict for which there are no easy answers. Building strategies of resilience is key to the facilitator's survival and efficacy in difficult times. So where facilitation has been explored in relation to the extent to which it can be framed *as* performance, this discussion also considers where *being* might become the optimum, facilitative stance to enable a critical facilitation practice.

A personal reflection

My intention in this longer first section has been to offer a critically informed, practice-based and honest insight into practice (drawn from my own experience and inspirations from the work of others) that will resonate, in part, with the reader.

Dorothy Heathcote stated of her practice (which altered significantly over many years working with children) that she was 'only ever in the same room'. This statement sums up the way I feel about my own practice. Although my practice has shifted significantly over twenty or so years as I have gathered more experiences and read more widely, there are some aspects that remain constant for me. I still feel that *I am* also 'in the same room' – politically, ethically and pedagogically – in terms of what I believe about the possibilities of pedagogy and practice. I like to think that the *means* of achieving this remain fluid and keep shifting as I encounter situations, experiences and people, and as I think about these moments I am sometimes jolted to reflect. The ability to be adaptable and responsive to the changing world (or at least be aware of this need) is key for the cultural worker/practitioner/facilitator/teacher and chimes resonantly with Brecht when he says 'Methods wear out, stimuli fail. New problems loom up and demand new techniques. Reality alters; to represent it the means of representation must alter too' (Willett, 1964: 110). I feel that now, more than ever, there is a need for the facilitator, committed to social justice, to be adept and resilient in negotiating the ever-shifting terrain of dilemmatic spaces.

As the writer of Part 1, I have attempted to bring myself into the discussion. Where appropriate, I have offered small examples of experiences and observations from my own practice. I hope that this will be useful for the reader and offer a contextual insight to where my influences have arisen, such as practice with Applied Theatre undergraduate and postgraduate students, with participants in mental health settings, with young people in a range of informal and formal educational settings, and in learning disability contexts.

My approach, which has always been multidisciplinary, has also been influenced by scholarly engagement with a wide range of sources: development studies, educational philosophy, disability theory, political theory, feminist theory, cultural studies, social psychology, critical race theory, mediation/counselling theory and, of course, approaches to facilitation and group work. My approach to the use of theory has been wide ranging and responsive to my dual needs as academic and practitioner – utilitarian at some points and conceptual at others, each responding to the issues that are thrown up from contexts that I have found to be involved, helping me to draw on new inspiration that I can bring back into my work.

There are dangers that, in the crossing of epistemological, cultural and disciplinary borders, my own (and others') anxieties are sharpened; we can never be 'expert' in all the fields we encounter. This is the occupational hazard of the Applied Theatre practitioner, who will find themselves in many different contexts, in challenging settings, both in the field and also in academia. Being in the place of 'not knowing', even 'feeling at a loss', the struggle in finding a 'home' with those like-minded, is indicative of the reality of working within 'dilemmatic' contexts and across disciplinary borders.

Laying one's practice on the line feels vulnerable and risky, but this in itself demonstrates a key proposition of the framework that is being conceptually offered: that, in the context of working in the uncertainty of dilemmatic spaces, the facilitator undoubtedly will be faced with working outside of their comfort zone of existing experience, practice and knowledge. No matter how well 'armed' with techniques, training and experience, there will be moments (often when one expects it least) that are confounding or bewildering (as James Thompson aptly puts it) or disturbing, even upsetting. No matter how one might try to control what happens, one cannot always presuppose, pre-empt, or pre-plan what will actually occur. We can of course prepare as fully as we can, but we cannot always 'know' what will happen next in the moment of working with real people in real contexts. The education of facilitators might therefore consider preparing for the reality of this unpredictability and uncertainty, and the resilience required as the way forward. I believe that practitioner and academic resilience depends on openness about the real difficulties of being a practitioner in the real world, no matter how 'knowledgeable' or 'experienced' we are. As a contribution to an Applied Theatre education practice, I hope the discussion will be useful for the emerging or experienced practitioner as well as for a scholar in this field.

Part 2 overview

Part 2 extends the discussion around facilitation through analysis of a range of perspectives *on,* *by* or *about* practices in various local and international contexts. Seven chapters written by practitioners and scholars present reflections on facilitation in relation to their own practices and/or the facilitation practices of others that resonate with the themes and issues of Part 1. Paul Murray conceptualizes his facilitator role as a clown. Embodying the role of clown enables and frees him from fear and performance anxiety as a facilitator and gives him the confidence to be 'in the moment'. Furthermore, Murray believes his clown role reconfigures the role relation between participants and facilitator, as he invites participants merely *to play* with him; this acts as a deliberate strategy to resist normative relations of drama facilitation built around 'lack', helping, fixing, or saving constituencies. Murray describes his highly responsive approach, in which he enters the space without a preconceived idea of what he will do; the clown persona enables him to be in the moment, to stay in a place of 'not knowing' to enable him to be fully reactive in the moment and to 'look again'. 'These clowns are not afraid to flop' Murray says, '[t]hey are the first to laugh at themselves and invite others to do so to a point where the game becomes ridiculous, more extreme as it goes around the circle. People seeking to out-flop each other. It is ridiculous, raucous, playful, new' (p. 99). In Murray's practice, politics (which I would argue are ever present) do not directly override the fundamental process of playing with his participants.

Play features in most Applied Theatre work and, as Sarah Woodland's work with participants from Balund-a also demonstrates, is key to forming groups and the motivation to work together. Woodland's chapter gives a rich insight into the highs and lows of a theatre project for facilitator and participants happening in Balund-a, a residental programme designed to divert Aboriginal people from the fact of custody. She discusses how the drama project offered an alternative, 'third space' or antithesis to the 'correctional' context of the programme. Happening in the evening, the drama project created moments for laughter, play, spontaneity; the 'buzz of drama' provided an effective release from the fraught personal and day-to-day issues that group members faced. In a changing and uncertain context, which Woodland identifies as a dilemmatic space, she captures the real struggle facing facilitators to make a performance with the members and reveals the complex negotiations that emerge: between ambitious visions (often envisioned by the facilitator, funder or other stakeholder) and what is possible, feasible and 'safe' within a space which may feel to participants as volatile and vulnerable.

Liselle Terret directly explores the political imperative of affording learning-disabled students the opportunity to engage in critical analysis of their location in culture. In this example, members of a learning-disabled community are enabled, through their participation in a performing arts training course, to occupy the space of a drama conservatoire. Terret discusses how a range of performance forms (including working in role) can become the vehicle to open up what has been previously unsaid or perhaps even unconsidered. What is apparent is the heightened awareness of the artist-facilitators who engage participants in this work and their capacity to be sensitive to the participants' sensibilities, yet their ability also to work *with* this and move them beyond the therapeutic and personalized engagement to address the politics of their disability. Furthermore, Terret explores the emancipatory potential in enabling learning-disabled participants to begin to conceptualize the facilitator and their potential role.

Michael Balfour's chapter, aptly titled after the 1930s jazz song 'T'ain't What You Do (It's The Way That You Do It)', points to the importance of the *how* in facilitator practices, which involves the synthesis of one's artistic craft, personal qualities and skills, and social attunement. He reflects openly on his own theatre facilitation experience and remarks on the challenges of training non-arts practitioners to work in theatre facilitation, especially the nurturing of an *aesthetic instinct*. The aesthetic instinct that Balfour identifies is about 'fostering the imagination of participants' (p. 153) and synthesizing such contributions into a group activity though the employment of an aesthetic form. Balfour offers an honest account of his 'failure' to engage participants in a probation centre where, on the surface, they participated but the work soon got stuck because, as a relatively young facilitator at the time, he lacked the social instinct to understand and connect with the group, who were older than him. Drawing on insights from group management and drama therapy, Balfour also talks about engaging with resistance as key to the attunement process of facilitation.

The theme of attunement resonates with Kay Hepplewhite's chapter through her research with a range of established facilitators. Through a collection of dialogues, her research reveals the role of *planning* in creating the framework to be spontaneous or 'in the moment'. She explores how practitioners understand and use planning to enact responsivity differently.

Hepplewhite develops the theme of responsivity and 'respond-ability', where the facilitator demonstrates in action the capacity to change the plan, to respond instinctively to needs and decisions in the moment. Responsivity is articulated by Hepplewhite as a skill developed by the facilitator after several years of experience.

Ananda Breed's chapter reveals the complex self-reflexive questioning that goes on in the moment of facilitation. The question 'What do I do now?' is not about exposing competency (as our judgemental sensibilities often assume), but an attempt to articulate a reflection-in-action that takes into account, in a moment, the cultural significance of the work, the myriad of choices available and previous experience, whilst constantly questioning the appropriate significance of form and practice *in that context, in that moment.* When the unexpected occurs, a further challenge emerges for the facilitator, who needs to deal with her latent critical voice asking 'Has the exercise gone wrong?' whilst needing to respond in the moment to what is happening.

Finally, Cynthia Cohen reflects on facilitator practice in the field of peace-building through a dialogue with two experienced practitioners with whom she has often co-facilitated: Farhat Agbaria, a Palestinian–Israeli coexistence facilitator; and Jane Wilburn Sapp, an African-American musician, educationalist, cultural organizer and activist. What emerges from the observations of these practitioners who have similar intentions – in terms of social justice and of the transformative possibilities of bringing different communities to work together – are differences in their practices that has a direct influence on the 'feel' of the groups. Farhat takes an active, more confrontational role in addressing power imbalances; re-presenting to participants what he notices about what they 'do' and say, including reflecting back how/what they communicate with their bodies. The intention behind this approach is to enable the individuals of a group to understand themselves better and in the context of coexistence and peace work, where different groups are brought together to understand how each of us will embody 'the dynamics of a conflict' (p. 222). By contrast, Jane Wilburn Sapp focuses on what brings communities together, building the circle, composing a song, eating together, all helping people 'to understand they are a part of something' (p. 211). Despite some differences in the feel and approach of the work, both practitioners draw on a direct approach to conflict transformation; they embody a courage to 'sit in the fire', whether this is addressing race or national conflict, and support others to also go 'towards the conflict' (p. 214) and affirm the courage that this takes.

Part One

A Conceptual Framework

Pedagogies: Critical Facilitation

The influence of critical pedagogy

At the heart of this first chapter sits an intention to offer a nuanced approach to thinking about pedagogies of facilitation by explicit framing as *critical* facilitation, thus locating it securely within the discourses of critical pedagogy. *Critical* facilitation, therefore, tends to avoid generalized judgement or isolated claims regarding what constitutes binaries around a good/bad or novice/experienced facilitator, or the 'methods' of a great/flawed practitioner, by considering what is done *relationally* – in context, between people, and against a socio-political backdrop. Critical facilitation is, in essence, *critical*, but not in an isolated or individualized way. Rather it critiques through a wider lens, interrogating the contradictions of theory, practice and human action that will ultimately emerge through the interface with the cultural context. From this perspective, facilitation and practice can never escape critical attention or avoid the problem of the paradoxes of intentions versus reality for the practitioner – whether they are emerging or established in their field and no matter how experienced or proficient they may be. A critical approach, always challenging and sometimes uncomfortable, needs to be considered in this broader context and not reduced to a single variable. A critical approach engages in a self-reflexive analysis of its own modes of reflection and critique, for example, noticing the common tendency to moralize the self and one's practice. A critical approach thus reveals its own ideological limitations in a constant struggle to transform practice.

Consideration of the reality of facilitation as a critical and pedagogical act or *intervention* means considering the dialectical relationship of practice with context in relation to our pedagogy *with* participants. For example, we need to remember that the room, classroom, corridor, library or wherever a drama workshop is happening exists as a cultural space that will carry multiple meaning(s) ever circulating and preceding any intervention happening right now. Those involved in the work, either directly present and physically participating, or behind the scenes, are also part of this context, offering different interests that manifest in the playing out of power relations either in the room or from afar. Critical pedagogy (closely aligned with the preoccupations of critical theory) offers the framework for such an analysis, as observed by Henry Giroux:

> One of its [critical theory's] central values was to penetrate the world of objective appearances to expose the underlying social relationships they often conceal. In other words, penetrating appearances meant exposing through critical analysis the social relationships that took on the status of things or objects. For instance examining things like money, consumption, distribution, and production, it becomes clear that none of these things represents an objective thing or fact, but rather all are historically contingent contexts mediated by relationships of domination and subordination. (Giroux, 2008: 27)

The historical, social, cultural and material conditions of context also feature directly and sometimes silently, acting as a direct presence or invisible force on the work created and facilitated with and by participants. While communities may well have social and interpersonal factors in common that bind them together in their various ways, it is also important to look at community not as purely homogeneous but also made up of heterogeneous individuals who are constituted as such through their differences. As key writers on community articulate, communities might be characterized through difference as much as similarity, identity and cohesiveness (Cohen, 1985; Delanty, 2009). The inclusive and exclusive nature of community is therefore also related to the politics of its construction, but also the *feeling* of commonality and difference both within and outside the community. Locating a community purely in terms of having something in common, or, in terms of lack, as Law (1997) identifies, potentially sets up a problematic deficit model. The following example, referring to a drama project developed with people with mental health referrals who attended a day centre, reveals moments where I became aware of the members' difference and resistance to the defining nature of the 'labels' that had brought them together.

Example from a mental health setting
The fact that all members at the Centre have been referred by mental health services does not necessarily mean that this is the members' only reference point. Tensions in values and outlooks on life were present between some members although not always apparent. When, after several months of working peaceably together, one man refused to sign another's petition on fox hunting, a vocalized disagreement emerged over animal rights, which created a tension within their working relationship. Because people may appear to do activities together it does not mean that they share common values, either with each other, or with the social structures within which the activities occur. This feels like an obvious point on reflection, but crucial differences can sit beneath a veneer of compliance and harmony. On one occasion a member took me aside and expressed his disquiet at the idea that other members of the group were happy to perform, in public, a play about the experience of mental illness. He felt uncomfortable with the association and that they would be representing 'him'. In these moments commonality assumed through the presence of a mental health 'condition' was resisted. Having the tag of mental health with all its stigmatizing associations meant that several of the members were very sensitive and anxious about whether other people knew about or could 'see' their 'illness'. (Preston, 2000)

Similarly, when I was working on another project involving people with learning difficulties who also were members of a self-advocacy group, the group seemed ambivalent about finding commonalities with one another, sometimes preferring to talk directly to the project workers and facilitators of the group rather than to each other. For most of the time (apart from a few exceptions) this unwillingness by the members to self-identify as a community or a group (even for the duration of a workshop) cast doubt in my mind as to whether meaningful drama activity would be possible.

Refusal to engage with the social label, and with those others who may serve as reminders of this, even just by being present in a room together, could be seen as denial and/or alternatively an act of resistance. From my observations, because of a lack of societal acceptance, participants often felt ambiguous about their membership of a community group even though they had aligned themselves with it voluntarily; the day centre seemed to represent a haven of safety even for those who were uncomfortable with the label of a mental health disability.

> Since the Centre attempts to provide a service for diverse groups of people referred with mental health problems, there will inevitably be struggles for different needs to be accommodated. Such divisions become conveyed in the drama process when, in one of the drama groups I struggle to accommodate everyone and their differences. It seems that some people welcome the opportunity to discuss issues of mental health whilst others want to avoid the subject. Of the two groups that I have been facilitating in the day centre, the different foci emerging from each group seem to represent the majority view of each group. This feels problematic as taking the course of action to go with the majority means that others may be excluded. In the first drama group (made up of mixed ages between sixteen and sixty, and gender) we devised a play (which evolved into a short film) about a story of a man with depression, with the aim of challenging [the] stigma of mental health, and with the second group (a women's group with mixed ages), we created fantasy stories with no direct connection to mental health. (Preston, 2000)[1]

As the example reveals, all participants were implicated in the cultural context of the work, either through denial, resistance or acceptance, which inevitably had a bearing on the kind of practice that could be facilitated. What becomes apparent in most workshop settings is the plurality of identifications and subject positions that can exist in a room and the difficult choices that a facilitator may need to make in moving the work forward. Whether acknowledged directly through the work, or not, the cultural context that has brought the group together becomes a challenge for the facilitator.

Critical pedagogy questions and draws attention to social constructions of knowledge and the institutions or sites that produce 'common-sense' practices or ways of thinking as part of their systemic organization (schools, mental health settings, prisons, hospitals and so on). Critical pedagogy analyses contexts in terms of the way in which they (re)produce values and systems or enact regimes of truth that benefit certain groups over others. In the example of the women's group, critical pedagogy unearths a way of understanding the politics of the context and the identities involved, rather than it necessarily becoming a major theme of the work or content itself. In contrast, the other project in the same setting evolved more politically to address the theme of mental health and societal attitudes, by deconstructing these issues with the participants, who then attempted to create an intervention through a film that they developed. These contrasting examples of practice happening in the same cultural setting but with different community members reveals the significance of process and of the particular group dynamic in shaping the intentions and direction of the work. Critical pedagogy therefore informs the scope of what might be possible politically, but also draws attention to the politics of *process*. The overtly 'radical' educator/practitioner therefore needs also to have clarity about *how* their intentions and processes will enable groups to articulate and develop a critical consciousness of their personal and social circumstances but also how they might enable and disenable. If the ultimate intention of radical education is commitment to social justice via a social intervention into systems and practices, critical pedagogy enables the theorizing of the modes of practice that intend to enable and empower those who may have been marginalized, excluded or denied a voice. Conversely, there is room for critical pedagogy to inform subtler and nuanced practice, less overtly radical in content but no less political in other ways, not least in the enabling of agency and alternative voices.

Critical pedagogy, as a philosophical and political theory, therefore, is a natural bedfellow for the Applied Theatre practitioner attempting to apply theoretical agendas of social justice and transformation into practice, but in a critical and reflexive way. The radical roots of Applied Theatre have always been grounded in the 'premise that the world needs change, can be changed, and the means of making change is human agency' (Prentki, 2015: 16). Prentki articulates a radical intent for practitioners who adopt a view, influenced by Marx, that 'change itself arises from a dialectical encounter between the understanding developed through lived experience and the capacity to construct alternatives; that inherently theatrical process of an encounter between reality and imagination' (Prentki, 2015: 16).

Practitioners committed to the more radical intentions of Applied Theatre could sit quite comfortably within the frame of a critical pedagogical analysis and practice that draws attention to the social and material contradictions of context. A key dimension of critical practice is not only to embark on a cultural analysis but also to respond critically and dialectically with this analysis in order to transform the conditions and pedagogical approaches being 'applied' in context.

Dilemmas and contradictions

A critical pedagogy perspective, therefore, while being committed to radical ideals, enables a critical analysis of the challenge of achieving such aims in the face of the social and material conditions. It also draws attention to the problems of actually achieving such aims, which have in turn compelled pedagogical practices attempting to engage with the contradictions of society. As a self-reflexive theory and practice, therefore, critical pedagogy engages with the problem of the pursuit of its own intentions. To return to the women's group in the mental health setting:

Today we spend most of the session telling stories as a group. Jun, who is Japanese, is quite anxious about this because of her English language skills and refuses to participate at first. However, she eventually becomes drawn into the storytelling. We create three stories, quite obscure and seemingly unrelated totally to the lives of the people present. There is lots of romanticizing of people meeting gorgeous Spanish lovers and living happily ever after with 'him' in a big mansion with ten children etc. It all seems good fun and we all laugh a lot at the ridiculousness of the stories. After the stories, the women talk generally about how most families don't take this structure, how in their street there isn't a father in sight, how the women just gossip about each other. There is a judgmental tone to the conversation. I want to challenge this, yet I feel cautious about upsetting the comfortable dynamic that is emerging as the women grow more confident and expressive. Amy talks about her relationship with her husband and how 'because of his illness' he gets violent. Chris enters at this point and gets into a discussion around a women's refuge she wants to set up, (Preston, 2000)

Within this group, storytelling became a popular form for the women as a space to indulge their romantic dreams. It is also notable that, although popular, the strategy of building a group story, word by word or line by line, can potentially operate to exclude people who do not feel confident with their verbal skills. In this context there were several people for whom this exercise was possibly problematic, either because English was a second language, or because of their literacy skills and not being confident expressing themselves with 'correct' sentence construction. Although most participants seemed supportive and would encourage others who found it difficult, I still picked up a sense that some felt exposed by having their verbal skills placed on the spot. Despite these problems, storytelling was unanimously chosen by the participants and gradually those who felt unable to contribute began to gather confidence and join in.

In creating fantastical fictional representations of how life *is not*, avenues emerged afterwards to discuss the material reality existing around them. However, in a discussion around the reality of single parents, they began to reproduce existing dominant, moralistic representations about non-traditional family units. The women were reproducing dominant narratives, from the mythical romance of a 'Hollywood' style relationship in the story, to the conservative rhetoric about alternative families as single parents who scrounge off the state. The romantic text was placed in opposition to the reality of those who do not fit the stereotype, which was in danger of turning into a moralizing attack on single parents. As the vignette describes, a facilitation dilemma emerges that reveals the contradictory intentions of participatory and critical pedagogies. Does the facilitator nurture and celebrate the community building and agency that emerges through the women's collective sharing of their observations and laudable plans to set up a women's refuge, or find ways to extend their critical awareness of the construction of stereotypes by challenging their statements and the texts created, but in so doing running the risk of closing down the conversation?

For the purposes of furthering thinking about dilemmas of facilitation practice, this discussion proposes that critical facilitation directly acknowledges practice to be inextricably bound up in a relationship with society and culture. For the facilitator, a critical standpoint therefore articulates the need for interrogation of the ideological influences surrounding facilitation practices that we take for granted as 'common sense'. Within this frame, we can engage in a critical analysis of the power relations of the facilitator embarking on practice. Understanding the political relationships and pedagogical dimensions of one's practice is an important yet often neglected area. Rather than forcing any one agenda, which would be contradictory to its aim, critical pedagogy acknowledges the tensions that exist, say, in Paul Murray's playful work with participants in a Serbian workshop (in this book) and with the Spanish lovers example (above). Neither of these (very different) practices seeks, actively, to politicize the process or to bring the social context of the setting *into* the work, but a critical pedagogy approach sees these practices as inherently political in their different ways. Facilitation choices that foreground the need to play and clown with people displaced from their homes, or that encourage participatory agency with vulnerable women despite (perhaps) the articulation of some questionable views, exist in themselves as productive, political tensions, by their nature subversive in their challenges to established orthodoxies of practice.

Performing culture

Critical pedagogy enables awareness and understanding of the cultural forms that are in play within culture. People's artistic expressions, their vernacular and their ways of talking, moving, being and feeling are all cultural practices (McLaren, 2008). People's behaviours and actions can also be articulated as signatures of culture and representations of cultural capital. Understanding how culture is emblazoned on our everyday doings, expressions and practices enables the practitioner to engage in a multilayered pedagogical process of reading the self, observing the complexity of practices of expression and behaviours of others, whilst working to enable a parallel process with participants. The example cited earlier, regarding the ambivalence of group members towards labels of mental health, illuminates this discourse and will have been played out performatively in all its contradictions in the daily life of the centre. The same analysis applies to the facilitator/ artist/practitioner as they enact, perform and/or socially interact in the moment and in context with people. Capturing the texts and stories of the everyday through devising, improvising, writing and performance enables an ongoing process of interrogation, reflection and physical exploration that can enable the growth of a form of intuitive development. The facilitator is of course subject to the same ambivalences, as politics of their own identities and belief systems will also be present, inscribed in their practice and on their bodies. A practice informed by critical pedagogy enables the drawing of attention to the politics of one's own and others' performativity in different spaces, thus representing the emergence of critical awareness.

Throughout this discussion it becomes increasingly difficult to disentangle the process envisioned for the participants, or constituencies of a practice, from that of the facilitator. Although the emphasis in this book is to focus predominantly on the practice of the facilitator, it is not possible to identify this practice as separate from the process one might want to achieve with participants, particularly as one will impact on the other. The journeys that participants and facilitators are going on may be different, occurring in different moments of time and space according to different needs and circumstances. They are, however, in essence, pedagogically similar in principle. Facilitators and participants are, in effect, operating through the same processes; every new experience or interaction potentially generates transformative understanding if one is open to these possibilities. To different degrees, and variably so depending on the experience of the facilitator, the facilitator *may* or *may not* be at a further stage of critical awareness to the participants (see Mda, 1993), though I would be cautious about making such assumptions. The crucial difference, obviously, is that the facilitator is charged with operating on a dual level, their primary role being to enable others (even if, from a self-reflexive position, the process is and should be bringing about new awareness for others). This is potentially challenging as the cultural (identities and context) *will* impact on the facilitators' identity and values.

The employment of a critical, informed pedagogy for facilitation also influences the choices that are made through the aesthetic and creative processes that are offered, and the ways in which the facilitator responds to the material created, directly informing a facilitator's practice *with* participants. To explore in a direct way with participants the informal cultural practices that emerge from the everyday – such as the street, the home or work; that which is often enacted indirectly in the workshop or classroom setting – might be an appropriate pedagogical strategy. As McLaren outlines, 'what can be seen as "natural" and personality based behaviours; tardiness, sincerity, honesty, thrift, industriousness, politeness, a certain way of dressing, speaking, gesturing … are, to a great extent, *culturally inscribed* and are often linked to the social class standing or cultural capital available to those individuals who exhibit them' (McLaren, 2008: 81; italics in original). As a pedagogical strategy, adopting creative opportunities that might enable participants to reflect on the practices that they observe as well as perform; as cultural markers (of conformity, agency or resistance) rather than individual and pathological behaviour, enables a growing critical awareness and potential empowerment. For example, in a project working with young teenage women in an urban school, a playful exercise exploring status and the 'roles' we adopt in certain situations, in which the participants were asked to act out arriving at a fictional party, led the way to discussions around the different 'fronts' we put on depending on the situations we are in

> Lisa said: 'when I go into a classroom, especially if it's a teacher I don't like, or don't know, I put on this face'. She composed this deadpan, lightly sullen expression and then smiled. (Preston, 2011: 258)

These young women, through the playful exploration of the cultural practices of *their* everyday, were engaging in their own self-reflexive observations, the starting place for an emerging, intuitive process of understanding of the relationships of their performative responses in different situations and to their cultural contexts.

A critical pedagogical perspective challenges facilitators to challenge their own cultural and moral expectations of what they see being 'performed' in the room, choosing not to view it only through the dominant behavioural lens which might define it as 'bad' or 'compliant' behaviour. Interventionist practices, often dressed up in all sorts of guises, commonly seek directly or indirectly to 'change' behaviour with a view to enabling socially 'acceptable' behaviour. Moreover, many applied drama projects are funded on the basis of their potential to address a pro-social agenda of some kind and a critical approach draws light on the subtle (and not so subtle) agendas that inform these practices.

A performative analysis affords the facilitator a self-reflective, gestic social criticism, enabling them to read the workshop space, the classroom, the participants (and themselves) as historical, cultural and social constructions. This angle has the potential to radically alter approaches to pedagogical practice and to draw attention both to the hidden curriculum in schools and other institutions and the 'performances' of people as they negotiate, conform to and resist their social experience, enabling the facilitator to adopt processes that respond to this; this also invites us to consider the performative practices that the facilitator plays.

The cultural worker

> It is important for critical educators to take up culture as a vital source for developing a politics of identity, community and pedagogy. In this perspective culture is not seen as monolithic and unchanging, but as a site of multiple and heterogeneous borders where different histories, languages, experiences and voices intermingle amidst diverse relations of power and privilege. (Giroux, 1992: 169)

Writing about and reaching beyond the context of schooling, critical pedagogy theorist Henry Giroux advocates the idea of the cultural worker. This notion extends the role of a 'teacher' to critical educator but even beyond, encompassing the whole range of practitioners who work in service in the community, such as artists, lawyers, doctors, teachers, adult educators and community workers; it signals the need for practitioners to recognize their potential multifaceted role, one that extends from a merely procedural function to the contribution of the production (or re-production) of culture. Recognition that our identities, our history and our contemporary practices sit in dialectical relationships with social, cultural conditions and power relations is an important basis for understanding one's location in culture, as well as realizing that this problematizes the pursuit of liberatory processes. The realization that the *mélange* of stories, histories and realities offered by communities both within and around the work potentially brings about possibilities to reconfigure and challenge existing social and cultural relations is vitally important, as is, of course, an awareness of their potential to perpetuate oppressive narratives.

Recognition, therefore, that any artist and facilitation practice, as well as practices taking place in more formal educational contexts, are embroiled in pedagogical and cultural relations, creates important possibilities: first, the enablement of one's own cultural awareness and agency, and second, a critical engagement with one's practice as an *intervention*. In the context of this discussion, critical pedagogy plays an important contribution to our understanding of the facilitators' *raison d'être*, practice and influence in particular contexts and settings.

Critical pedagogy can offer a discourse and frames of reference that can help the facilitator to situate themselves in the field of culture and pedagogy in order to help them understand what they do, why they do it and what forces are influencing this. As McLaren articulates, 'We do not stand *before* the social world; we live in the *midst* of it' (McLaren, 2008: 63; italics in the original). Importantly, our experience of what is happening as we facilitate and how we respond to what happens has a crucial influence on the work and this is socially and politically nuanced. Although the facilitator role implies a *performed* neutrality, it is not possible to stand outside of the work and facilitate as an impartial observer – we are implicated before we even enter the room with the participants. In the light of our presence, we need to attempt to under-stand the moments that emerge for us – in their complexity, messiness and difficulty – without letting our ego result in an unwitting reframing of the work around *our* sensitivities and sensibilities. The ability to listen to our own thoughts and feelings in order to understand their cultural 'locatedness' enables us to work productively with others with a heightened awareness of self and others.

Regimes of emotion

So what are the social and cultural circumstances that sit around the experience of facilitation, making it feel 'real' and 'right' at one moment, 'fake' or 'performed' in another context, unsettled and disturbed in another? What is it that causes us at times to feel at odds with how we are expected to feel? And what sorts of choices will be made by the facilitator in the light of this? Arlie Hochschild's coining of the term *regimes of emotion*, which evolved from her seminal work on emotional labour (Hochschild, 1983), explains how the 'feeling rules' that exist at all levels of social discourse are a way of articulating the political uses of emotion: in public and media discourse around the framing of key events, such as 9/11, in relation to public service industries, and even the home and family life. Feeling rules frame 'how we should both see and feel reality ... Such regimes require us to do emotion work in trying to live up to them' (Hoschchild quoted by Smith, 2002: 99). Megan Boler also argues that we need to engage in recognition of the extent to which 'the politics of emotion shape our lives' (1999: xiv). As emotional narratives feature constantly in the media and circulate in our minds, socially and culturally influencing our own feeling responses in each moment, to circumstances, people and places, we need to consider how this also influences our pedagogical practices with young people:

> The risky business of addressing emotions within our classrooms is a productive and necessary direction for the exploration of social justice and education ... In order to name, imagine and materialize a better world, we need an account of how Western discourses of emotion shape our scholarly work, as well as pedagogical recognition of how emotions shape our classroom interactions. (Boler, 1999: xii)

For Boler, emotions are intrinsically connected to culture, social class, race and gender, and working with this reality represents an important pedagogical intent for work in schools hoping to transform existing social relations.

Similarly, for the facilitator, consideration of the impact of how regimes of emotions act on the self, acts as a signifier for understanding how one is responding and goes beyond the tendency to engage in a personalized, individualized analysis. The impact of emotional labour on facilitation practices is raised in Chapter 2, and in Chapter 3 we get to the heart of the tensions and possibilities of working in the dilemmatic space, where a cultural application of feeling, although challenging, can open up pedagogical possibilities.

Summary

Acknowledging the influence of critical pedagogy as a core philosophical framing of the critical facilitation progresses the discussion to enable a theoretical understanding of facilitation politics, practice and function in contemporary community and educational practices. By engaging in the philosophical, political and performed possibilities of the role in context (and therefore moving beyond technical or instrumental notions of facilitation), the chapter has developed a theoretical analysis that contributes to facilitator praxis. Countering tendencies to frame discussions about human action and emotions within dominant psychoanalytical or individualizing and psychological frames that remain at the micro, personal level, the discussion considers these narratives critically through a broadly socially constructivist approach that embodies, at points, the psychosocial but is always framed in the cultural.

In summary, critical pedagogy enables us to locate acts of facilitation as a *political* project. In so doing, *critical* facilitation, just as critical pedagogy might approach the act of teaching, analyses (Applied Theatre) facilitation not as technique but in terms of its potential contribution as a social and cultural project that can potentially transform existing social and cultural relations. *Critical facilitation*, therefore, enables us to have a heightened awareness of the politics of the choices that are available to us as we notice how culture is performed, enacted and practised.

Practices: Doing and Performing

This chapter seeks to extend thinking about critical facilitation as a creative practice. The discussion focuses on selected *approaches* to practices of facilitation rather than detailed facilitation techniques or aesthetic strategies. The strategy of this discussion in resisting the tendency to describe practices instrumentally by offering a description of operational or aesthetic approaches or a range of drama/group work techniques is not to negate the value of such approaches, but to articulate a broader understanding of facilitation practice that encompasses the critical and cultural (as outlined in the previous chapter), while considering the facilitation choices that emerge *through* the varied roles that are taken. These choices, which may or may not be intentional, are decisions that are made beyond the technical or conventional approach to the work and offer possibilities for the facilitator; they are, arguably, a dimension of Applied Theatre facilitator education that is often lacking in the preparation of emerging facilitators.

The problem of doing: 'Applying' and 'delivering'

In mainstream educational settings, formal, technicist approaches dominate against the backdrop of a neoliberal hegemony, with its growing pressures to meet targets and drive up standards, as well as the 'measurements' of success via league tables. Such cultural factors have had an impact on the development of Applied Theatre practice. For example, since the National Curriculum was introduced in the United Kingdom in 1988, drama has been sidelined as a taught subject in state schools, leading, over the intervening twenty-five years, to a serious decline in the number of teacher training places and dedicated courses focusing on drama pedagogy and the training of drama teachers. As Davis points out, 'teacher education courses have been stripped bare of the possibility of giving new teachers a thorough grounding in pedagogy, which is a vital basis for any teacher who wants to educate rather than deliver a prescribed curriculum' (Davis, 2005: 163).

As a curriculum subject, drama pedagogy has been subjected to a technicist approach. As an example, Davis contends that the Edexcel GCSE Drama Curriculum has ultimately reduced a 'complex art form to a list of things that can be practised, learnt and tested' (2005: 165). Davis critiques how practices of drama – forum theatre, thought tracking, tableaux, role on the wall or hot seating – have been hijacked, stripped of their contextual and philosophical underpinnings and described instead as '*methods*'.[1] Davis identifies how the formalization of drama processes through the popular textbook *Structuring Drama Work* (see Neelands, 1990) 'inadvertently led to this "bits and pieces" approach to teaching drama for a whole generation of students' (Davis, 2005: 165). Similarly, it is possible to see how equally popular texts such as *Games for Actors and Non-actors* (Boal, 2002), *The Geese Theatre Handbook: Drama with Offenders and People at Risk* (Baim, Brookes and Mountford, 2002) and *House of Games* (Johnston, 2005), designed for their accessibility and distilling of established 'canons' of practice such as forum theatre, and other manual-based books might have similarly contributed to a delivery-focused approach. As Davis implies, the 'drama conventions' approach succeeds in reducing complex aesthetic-pedagogical processes to mere techniques which become foregrounded at the expense of deeper engagement with the socially transformative potential of drama in enabling a process of critical engagement with the world. We are reminded by Gavin Bolton (a key pioneer and theorist of the drama in education movement) of the purpose of drama in education: 'to help the student understand himself and the world he lives in' and importantly 'to help the student know how and when (and when *not*) to adapt to the world he lives in' (Bolton cited in Davis, 2014: 22; italics in original). Bolton's positioning reveals the politics of social justice that sits beneath the aesthetics of his own approach to educational drama. Davis reinvigorates the contemporary relevance of these words in *Imagining the Real: Towards a New Theory of Drama in Education* (2014), where he argues that current social and material conditions require that (drama) education has a fundamental responsibility to play this role to enable young people to make sense of their world and to make choices in it.

Students, academics and practitioners frequently articulate the very real-life problem of applying theory to practice and the contradictions that emerge between the ideals of theory and the reality of working with people in diverse contexts and circumstances. The challenges of meeting the ideals of practice are often expressed through frustration, disillusionment and even rejection of these ideals. However, an educator 'training' that focuses mainly on techniques of becoming a 'process expert' may mean that the core values that underpin the work are never fully engaged with and thus the work never reaches its full potential.

Applying 'ends' first

A significant problem inherent in the 'applying' delivery mindset (and a problem with the Applied Theatre term itself) is the belief that an idea or aesthetic practice that 'works' in one context can be uncomplicatedly translated, like a recipe, into a new context and situation. Thought-systems that consider 'application' or the idea of 'applied' as the translation of standardized technique or knowledge reveal positivist epistemologies that are based upon technical rationality and scientific approaches and represent a central contradiction of the intention of 'counter-cultural' pedagogies. As Donald Schön articulates, the fundamental flaw in the use of applied terminology is that it 'depends on an agreement about ends' (Schön, 1984: 39). He says, 'When ends are fixed, and clear, then the decision to act can present itself as an instrumental problem' (ibid.). The uncertainty, messiness and dilemmas of context and values requires instead a 'non-technical process of framing the problematic situation that we may organise and clarify both the ends to be achieved and the possible means for achieving them' (ibid.).

Where facilitation and/or the arts are applied instrumentally, or the ends determined at the outset, practitioners are faced with this contradiction. They either measure the success of their intervention in terms of the perceived outcome intended by the exercise (like a learning outcome) or, if the exercise then 'fails', the cause is attributed to facilitator (in)competency, the participants (or their behaviour) or the theory/method/educational practice of delivery that somehow missed the mark. Each and all of these factors may well be implicated, and triangulation across variables may be useful in analysing the 'success' of an intervention, but an ends-focused approach may blind facilitators to the possibilities of gaining a fuller understanding of the dynamics and interrelations of process and a deeper clarity about the intentions of the work.

Competency-based facilitation education tends to emphasize the instrumental, technique-based nature of facilitation. Within this frame of thinking, the focus is upon delivery of technique and skills-based learning. This idea of a (drama) facilitation approach as a form of delivery or application can be aligned with what Thomas (2007, 2008) identifies as *technical facilitation*, which tends to focus on skills and strategies in isolation (see Thomas, 2008). As a stand-alone approach, technical facilitation 'dumbs down the real complexity and challenge of facilitating groups and does not accurately illustrate what is required to facilitate effectively' (ibid : 7).

According to the research Thomas has conducted into facilitator education, the frame of technical facilitation, akin to delivering exercises, games and techniques, tends to be the starting approach for the emerging facilitator. However, as Thomas's research with experienced facilitator interviewees explains, 'It's what's between the techniques that is more important. Often people want more and more techniques to cover up for inadequate awareness and these over-structured facilitation sessions remove uncertainty and allow them to feel competent ... Techniques are often used to overcome uncertainty and awkwardness' (Thomas, 2008: 8).

Schwarz distinguishes between basic facilitation and deep facilitation. 'Basic' facilitation might also be analogous to an ends-orientated or delivery approach, where the task or the process is developed to meet the goal, although the way that even basic facilitation is described by Schwarz seems to offer a more open-ended approach that potentially can move beyond the technical:

> In basic facilitation, the facilitator helps a group solve a substantive problem by lending his or her process skills. When the facilitation is complete, the group has solved its substantive problem but, by design, it has not explicitly learned how it improves its process. (Schwarz, 2002: 24)

By design, a workshop will often involve a series of task-based participatory exercises with a developmental goal in mind. However, as Schwarz identifies, although the goal may be open-ended, that is, involve some negotiation and ownership of the process with participants, the process remains a temporary one, as the facilitator 'lends' their skills.

'Doing' a workshop

In drama facilitation, possibly because of the existing array of imaginative and creative approaches and exercises available to the facilitator, the urge to engage in 'doing' is strong. Both drama practitioners and students like to 'do' and 'make' work: it is the kinesthetic, learning through the body, 'doing' feeling of enjoyment that drama students and practitioners are drawn to and which is also admired by those outside of the drama fields.

Flow

The enjoyable, creative feeling of absorption in the experience of 'doing' has been described as 'flow' by Csikszentmihalyi (1997, 2013). Also described as being 'in the zone', flow moments represent a state where what we feel, wish and think are in harmony. We have the flow feeling when we are absorbed in a task, a game or an activity that we are doing in a particular moment in time. Csikszentmihalyi argues that experiencing flow is of crucial importance for good quality of life (ibid.) It is also not particularly the feeling of happiness that produces a flow effect but rather a feeling of motivation and enjoyment that comes about from the experience of being creative and challenged; and it is the latter that can bring about release of stress and feelings of well-being. Csikszentmihalyi cites a range of activities – rock climbing, dancing, sailing, and chess – as examples of flow-producing activities that occur through the optimum balance of a person's skill set and challenge (ibid.) He also points out that flow activity can even involve pain and risk if they stretch a person's capacity. If the activity of a particular task is too easy then boredom can set in, the activity ceases to become enjoyable and creative, and disengagement ensues or, at worst, anxiety sets in.

Drama games potentially fulfil this function if facilitation can enable the right balance between structure and safe boundaries, and high levels of mental and physical energy, along with the thrill or excitement of suspense, anticipation and/or competition. This 'right' balance of challenge, skills and goals is important, as Csikszentmihalyi notes that 'In a really enjoyable game, the players are balanced on the fine line between boredom and anxiety. The same is true when work, or a conversation, or a relationship is going well' (Ibid.: 113). If the challenge is too great, worry, anxiety and frustration will diminish the well-being effects of the activity.

Csikszentmihalyi outlines the following essential elements for flow and creativity, which provide a useful guide for the goals of workshop facilitation:[2]

1. Clear goals: we always know what needs to be done.
2. Feedback on our actions: we know how well we are doing.
3. The right balance between challenge and skill is created: our abilities are well matched with the activity required of us.
4. Action and awareness are merged: when thought and action become one 'the creative process begins to hum' (ibid: 119).
5. Avoiding distraction: protecting the focus of concentration so that one can stay involved in the creative process.

The premise of a workshop structure, beginning with the making of the circle, enables democratic participation, rebalancing previous hierarchies where everyone can assume an 'equal' place. Ananda Breed's chapter in this book points to the inimitable capacity of applied performance to create a shared communitas or 'community spirit'. Facilitator Jane Wilburn Sapp (in Cynthia Cohen's chapter in this book) pinpoints how her African-American heritage is a core part of her practice in peace work and has influenced her belief in the importance of the circle for participatory community building, where 'every voice counts' in the creation of a group energy through play.

Participants of a drama workshop may experience a range of feelings about 'doing' drama and this will depend on how the facilitator is able to match the level/kind of 'doing' required with the group's need to feel *safe enough* to step outside their comfort zone a little. If the balance is struck, participants find the experience involving and enjoyable, creative and opening up of new possibilities and ways of thinking, experiencing and collective learning as a group.

Considering critically the conventions of the workshop as a working structure for groups enables interrogation of the assumptions of co-intentional participation. Although having fun 'joining in', participants may be, in effect, taking on a passive or procedural role in the process if the 'game'/exercise/activity is controlled too fully by the facilitator. As participants we may feel very safe in this, being led by the facilitator from one task to the next; we may find this very pleasurable – our flow experience resides through the freedom to engage fully with a task.

However, from this perspective, participation is operational, functional and task based: there can be little co-intentionality possible at this point beyond the compliance and experiential act of joining in the game, unless the facilitator can create spaces around the structures for negotiation. The ambition of enabling participants to take more ownership over the process as co-workers is limited if the 'ends' or the outcome of the work have been predetermined through the rules of the game and/or the workshop structure itself. But can co-intentionality coexist with flow? Would the experiential pleasure of immersion and absorption in an activity be lost if the facilitator attempts to do more than *lend* her process skills or presence as workshop leader and, instead, involve participants in a negotiation with the content and intentions of the work? I would suggest that an evolving, generative process will inevitably require transaction shifts. Participants may, depending on their needs (and goals), require more than to be a passenger transported to new possibilities through the creative process. As Csikszentimahalyi points out, the need for greater challenge matched to one's evolving skills is ever present in terms of achieving fulfilment. The possibilities for a constant renegotiation of the terms of the transaction potentially emerge and are perhaps why dancers become choreographers, actors become teachers, young people become youth workers, participants become facilitators. Terret's chapter in this book articulates how, in a performing arts training course for people with learning difficulties, this shift from being facilitated to make performance to becoming a facilitator represents an important political intervention.

The following example outlines a different sort of challenge that emerged in the facilitation of drama, whereby it became necessary, politically, ethically and personally, for the participants in the context of a self-advocacy group for people with learning difficulties to retain control over the structures of the weekly meetings; therefore the taken-for-granted conventions of the workshop were rejected. This draws attention to the challenge of facilitation to be responsive and adaptable to the needs of the context.

Example: a self-advocacy group

Challenges around the negotiation of ownership through drama workshop structures became apparent when I worked within a self-advocacy group with people with learning difficulties. I was invited to work with the group by the participants, on their terms and into a pre-existing structure. This experience questioned my previously taken-for-granted assumptions concerning the conventions of workshop rituals. In this setting I realized the necessity of introducing drama in a highly negotiated way, offering it as a strategy for the group to explore an issue as it became appropriate and as they consented to do so. As I was entering a pre-existing group and set-up, I felt sensitive about the potential to dominate the existing structures because it would risk the hard-earned ownership over *their* group, thus contradicting the self-advocacy purpose. I felt that if I were not careful, I would represent yet another non-disabled person coming in and redefining their group because 'I knew best'. It subsequently became very difficult for me to get drama started in the first instance to give the group enough familiarity with the medium of drama and the building of confidence that needed to be developed through workshop processes. Drama eventually was utilized in this context but the process was tentative, used only when the need arose and never arrived at through the conventional workshop structure.[3] For example, drama often became useful as a medium to role-play challenges the group were finding in their day-to-day lives. A simple 'forum theatre' style practice emerged as the participants brought real-life experiences of injustices, and drama enabled the group to explore and try out ways to challenge difficult experiences for the future. Drama was helpful to enable participants to 'see' their experiences presented in front of them and to help each other to explore possible ways of addressing a problem. As well as having a sound operational understanding of forum theatre as a process, so that it could be *made easy* for the participants, a further facilitation *capacity* lay in the discussion with participants regarding the selection of stories that were appropriate to the group (and redirecting other more personal stories to another setting), and enabling a non-judgemental and safe exploration of a story where all could participate freely with their opinions and ideas.

As the above example describes, the development of drama skills was held in a complex balance between enabling participants to acquire an effective communication form through the medium of drama and a workshop format, and the danger of imposing new processes, thereby temporarily preventing full participation and co-intentionality. Every offer made with respect to the introduction of drama needed negotiation and this was a constant reminder that it was not *my* space and the participants were not present on my terms; rather, it was the reverse. It was as if I was working at the service of the group, 'lending' the group my drama process skills as and when they were required, but the facilitation process felt more *developmental* than basic in that the activities that were offered were intrinsically connected to their lives and their future relationships with one another. As Schwarz says:

> In developmental facilitation, the facilitator explicitly helps a group solve a substantive problem and learn to improve its process at the same time. Here the facilitator also serves as teacher, so the group can eventually become self-facilitating. Developmental facilitation requires significantly more time and facilitator skill, and it is more likely to create fundamental change. (Schwarz, 2002: 22)

In the self-advocacy group, participants weren't being explicitly 'trained' in the use of drama approaches but the work was becoming embedded into their working structures. The development possibilities of facilitation could be demonstrated in the work *around* the drama.

Giroux reminds us that pedagogy is a political and moral practice and 'not ... a technique or a priori set of methods' (Giroux, 2008: 18). In the example given, with two layers at play here – the context of a self-advocacy setting working with young people defined as 'vulnerable' *and* an external facilitator entering an established set-up – the negotiation of drama as a potential political and moral pedagogy was provisional, contingent on moment-by-moment negotiation with participants in the space. The purpose and intent of the work was to enable self-advocacy and the working processes needed to be aligned with this intent, not contradict it. The forms and exercises employed were not predetermined but evolved from the facilitator needing to listen to the needs of the group, responding, and generating a process from this.

The following section explores the possibilities of practice as a generative encounter and has been inspired particularly by the use of drama by education pioneers who developed forms of process drama. Aligned to process drama, the concept of teacher-in-role draws attention to a range of fluid performance and/or role possibilities that can be taken by the facilitator, from within and alongside a drama. In the example that follows, aesthetic practices drawn from drama in education are referred to, but it is the concepts of *living through* and *generative* approaches that potentially inspires insight into the possibilities of facilitation, whatever one's preferred practice.

'Living through' – generative approaches

Within drama in education, the use of role play in primary school settings evolved as an explicit dramatic and pedagogical device for the teacher, who was able to facilitate and deepen the child's learning in the classroom by working alongside them. The use of teacher-in-role (brought to attention by innovators such as Dorothy Heathcote, Cecily O'Neill and Gavin Bolton) exists in the practices of process drama, drama for learning, classroom drama and 'mantle of the expert' (all with their different associated nuances). As a simple summary, teacher-in-role represents skilled facilitation by a practitioner who takes on a role within the fiction world of the drama with children, often with a whole class. From the place of *experiencing* from *within* a fictitious moment, and facilitated by a practitioner, children discover a place of 'deep learning' and encounter a whole range of challenges: about curriculum topics, working together and the solving of human dilemmas (see the example that follows on p. 53, 'What is happening here').

Through the playing of an aesthetic role within a fiction, the teacher's presence within the drama services a range of facilitative intentions which include the following:

1. Deepening the children's engagement with the themes and the dilemmas of the fiction that they are involved in by being *in there with them.*
2. Questioning, provoking, wondering, setting up possibilities *through the fiction.*
3. Retaining the structure or form of the drama for the children to work within and affording children an experience of 'living through' a dramatic moment so that they might have a *real-enough* experience of what it might be like in that context (without the intention for children to get 'lost' in the experience).
4. Protecting the children in their roles and giving them enough power and determination to succeed and be 'authorities' of their roles 'in the play', whilst learning from each other and about the world they are in.
5. Creating opportunities for reflection on that experience by the teacher stepping in and out of role (and enabling this for the children).

Drama in education, or process drama, enables children to encounter a 'living-through' experience that involves them in *'being themselves* in the role they are taking' (Davis, 2005: 167; italics in the original). The feeling experienced by participants, of *making drama*, enables a dual experiential and reflective experience in the moment, aptly phrased by Bolton as a strong sense of 'it is happening now; we are making it happen; we are watching it happen' (Bolton, 1999: 272).

Enabling an experiential process with a high level of possibility for autonomy by participants requires the careful structuring of participation and ownership by the facilitator. Also referred to in its early days by Heathcote as 'man in a mess' drama, these kinds of experiences are structured to enable children a safe (but not too safe) opportunity to experience being in and inhabiting different worlds, to be confronted with dilemmas where the path is not always clear, and to take risks.

Cecily O'Neill points out that 'When drama techniques are valued only for their capacity to promote specific competencies and achieve precise ends, and remain brief, fragmented, and tightly controlled by the teacher or director, the work is likely to fall far short of the kind of generative dramatic encounter available in process drama' (O'Neill cited in Bolton, 1999: 231). Here, O'Neill points to a *quality* of experience that might be possible through a *generative* approach. A generative approach is akin to co-intentional learning whereby outcomes are not fixed at the outset but are process orientated, with the content negotiated. O'Neill particularly refers to the drama process itself which, when facilitated with this understanding, might offer the participant new ways of imagining, exploring, discovering and experiencing. Such a process, rather than being ends-based, is open ended and potentially led by participants. It is also not solipsist but grounded in the experience of human and social dilemmas. Working, playing or 'living through' drama creates a unique layer of creative possibilities brought about by the aesthetic form itself.

Akin to Schwarz's idea of 'deep facilitation', a process-based approach to working presents similar challenges for facilitators and requires skill with the procedural elements of the form, an 'artistic' insight (see Duffy, 2015) *as well as* the facilitation of processes. However, like the enjoyable 'flow' feeling of the experiential workshop, it is not necessarily *developmental* (as described earlier) since the structure relies on facilitation by the teacher who has temporarily lent their 'process skills' of drama for a particular purpose. However, there is capacity for this process to be developmental for participants in terms of content, depending on how 'task-based' the process is (too task-based and the process is in danger of becoming procedural with limited scope beyond the activity itself). As O'Neill suggests, facilitating a 'generative dramatic encounter' sets out the possibilities for growth, but this is only possible if the fictive moments emerge through a genuine engagement with what happens 'in the moment'.

The capacity to improvise, working spontaneously with the offers made and being able to call on one's aesthetic knowledge in order to respond *through* the form, is challenging for the facilitator and relies on a secure knowledge of the dramatic form one is working with in order to be able to respond to participants and to shift and move within the aesthetic frame. Peter Duffy recalls (2015) that as a young drama teacher he had the procedural knowledge of techniques and practices but it was 'artistic insight' that eluded him at that time. Referring to Dewey and Schön, Duffy distinguishes between the need to acquire procedure *and* craft. Being able to draw on one's artistic vision is the missing 'something' for the practitioner and, as pointed out via O'Neill and Davis, is in danger of vanishing from the teacher's skill set. Artistic insight and craft involve a deep understanding of the purposes and intentions of the work that will then become embodied in process. Over-reliance on technique and form will not enable a generative approach to facilitation, which requires the facilitator to be *in* the work with participants, experiencing, noticing and responding.

Whatever one's preferred aesthetic practice, core elements of process drama – the concept of 'living through' and being 'in a mess' and in a place of questioning and 'wonder' – are powerful metaphors for the optimum facilitator positioning. When the facilitator can experience that 'strong' sense of 'it is happening now' and that s/he is also 'making it happen' (Bolton, 1999: 272), s/he is experiencing a mindful facilitator *flow*, which makes openness to a generative approach possible.

Facilitation *as* performance

Considering the facilitator's *doing* as a form of performance takes us straight to the 'it is happening now' moment and enables us to understand how facilitation as practice evolves in a nuanced, generative way, which extends procedural approaches to dramatic forms such as forum theatre, teacher-in-role or mantle of the expert. Facilitation *as* a form of performance enables us to take a multifaceted view of the facilitator 'doing', and other aspects of their behaviours, qualities and utterances that emerge can also be considered alongside the application of a particular methodology or approach. Considering the facilitator's action and responses as a dialogic form of performance enables us to consider what is done in a *gestic*, relational and socio-political way, but also intimately connected with our sensibilities, our previous experiences and our decisions in the moment.

Considering facilitation as a form of social performance enables us to take a self-reflective view of our action in context during or after an event. In other words, reflection on doing *as* performance gives us a critical distance to re-examine the nuances of our intended practice and what actually happens as a result of a negotiation (or struggle) of intentions in context. Analysis of our practice-as-performance becomes, therefore, an act of reflectivity, enabling us to have the critical distance to consider what might be possible in future as we aim towards generative, co-intentional encounters. The performative aspect enables us to draw upon the idea of facilitator performance as a form of 'restored' behaviour, with elements of previous actions, behaviours, presentations all contributing to a 'persona' enacted in the room (see Schechner, 1988). This might help us to understand the different facets of the roles being played out by the Applied Theatre facilitator working in the moment, in context and *in situ* with participants. A heightened sensitivity around when we are consciously performing and when we are not becomes a useful strategy for understanding the cultural rules of a setting and our approach to it. In this way Schechner's notion of the Goffman performer, which draws attention to ordinary people playing their 'life roles' as waitresses, doctors, teachers, people on the street (ibid.), becomes a useful frame for identifying the different levels of performance that emerge in a context. As Schechner identified, there are those who intentionally conceal (as he says con-men do) and those who don't know they are performing (ibid.). There are times when we perform any of the following roles, such as carer, teacher, director, social worker, parent, friend as well as artist and facilitator, and it is useful to notice how we play out these transactions in different contexts, and to reflect on what happens, as this sharpens our awareness for future roles and choices. Therefore, the facilitator's performance in a context may represent a complex mix of tactics as one adjusts to the needs and expectations of the setting.

Within this frame, the facilitator is sometimes unaware of his/her performance but at other points becomes acutely aware of how s/he is performing or, in other words, engaging in *impression management*. Impression management involves the suppression of 'spontaneous feelings in order to give [an] appearance of sticking to the affective line, the expressive status quo' (Goffman, 1990: 211) and contributes to the *front* one presents. For the facilitator, awareness that our performed persona or *front* has been influenced, even constructed, by the cultural 'rules' of the context is important, as is awareness of the expectation of what those rules are and how s/he feels s/he *should* be positioned in relation to them.

Emotional labour

There will be times, in the facilitator role, when one feels 'fake' and even disingenuous; when our actions feel incongruent with our feelings. We may stray into performer modes that feel less comfortable for a range of reasons, including self-preservation, when we are trying new skill which we have not yet embedded into our being, or crucially, because the topics of the work moves us into unfamiliar areas. Additionally, according to our mood or the challenges we are facing, we may feel we need to summon up feelings that aren't readily accessible or spontaneously felt in order to work effectively with participants. Moving between roles that feel authentic and inauthentic cannot always easily be reconciled and can create dissonant feelings that are difficult to manage. Awareness of practice as social, constantly performative and responsive enables a critical reflexivity which monitors and *notices* rather than moralizes about the impact on the self.

Hochschild's seminal work on emotional labour has influenced the way in which we understand public sector work and the multiple roles that are played in order to survive when engaging in emotionally challenging work. Hochschild's early work with flight attendants, and the further research in public-sector contexts of development work, teaching, nursing and policing, reveal the range of performance strategies that workers employ in order to provide a necessary service *and* to prevent burnout. The idea of the containment of feeling for productive as well as self-protective purposes is key to Hochschild's thesis on emotional labour, but crucially a critical frame extends to how the management of feeling can be used for commercial purposes.

Emotional labour 'requires one to induce or suppress feeling in order to sustain the outward countenance that produces the proper state of mind in others – in this case, the sense of being cared for in a convivial and safe place' (Hochschild, 1998: 7). Therefore the labour involved in creating and maintaining the 'convivial' and 'safe' space of the workshop can be challenging and may involve the facilitator performing a desired state rather than one that feels authentic at the moment in time. Referring to the craft of acting, Hochschild draws attention to how the performance of emotion becomes a form of impression management. In this vein, Hochschild refers to *deep acting* and *surface acting* as crucial states between how one approaches one's outward presentation to others. Surface acting, as its name suggests, is where the mind tends to remain separated from what the body does; where one tends to experience going through the motions, acting and responding in a manner that is 'appropriate' and 'expected' in that context, where we do not fully embody our actions. Although, initially, surface acting might operate as a self-protective strategy, caveats emerge; as Hochschild says, 'in surface acting we deceive others about what we really feel, but we do not deceive ourselves. Diplomats and actors do this best, and very small children do it worst – it's part of their charm' (1998: 33). As well as potentially not managing to convince others and running the risk of appearing fake or inauthentic, the cognitive dissonance that results means that maintaining such a performance is exhausting and tends to result in a deep emotional cost.

Alternatively, in *deep acting* the worker, like a well-trained, professional actor, commits fully, imaginatively and emotionally to the role that is being taken. In deep acting, 'we make feigning easy by making it unnecessary ... By taking over the levers of feeling production, by pretending deeply, she alters herself' (Hochschild, 1988: 33). Hochschild's approach therefore offers an important layer in our understanding of the contribution of performance to facilitation through the acknowledgement and uses of our feeling and emotions. Although performance can enable us, as discussed earlier, a gestic, critical distance through drawing attention to 'doing' at all levels, conversely the notion of deep acting enables the facilitator the important potential to commit fully and to *embody* the doing (as in the practice) and to respond emotionally and genuinely in the moment. This is helpful in terms of thinking through the breadth of role registers that the facilitator may adopt. Whether directly in role in an *as if* scenario, or in a more nuanced performative and fluid role-taking, the facilitator needs to embody something akin to *deep acting*, also aligning with Rogers' notions of being genuine.

Furthermore, the consideration of emotional labour and the possibilities of a *deep* approach to facilitator performance enables a productive approach in the use of emotion. Hochschild's work is applied in many ways to explain how public sector workers cope with the feelings of others and find strategies to avoid burnout. This is a crucial issue, especially in the discussion of facilitation in dilemmatic spaces. However, what is also present in the notion of deep acting is the active and resilient use of feeling as a pedagogical tool. Emotional responses can be induced and can transform feeling (not only suppress it) through the doing and committing to whatever activity or role is demanded. The emotional labour of the facilitator can be generative and transformative (rather than passive or reactive) through the bringing of physical energy and focused commitment to the participative space that can infect the participants in a very positive way.

Not least, Hochschild's work reminds us that a productive use of emotional labour is always in tension with its potential function as a commercial product. Rather than individualizing and pathologizing the individual, which tends to be the focus of literature on emotional intelligence (see Goleman, 2006, 2011), emotional labour critically reframes personalized and individualized narratives to locate their material function as *work* involving the labour (sometimes low and unpaid) of paraprofessionals, providing important social work in communities. Acknowledgement that engaging in emotional labour is a real, challenging dimension of critical facilitation can go some way to sharpening the senses of our practice.

Reflection on facilitation practice as performance can sharpen our 'professional knowing' of the roles we play in context (Schön, 1987: 39). As a form of reflection-in-action (ibid.), a heightened awareness of the performative roles that we play in different contexts opens up possibilities for our interaction in uncertain and new settings. For example, a freelance facilitator, Annie, told me how she self-consciously accesses a tone of voice and a persona drawn from a London/Jamaican vernacular in order to find a reciprocal connection with her participants. This 'convivial', playful 'performance' is what Annie calls 'a code' that enables her to make connections with her participants; she describes it as 'a joining, it's like "I know, you know"' (Preston, 2013: 236). In this example, Annie, through her spontaneous performance, is inducing and producing a playful and positive emotional state in others but also a focused state where participants commit to working together.

Consequently the use of the dramaturgical metaphor frames a self-reflexive analysis that considers the 'roles' and 'behaviours' played by the facilitator as dynamic, intuitive and sometimes playful performance, potentially releasing an honest, non-judgemental set of possibilities with which the facilitator might be resourceful and thus reflexive. The notion of the performing facilitator therefore transforms dominant (moral) perceptions of performance that are often based on value judgements and meeting 'standards', the antithesis of which is of course an ideologically influenced notion of failure.

Failure, seen through a moral lens, is debilitating, shaming and unproductive, leading to internalized self-judgement. Reflective practice by practitioners tends to veer towards stories of personal failure. Those who 'survive' their 'cringing' experiences put this down to lack of experience and offer individualized redemption narratives through which they 'transformed' into experienced practitioners now able to do the 'right thing'. I hope that the first section will have worked to problematize this tendency and to point out the more productive possibilities of challenge and 'failure' by subjecting 'feeling' to a cultural analysis.

Facilitation roles

A continuum of performance roles exists for the facilitator, from the informal nuanced performances of day-to-day practice to more formalized, heightened performances of teacher-in-role, opening up a range of aesthetic resources that can bring another quality of role playing to facilitation. As an example, the following register of roles[4] offers the facilitator frames of reference for thinking about the different stances one might take whatever one's practice.

Register of facilitator roles
1. The deliberate opposer of the common view in order to give feedback and aid clarity of thought.
2. The narrator who helps to set mood and register of events.
3. The positive withdrawer who 'lets them get on with it'.
4. The supporter of ideas, as a group member.
5. The 'dogsbody' who discovers material and drama aids.
6. The reflector who is used to assess their statements.
7. The arbiter in arguments.
8. The deliberately obtuse one, who requires to be informed.

(Sandra Heston)[5]

Such role titles offer examples of the possibilities of flexible and playful changes of 'register' available to the facilitator in the moment of working with a group. As performance roles, signalled by changes in voice and tone, presence, energy and status, and emotional register, they are often applied as forms of restored behaviour and fully embodied. As we have discussed earlier, many of us will find ourselves in a range of similar (Goffman) performer roles at home, work and in a range of contexts as we intuitively perform for certain responses. Significant for this discussion is the consideration of the pedagogical possibilities that sit beneath the roles that are played in moments of intentional facilitation. The following example offers insight into the nuances of facilitation registers played out in the taking on of roles within a process drama.

Example: *What is Happening Here?* (1980)[6]

In this example of a fictional drama in an infant school, a pilot, Amy Johnson (one of Dorothy Heathcote's students in role), has just crash-landed her airplane in a lady's rose garden (the school classroom). Sandra Heston explains that one of the lesson's aims is to identify *what children already know but don't know they know*:

> One child said, 'It'll be a long way up there,' pointing to the sky. Heathcote answered 'It will.' She turned to Amy Johnson and pointed at her padded trousers, 'Do you always wear those?' she asked. Then, she turned to the class and commented, 'It looks like she's wearing them for the cold.' Another child asked, 'Do they keep you warm?' Amy Johnson replied, 'I always travel with them, they keep my feet and legs warm.' Heathcote retorted, 'It must be cold up there.' Amy Johnson answered, 'It is.' A little boy said, 'There's clouds up there and the wind blows up there.' Heathcote looked astonished and said, 'I didn't know the wind blew up there. I thought it only blew down here. You mean the wind blows up there as far as you can see?' The little boy replied, 'If you go up higher than the clouds there's no air. You need oxygen.' 'You'd better tell that to Miss Johnson,' suggested Heathcote. 'You need oxygen when you go up high, higher than the clouds,' the little boy said to Miss Johnson. 'Has she got any oxygen?' inquired Heathcote. 'Does anybody know what oxygen looks like? How can you tell when you've got oxygen?' 'You breathe it,' said a

child. 'I'm breathing oxygen?' said Heathcote surprised, 'Everybody breathe and see if you can tell there's some oxygen.' All the children started breathing in to check. 'Would you say that's oxygenous,' said Heathcote. 'Yes,' answered the little boy. 'How can you tell when it isn't oxygen?' said Heathcote. The little boy replied thoughtfully, 'You can feel air going into your mouth. When you go up higher than the clouds. You don't breathe out air to your mouth so you know you're going to die quickly so you're going to need oxygen very quickly.' Heathcote said to the children, 'You realise that this man is an expert on all the dangers of the world.' (Heston: 57–8)

From this rich example of a process drama moment, it is possible to see a range of role registers being employed in enabling the children to experience and discover what they 'already know but don't know they know'. The mood of the room has been established, a crash-landing in a rose garden. This is serious and committed, but the tone is also clear (there's no panic or hysterics). The children and the facilitator are improvising in role carefully and thoughtfully and focus is on under-standing through the fiction what has happened. In performing the role of the 'deliberately obtuse', Dorothy Heathcote 'performs' a shift in power through the performance of astonishment and withholding of her expertise – 'I didn't know the wind blew up there' – which enables the children the opportunity to heighten their status as she values and 'prizes' the knowledge and the contribution that they bring. Dorothy Heathcote is in role, not as an explicit character, but more characterized by what *she is not*: she has put aside her teacher role. If she were to remain in the role as teacher, the potency of *being in the fiction* would have been lost and the children would have returned to the classroom and would be once again in their teacher–pupil roles.

The prizing of participant responses can be aligned with Carl Rogers' ideal of the facilitator who demonstrates unconditional positive regard. Sandra Heston cites Betty Wagner, suggesting that 'Heathcote is a master of withholding her factual expertise, at building a need for information before she loads it on the child, and in some cases, of simply leaving the implications unstated, the end untied, so the class goes on wondering' (Betty Wagner, cited in Heston: 58). To leave the class in a state of 'wonder' with 'ends untied' is at odds philosophically with outcome-led approaches to education but is crucial in engaging and inspiring children to question further. It also requires the facilitator/teacher to be aware of the implications of their knowledge and the timing of when to share it, or whether to withhold it. This translates to facilitation in any context.

Summary

In summation, the potential and range of critical facilitation *practices* can be glimpsed through paying attention to the different conceptual frames of *doing*, which, far beyond the instrumental or methods-based approach, actually encompasses *performing* and *responding*. Analysis of each of these interrelated 'doing' states offers the facilitator a framework for seeing, thinking and understanding, as follows.

Facilitation *as doing* has drawn attention to the facilitation choices (including aesthetic decisions) that lay behind the action that can move us from the paradigm of the instrumental to the interactive and, subsequently, the critical. Here, *facilitation* and *intent* are crucial in moving what is being 'done' onto a deeper level. This is challenging for the practitioner if they are not yet practised at the *other* skills of facilitation needed in the real world, such as listening, responsiveness, resilience, and so on, which could be articulated as emotional literacy skills.

Facilitation *as performance* focuses attention on the 'role', persona and action played by the facilitator acting in contexts, situation and with participants. This can enable the facilitator access to different roles that can be employed tacitly and overtly in response to the context. Analysis of facilitator action as performative potentially provides us with a resilient response to the challenge of facilitation. Awareness of the performative possibilities of the facilitator can become useful as a pedagogic, aesthetic strategy as well as an important tool for reflection.

Finally, facilitation as *emotional labour* draws attention to the multilayered uses of feeling for a facilitator performance and practice that is genuinely engaged and responsive. In the example *What's Happening Here?*, we can see Dorothy Heathcote engaged in deep acting, fully committed in-role as facilitator and sincerely engaged in the fiction with the children. The effect is the successful inducing of feeling in herself, which is then expressed externally, engendering committed engagement by the children. Heathcote's deep acting appears effortless but requires personal investment, self-awareness and a clarity of intention. The alignment of the concept of deep acting with the performance of the everyday prevents any misunderstanding that to undertake 'deep' acting would represent an overidentified, individualized, self-centred performance (like acting in a bubble). For the facilitator, a commitment to deep acting potentially induces an optimum *flow* experience as s/he works in the present moment with participants, performing a range of roles as required. Deep acting signals the investment needed for the coordination of mind–body required for optimum achievement of a triple *living through* facilitation experience (or, being in three places at the same time), as facilitators (along with participants) experience '*being themselves* in the role they are taking' (Davis, 2005: 167; italics in original), making choices as facilitator/actor/participant.

The following, final chapter of Part 1 moves to consider the needs of the resilient facilitator in the context of dilemmatic spaces. The consideration of resilience needs to embrace the inevitability of upheavals that will be experienced by the facilitator. A recurring theme, which began with the influence of critical pedagogy at the outset, has been to acknowledge emotion and feeling, the difficulty and challenges of social conditions and to rearticulate what is often framed as personal and private, and/or an individualized struggle, as part of a broader cultural context.

Resilience in Dilemmatic Spaces

This final chapter of Part 1 completes a third layer in the articulation of a critical pedagogy of facilitation. So far, critical pedagogies informs intentions and practice (reflection on action), and practice has *become* performance (reflection in action). Now, the resilient facilitator works in the difficulty of the neoliberal cultural and political landscape, conceptualized here as the dilemmatic space. Where facilitation has been explored earlier in relation to the extent to which it can be framed *as* performance, this discussion also considers where 'being' might become an optimum facilitative, resilient stance.

The need for a resilient facilitator role is explored in the face of upheavals brought about by contemporary cultural drivers, imperatives and contradictory agendas. In these settings, the facilitator (whether teacher in an urban school, community worker, artist freelancer) commonly faces a lack of support, unrealistic expectations and competing demands. In this work, the shifting roles played by the facilitator and the kind of, or quality of, relationships forged with participants, pedagogical or otherwise, will be key. Self-reflexive awareness is key for the facilitator's well-being in the first instance, but also there are radical possibilities, where the acknowledgement of a 'pedagogy of discomfort' offers a possibility for the enactment of a critical, *political* facilitative pedagogy

Dilemmatic spaces

The growing 'anger and despair' expressed by troubled individuals and groups struggling with a whole host of challenges including the 'hidden injuries' of class and race, along with the 'social suffering' generated by poverty and exclusion, and displacement brought about by war and disputes over territories is compounded by the combined impacts of neoliberalism and globalization (Hoggett et al., 2009). The tendency to respond to the failure of social cohesion and harmony through the frame of 'poor behaviour', 'dysfunctional' or 'traumatized' individuals, families and groups can be reconceptualized through a deeper under-standing of the struggles experienced at the local level as placed in a tension with broader discourses at the macro level. Critical awareness of the wider context that produces the 'pressure cooker effect' (ibid.: 59) on individuals internalizing and externalizing frustration and anger gives the cultural worker a potential understanding of the complex and challenging circumstances within which they often find themselves working. Furthermore, the very same macro discourses place another structural set of contradictions that the cultural worker needs to negotiate within their working-life:

> The dispersal of state power to newly 'autonomized' agents seeks to de-politicize the spaces in which professionals, managers and organ-izations make decisions. In the process, responsibility for managing tensions and dilemmas becomes devolved to individual agents … Dilemmatic spaces tend to be experienced as personal, professional or ethical dilemmas. But they are rooted in wider tensions and contra-dictions, refracting the uneasy alignments between different regimes of governance … Each is also likely to privilege particular logics of decision-making and particular forms of practice. (Newman and Clark, 2009: 127)

Newman and Clark remind us that dilemmatic spaces, experienced, felt and struggled within, are contributed to by the organizational tensions and contradictions of neoliberal economies. These same social, economic and ideological circumstances have impacted across the public and voluntary sector, and on those professionals who work in paid and unpaid occupations as well as the more informal community and social development work occurring at street level.

The marketization of services and the 'outsourcing' of provision bring with them the need for measures of accountability. Professional languages that describe interventions as 'service provision' and 'delivery', with 'outcomes' and 'impacts' to 'service users' (see Hoggett, 2009) articulate technicist agendas where contradictory combinations of 'centralized control of targets and outputs' with 'increasing decentralization of responsibilities' (Hoggett et al., 2009: 147) put pressure on those working in the state and public sectors, specifically social, youth and community work, education, nursing and policing (see Hochschild, 2002; Mackintosh in Lloyd-Smith, 1999; Newbold, 2002; Rattue & Cornelius, 2002).

Applied Theatre projects operating in this complex terrain are often financially and competitively dependent on funding and public/third-sector grants targeted around agendas of civic renewal, health and welfare, and social inclusion. Against this social and material context and influenced by private-sector models and a marketized approach, the facilitator also becomes an 'autonomized agent' enacting the role as para-professional, delivering social work in community settings. The contradictory environment aptly characterized as the dilemmatic space seems far from being affirming and supportive for cultural workers to flourish in their practices.

'Acting for the best'

It is against the contradictions of the social and material context, and across the boundaries of state and civic life (Hoggett et al., 2009), that the dilemmatic space is experienced by and impacts on those living and working at in the front line. Hoggett (ibid.) describes how development workers, who face very tough decisions on a daily basis, often find themselves 'acting for the best' where there is 'no obvious right thing to do' (2009: 62). Similarly, in the context of education, teachers, working in deprived areas with high levels of need are also caught in a quandary of balancing cultures of inspections, targets and accountability with responding intuitively and informally on a human level to the urgent needs of the young people that they work with (Archer et al., 2010; Hargreaves, 1998, 2006; Preston, 2013).

When working in difficult conditions, a form of courage brought about by a critical resilience is crucial in order to feel able to make decisions, to work 'against the grain' at times, whilst being accountable to potential criticism when one needs to act intuitively 'for the best' in a particular situation. As Archer et al. suggest, 'for teachers to create spaces for their students to be heard and valued … relies, in part, on teachers feeling that they are heard and valued by others rather than being tired, stressed, and overwhelmed by their situation' (2010: 112). Hoggett et al. capture the highly skilled capacities and resilience required of the development worker 'to operate in shifting and ambiguous situations without becoming paralysed by the uncertainty, and to act and make decisions *and* to accept the risks accompanying this (including the risk that good decisions may have bad consequences)' (ibid: 68). As both Archer and Hoggett attest, speaking from the contexts of development work and education, effective cultural work requires a high level of mental and critical capacity that these workers and teachers need *besides* their official 'occupation' (as development workers, teachers, artists, nurses, etc.). Mental resources are never limitless: repeated experiences of conflicting situations and feelings of being overwhelmed and stressed will eventually take their toll if effective support is absent.

The critical facilitator working against this backdrop is faced with negotiating these very same personal and professional dilemmas of working in challenging settings where 'acting for the best' often sits in an uneasy compromise between a range of contradictory agendas and circumstances. The dilemmatic space *is* the inevitable context of Applied Theatre work. The reality is that the Applied Theatre practitioner, like the public-sector workers described, is often carrying responsibilities beyond their immediate remit; they experience little acknowledgement or support, often working in relative isolation, and furthermore exist on low-paid or voluntary contracts.

Critical reflection presents its own dilemma: the dilemma of colluding with an unacceptable situation. This is a difficult contradiction that is not easily resolved. We may agree that we have no real option but to acknowledge the uneasy compromises that are faced and to continue to labour in the dilemmatic space (despite its unacceptability). Politically this is problematic, as it colludes with neoliberal rhetoric (and resulting right-wing 'common sense' understanding) that there is no alternative. Acknowledging the contradiction means conversely to escape the potential double bind brought about by the no-win theory trap of the action versus non-action route that this could take us down. Paradoxically, the critical arts facilitator, however s/he practices – whether arts-led, play-led or issue-led – is driven by the belief in the possibility of finding (and facilitating) creative alternatives *for* and *with* the constituencies, or human beings, with whom s/he works. With this premise, the rest of the section attempts to offer some possibilities for practitioner resilience that engages the personal but goes beyond the individualized 'survival' or 'coping' mentality to consider a political economy of emotions. A critical resilience is born out of awareness of the wider challenges of working in dilemmatic spaces and unsatisfactory situations.

Although this feels negative, difficult, messy, and impossible, a critical resilience offers a positive way forward. Although, biologically and culturally, we like to imagine we should avoid pain and discomfort, and are 'sold' the idea that we can achieve perfection through comfort, this is a myth. As Brown[1] argues, humans are 'wired' for struggle and it is possible to find a courage to be vulnerable because this is what potentially enables us to grow. This final chapter of Part 1 aims to embraces a critical approach alongside the artistry that can be brought through a creative approach to thinking, reflecting and being in the dilemmatic space made productive *because* of difficulty, messiness and unpredictability.

The Artist-facilitator: The *art* of 'applied'

> What aspiring practitioners need most to learn, professional schools
> seem least able to teach. (Schön, 1987: 8)

Having previously identified in Chapter 2 the problem with the notion of
'applied' when approached from a positivist epistemology and associated
value judgements, I want now to return to Schön's point about the possibilities for *artistic relevance* in the dilemmatic space; particularly apt
in this context because of its easy alignment with the existing ethical
and moral concerns of (applied) theatre practices. The idea of artistic
relevance serves to argue for the importance of an explicit approach *as
applied* practice, particularly in the education of future practitioners.
Furthermore, as the quote above implies, the challenge of offering a
practice that is of direct relevance to the needs of the aspiring facilitator is an *artistic* struggle, and sits at the heart of an Applied Theatre
pedagogy. This 'artistic struggle', however, is less about the skills-based
competency of the aesthetic (which is a given), but rather, articulates
the resilience of the practitioner to respond creatively and dialectically
in the dilemmatic 'mess' of the real world. This notion of finding the
artistic relevance of the *applied* therefore has potential to reframe how
the practice of facilitation in dilemmatic spaces is professionalized and
ultimately how we teach and educate emerging facilitators.

In this vein, Donald Schön (1984, 1987) outlines the limited value,
or 'utility in practice', of scientific or positivist models that rely on
'technical rationality' and 'values of certainty'. When practitioners
enter the field, they:

> … find themselves caught in a dilemma. Their definition of rigorous
> professional knowledge excludes phenomena they have learned to
> see as central to their practice. And artistic ways of coping with these
> phenomena do not qualify as rigorous professional knowledge (Shön,
> 1984: 42)

As Schön identifies, the dilemma between rigour and relevance represents two different schools of thinking that circulate and that can be

seen in Applied Theatre where the professionalization of the field, and subsequent educational 'training' practice, sits within layers of contradiction. First, there is the contradiction between the methodology of participatory practices and the *knowledge* of that practice, which requires a context-based, case-study approach to understanding. Second, there can be ideological contradictions between theory and values, such as the aim of participation and the reality of dilemmatic spaces, for example the need to deliver outcomes, meet targets and 'fix' problems whilst responding to, and being 'real' with, participants and at the same time dealing with scrutiny by the commissioner of the work who can choose to discard the facilitator at a moment's notice. For the practitioner not to be totally overwhelmed by these paradoxes, to retain the core principles of working whilst being present in the work, one needs to embody preparedness for these contradictions and realities.

Schön outlines a conundrum present in teacher education where the academy privileges subject knowledge but then expects practitioners to know how to 'do' something with it; to apply knowledge in a context for a particular purpose. *Knowledge* and its *application* are clearly different entities. This can relate to a range of industries such as architecture and the fields of health and education as well as to theatre, where, in each context, the 'applied' represents a different sort of practice. Schön aligns this pedagogical dilemma as a contradiction between rigour and relevance and as akin to the 'high ground' and the 'low ground'. The high ground represents the skills and theories learned in the academy, where there is certainty and where theories are built via reliable and procedural approaches and techniques and where one can practise rigorously. The low ground is described as the 'swamp', where, Schön contends, exists the real-life problems of 'greatest human concern' (Schön, 1983: 42). He describes the practitioner as being presented with the choices:

> ... of remaining on the high ground ... or opting for the 'low ground' where one has to be 'willing to forsake technical rigor' ... There are

those who choose the swampy lowlands. They deliberately involve themselves in messy but crucially important problems and, when asked to describe their methods of inquiry, they speak of experience, trial and error, intuition, and muddling through. (ibid.: 43)

In contrast, those opting for the high ground are:

> ... devoted to an image of solid professional competence, or fearful of entering a world in which they feel they do not know what they are doing, they choose to confine themselves to a narrowly technical practice. (ibid.)

One can see how the temptation of aligning one's practice with the importance of 'professionalism' or 'aesthetic' competence creates a secure framework for understanding and assessing practice. As a professional artist, the 'certainties' that become agreed as 'good' practice become the prevailing mode of analysis but at the expense of being able to articulate the reality of uncertainty.

The capacity to draw on tacit, intuitive strategies, which are honed by working and talking with people of all kinds, are people-centred skills that are drawn from multidisciplinary sources such as, for example, counselling, group and community work, and adult learning. The subject-specific expertise of artists, not narrowly defined by 'artist method and skill', enables the honing of our artistic and creative capabilities for working with ordinary people in messy contexts. In this vein we are all artistic and creative when we are able to be flexible, able to view the ordinary anew with a fresh curiosity and be responsive to it. The *applied* artist potentially has this capacity in abundance, which can be embodied as a critical resilience that can equip her to deal with the swampy low ground of dilemmatic spaces. As Schön points out, 'it's no accident that professionals often refer to an "art" of teaching or management and use the term *artist* to refer to practitioners unusually adept at handling situations of uncertainty, uniqueness, and conflict' (Schön, 1987: 16).

In an attempt to express the capacities needed for a critical resilience, the following sections outline a series of alternative pedagogies which could be conceptualized, reframing them (applying Schön's thinking) *as* artistic qualities, for the facilitator working in the dilemmatic space. Such practices rearticulate sensibilities and qualities that are hard to express (and harder to hone as skills) but that are key for practitioner survival and crucial for enabling the practitioner access to the critical transformative possibilities of the role.

Keeping it 'real' – can I be myself?

> Children want the adults to give something of themselves. Be a human in this room. Give a little something … don't make it up. (Adam Annand – London Bubble. Speech Bubbles training, 2015)[2]

In a context of uncertainty it can feel risky for a practitioner to put aside the objectivity, distance and expectation that comes with the role of professional, teacher, artist and so on and let participants see her 'as a person' (Rogers, 1994: 23). Carl Rogers discusses the challenge for the practitioner (in his example, a teacher) who 'knows she is not as expert as she appears. She knows that … she has her good days and her bad ones … If she let her mask slip, if she showed herself as she is, there would be questions to which she would have to answer "I don't know"' (ibid.). Understandably, practitioners working in unpredictable environments may be more drawn to play it safe. Yet research with practitioners in urban settings indicates that particularly when working and forging relationships with participants where there is a high level of need, revealing one's personable, 'human' qualities in the facilitative relationship has been crucial for forging effective relationships with young people as it gets to the heart of people's need for recognition and respect (Lister, 2004; Archer et al., 2010; Preston, 2013). As Rogers points out, 'many a student has his façade too, and often his mask is even more impenetrable' (Rogers, 1983: 24), so in the moments when we 'show' some of ourselves in our work we are demonstrating genuineness and regard which might create the possibility for the risk of reciprocity.

Example: 'head on the block'

This is my first session with the women at the Willow Day Centre. We are all trepidatious and the women are initially reluctant to join me saying resolutely that they are not going to do any drama. Despite sensing some hostility, I summon up my confidence and enthusiasm in persuading people on to their feet to have a go. After a name game, I ask the group to mould each other as if they were pieces of clay to show the others how they feel today. Maggie shows someone crying, Belinda depicts someone with her arms crossed, at peace or death, I join in depicting someone quaking & scared, and Tania does the same as me. We laugh and talk about our images. I then try to explain how we can build a story through our actions. To demonstrate I enter the space and kneel with my head down. Tania then enters the image and ties an imaginary noose around my neck! Then Belinda comes in as the executioner! I think and then say out loud, 'Are you trying to kill me off already?' As I voice this thought to the group we all laugh and the ice begins to break.

From this short extract, insight can be gained into the dynamics of an interaction, a moment involving myself as facilitator beginning work with a group and the first tentative steps of making some drama. In the writing of the thick description I tried to offer an honest depiction of 'me' and the anxiety I felt as I negotiated my role as an outsider, enlisting the women's reluctant participation and attempting to transform a computer room into a workshop space. The women's conscious performing of metaphors of death and despair in response to how they were feeling that day speaks volumes regarding their feelings of reluctance to participate in this first session. Early on I take a risk, by participating within the drama *with* the group to demonstrate its possibilities; I literally and metaphorically put my 'head on the block'. As they build on the text created, which then depicts the execution of the facilitator, I decide in the moment without thinking that I'm going to verbalize this tension in the room. I amusedly verbalize this: 'Are you trying to kill me off already?' The response seems to have the effect of relaxing people and creating a moment of joint pleasure through laughter. Relief! The permission for laughter at the shared moment and at each other creates possibilities for the next step.

Whether or not this particular act was a 'good' or a 'bad' thing to do, as a strategy, describing what you see or reflecting on the moment in front of you is a facilitation choice that can be powerful. Furthermore, a capacity to reveal, in a very human way, one's own vulnerability, by using humour, to feel able to gently play with some harsh feedback, takes some courage but can effectively diffuse conflict and move us a step towards working together.

Of course we have many 'selves' we could employ (some more appropriate than others) so we still need to challenge the idea that there is one person who might represent *me*. Reflecting on my own habits, I know that *who I am* and *how I am* alters according to situations: I behave in different ways in certain contexts with different people. A secondary school teacher who works in an inner-city school put this very clearly when she said:

> I am very much 'me' with the students. [pause] I do remember, I think, putting on a persona when I first started teaching and now those two things are quite closely connected so I do feel like I'm 'me' but I do have a light distance. I want every student to know that I really care about them and where they're at and I want them to know that I know them, I really know them. So I always know their names, I always know something about them and I know that's what makes a difference; that they know that I know them and what happens to them matters. (Preston, 2013: 235)

As this teacher explains, being able to be 'me' signifies a will to make a genuine connection with the young people. Letting the young people get to know 'her' as she gets to know 'them' is key to establishing a reciprocal, working relationship with the students. There is, however, also a performed aspect to the parts of her identity/personality that she decides she will share, which is revealed when she also says 'I let them know the 'me' that I want them to know' (ibid.).

The acknowledgement of the 'multiple "me"s' that may be present and that are possible in a moment offers the facilitator potential for a reflexive analysis of the layers operating around his/her actions and simply to *notice* one's impact in a setting. Developing an analysis *between* the conscious act of knowing and performing, and our intuitive action or experiencing 'in the moment' with others might offer unique insights into the dynamic of facilitation.

'In a mess'

A teacher of arithmetic, listening to a child's question, becomes aware of a kind of confusion, and, at the same time, a kind of intuitive understanding, for which she has no readily available response. Because the unique case falls outside the categories of existing theory and technique, the practitioner cannot treat it as an instrumental problem to be solved by applying one of the rules in her store of knowledge. The case is not 'in the book'. If she is to deal with it competently, she must do so by a kind of improvisation, inventing and testing in the situation strategies of her own devising. (Schön, 1987: 5)

When in her element, the facilitator is able to draw on a kind of tacit wisdom of knowing what to do that occurs in the moment. This fluid combining of knowledge and instinctive response that occurs when things are working well is akin to a form of *facilitator flow* mentioned earlier. This understanding, brought about by an amalgamation of previous experience and knowledge of the situation is not in some textbook of games and exercises, but an effective bringing together of personal creativity and cognition. Like skilled improvisers, intuitive responses don't appear by magic – as on a wing and a prayer (although it might look like it). Intuitive understanding is action that arises *through* the capacity to listen, observe and respond *with* the 'confusion' of the moment – in that context, at that point in time. 'End-gaming' and ignoring 'the mess' potentially leads to misjudgement of a situation, bringing about the 'wrong' response for that moment. The following vignette reveals the impact of a facilitation decision through an exercise with young women in an urban school, some of whom had been referred because of their challenging behaviour. In this session we were looking at triggers to conflict through the stimulus of the question 'What happens when communication goes wrong?' The young women devised scenes of their own making in response.

Example: drama with Year 9 girls in a London school

A small group created a typical scene between a teacher and a pupil where the pupil seemed to be deliberately ignoring the teacher and talking. In the drama the teacher tells her off and ridicules her publicly. The situation escalates, both parties engaged in a battle of power and trying to save face. The teacher eventually wins the battle, belittles the pupil further and banishes her from the classroom. We introduced the strategy of 'feeling angels' into the exercise. Volunteers were asked to stand by the characters and after each statement an 'angel' voiced the character's feelings. The idea was to develop deeper awareness of the feelings that drive the position statements that people make. The group resisted the idea. Eventually, with cajoling, volunteer 'angels' reluctantly got up and complied with the task with half-hearted responses: 'I feel angry' ... 'I feel ridiculed'. When it came to the teacher character there were no volunteers for the feeling angel. The young women had disengaged, their gaze elsewhere. (Preston, 2011: 258–9)

In this moment where the facilitators make the choice to invite the young women to reflect on their feelings about a tricky exchange with a teacher, employing the strategy of *feeling angels* lets slip an intention to endgame by pre-empting the direction of the work. In an instant this was noticed by the young people, who collectively and immediately disengaged. Why? Perhaps they felt this was not what had been negotiated at the outset; the presence of the reluctant-feeling angels had shifted the goalposts and the facilitator was faced with a position of cajoling the participants to join in. However, we need to consider the intentions for the implementation of this strategy (remembering that the purpose here is not to berate or moralize about facilitation choices). I believe that, in that moment, we felt concerned that the content of the young women's drama was biased against the teacher. The scene as it stood could be read as a hard luck story by the young people who are treated unfairly by the 'bad' teacher, but in this scene the teacher was also being treated in a troublesome way by the pupils. The facilitators felt a duty to enable the young people to see different points of view of a situation that was very common to their lives and that was often replicated, outside the workshop space, in their classrooms. There was some evidence of this – in fact the learning mentor who attended the sessions had already told us that some teachers were scared of these young women. From the young women's response to the teacher within the drama, it is not difficult to see why a teacher might feel intimidated. A common, perhaps predictable, problematic teacher–pupil transaction had emerged, but one that was richer in complexity than it seemed. The feeling angel exercise required the young people to publicly empathize with the teacher and yet it appeared to them that this was didactic; they were not ready for this. My belief is that the young people had picked up a shift from an initially open-ended task exploring 'What happens when …?' to an exercise that seemed to have the learning objective of making the young women reflect on *their* actions. The young women reacted defensively to the task and its facilitation by refusing to engage. Elsewhere I have written that this defensive reaction could be conceptualized as a *moral anger* (ibid.). Because the situation felt unjust, the young women were not willing to engage with the feelings of the teacher.

Having noted that this strategy wasn't 'working', we moved on to the other scenes that had been devised. In contrast, the young women appeared to enjoy reflecting on these scenes and looking at moments of communication breakdown through the interactions between the characters. In the latter part of the session they 'forgot' themselves; we observed their participation as they re-engaged with the *flow* of the session, spontaneously engaging with the characters' life-choices.

However, reflecting on our actions as facilitators, it might also be interesting to think now about how we might have stayed 'in the mess' with the young people and their disengagement from the scene. There are several directions staying with the scene could have taken had we not felt the discomfort and moved on to the next exercise. The simple question 'What's happening here?' leading on to the explorative question 'Isn't it interesting that we don't want to be the angel for the teacher ... I wonder what that's about?' might have opened up some frank and open discussion about the topic. This was the potent scene, the scene that got to the heart of the issues that these young people were facing on a daily basis. Having noticed that the young women perhaps didn't feel safe (hence their disengagement), we might perhaps have found ways of making the exercise safer for them. Instead, because we felt uncomfortable that *they* felt uncomfortable, we moved on to the next topic.

Heathcote's metaphor of all drama being about 'a man in a mess' is a wonderful analogy for drama but also for the acknowledgement of the real-world, dual 'mess' of facilitation. If one can find the resilience to stay in facilitation chaos, it might be possible to tolerate the 'mess' of the dramatic fiction (and the apparent poor moral decisions contained in it) without feeling the need to rewrite the outcome. It might have been possible to introduce a stop-think moment for all in the room and to invite the young women's opinions on the process and the content of the drama. For the facilitator, having the courage to stay in a mess and to tolerate the confusion of the moment confronts the reality and potential that this might bring. It is a creative state of *facilitation flow* where the immediate 'not knowing' might bring about the 'right' direction, rather than a pre-conceived position of a knowing, endgaming, procedural approach which may not respond to the needs of participants. The example reveals how a facilitation approach, pulled from a toolbox of techniques that in theory might have seemed the 'right' strategy, in actual fact missed the mark with these young women, who were already wise to attempts to change their behaviour in other aspects of their lives. Even so, there were possibilities to stay in the mess and engage with the challenges of the situation.

A pedagogy of discomfort

Educators must deal with the messy issues that others cannot or do not want to address. (Megan Boler, 2004: 4)

Example:

Laura (*white student*):	Should we call it black theatre?
Mary (*white student*):	It's divisive, as these issues affect white too.
Jon (*non-white student*):	Eighty per cent of people in these estates are black people ... These issues affect us.
Marcus (*non-white student*):	There is a need for this. It's relatable. Most theatre is written by white males.
Laura (*white student*):	It's often about the negative aspects.
Kevin (*white student*):	I'd rather forget whether it's black or white.
Ben (*white student*):	It's been told many times. It's conforming to stereotypes.
Jon:	It's reality!
Eloise (*non-white student*):	People need to realize that playwrights are writing about what they have experienced.
Jon:	There *are* more black people on these housing estates; that's their life.
Marshall (*non-white student*):	Are black actors limited to certain roles?
Laura:	These discussions segregate society.
Marcus:	These plays are staged at the Royal Court; usually the majority audience have no experience of these communities.

These exchanges occurred in a lecture involving approximately 40 Applied Theatre undergraduate students, predominantly white, but with a range of racial and class backgrounds present. The students were responding to a question posed by visiting black scholar Lynette

Goddard, who had asked whether they felt new writing, and a recent increase of stories about black working-class communities, had been blighted by a 'ghetto' mentality. The scholar was referring to a provocative article on this subject that had been written by a journalist who described himself as a black British (mixed-race) Londoner, but also an Oxford-educated media critic who writes for *The Times* and the *Daily Mail.* As an observer I became aware that this article, along with the students' responses, seemed to be raising a significant range of problematic discourses around race and difference that presently circulate in society.

What felt striking about this brief exchange was the consistency, on this occasion,[3] with which the 'white' and 'non-white' students seemed, without exception, to be occupying polar-opposite subject positions within the debate. I noticed that statements that homogenized or invisibilized difference in terms of race – 'It's divisive, as these issues affect white too'/'Should we call it black theatre?'/'I'd rather forget whether it's black or white' – were expressed solely by the white students, whereas the non-white students emphasized the real-life, social context of the issue along with their own self-identification: 'There *are* more black people on these housing estates; that's their life'/'It's relatable'/'It's reality'/'These issues affect *us*'. Present in this latter discourse was the need for change: to redress the balance of *who* writes and *what* is written, and to draw awareness – 'There is a need for this ... Most theatre is written by white males'/'the majority audience have no experience of these communities'.

The arguments presented by the white students offer a stark reminder of continual hegemonic narratives of race that gain acceptance through a pseudo-political correctness achieved via the liberal rhetoric of 'We're *all* different.' As a subject position, this line of argument ignores the need for a particular acknowledgement of difference, which exposes historic levels of privilege and marginalization and the resulting standpoints. The counterargument by the non-white students was a political one, articulating the need to make visible the reality of black working-class experience. A third dimension of the argument was the provocation that had been presented by the columnist, himself a black man, in the first place, critiquing the Royal Court for creating 'theatre of the ghetto' where black and British identities had been characterized as exclusively working class and urban. This middle-class journalist took issue with the fact that, as a member of the minority, he felt at risk of being trapped in this 'urban' stereotype and was keen to disassociate himself. This latter discourse complicates any binary understandings of subject positions based purely on racial distinctions since, in this instance, class also becomes significant.

Reflecting on the pedagogical possibilities of this interaction in terms of facilitation draws attention to the difficulties of exploring powerful narratives on race and class with a heterogeneous group who will inevitably express the full range of contradictory personal, emotional and political responses to the issues.

To give a little more context to this discussion with the students, I had previously noticed that in conversations about race, black or non-white students were often silent on the issues even when other students took controversial positions that seemed not to represent their interests. It was myself as (a white, middle-class) lecturer who tended to be the one to challenge, provide alternative perspectives and attempt to generate knowledge and deepen understanding of the topics. I expect the black/non-white students didn't feel safe enough expressing views that contradicted their peers at this point, and perhaps felt that they should not be called on, by default, to speak for the black community. Although I understood this, I felt uncomfortable speaking on behalf of the non-white students and often educating black students about their history and assuming, despite my own background, a position of authority on topics of race and class. However, at the same time I felt it was necessary to do so, as I was explicitly trying to de-invisibilize race and class and enable these issues to be discussed openly.[4]

To return to this particular example, on this occasion the non-white students were more vocal than they had previously been. This felt positive, a contrast to previous scenarios, and I concluded that some might be feeling a sense of permission or confidence owing to the presence of a black visiting scholar. However, their views thereby came directly into conflict with what was arguably a hegemonic position taken by some of the white students: that there was no need for black theatre. This was an inherently problematic position because it didn't take into account the politics and histories of inequalities of representations of race and hence potentially jeopardized the voices of the non-white students in the room. This jeopardizing of voices needs to be put in the context of an 'historicised ethics'[5] (Boler, 2004: 4).

For a critical facilitator the collective subject positions represented in the room by these students offered rich material and there was a clear opportunity to draw attention to these discourses. In such situations it might be argued that the facilitator has a responsibility to facilitate a critically informed discussion and to respond to these comments by framing them in the context of the wider discourses of race and difference present in society. By reframing the students' statements as 'positions' within a wider ideological discourse they would be, in theory, protected from feeling personally attacked and thus be more open to encountering a different view. Facilitation, or teaching in this context, acts as a 'disruptive pedagogy' that draws attention to the habits, emotions and common-sense views that inform our understandings (see Faulkner, 2012), in this case, of race and class. It is possible to see how, *in theory*, one might address these issues from a critical pedagogy/facilitation position, but this is always more challenging in practice. I would like to draw attention to the issue of *discomfort*, which I believe was present in the room, and the role that our emotions play in the pedagogical choices that are made in such moments of facilitation.

In this particular moment, faced with this disparity of views from the group, the lecturer made a choice not to comment directly on individual statements, responding instead in a non-committal, but open way to each as in 'Mmm … that's interesting, what do others think?', thus opening up the floor to take another opinion. In this moment she performed the role as listener, witness (as we all did), but also curator of a range of voices and subject positions to be expressed in the room. This is a good example of the facilitation of an inclusive, participatory discussion where a sense of balance was created in an 'equality' of views expressed. Arguably the lecturer did not need to say much, as the students presented their own counterarguments to the problematic positions taken. There may be a number of reasons for making the choice not to intervene any more directly than this, the most obvious one being that, as a visiting lecturer speaking with a relatively large group, she may not have felt it judicious to raise contentious issues in her transient professional role. One might argue, however, that this approach enabled students' personal opinions to dominate the discussion without being framed in a wider context. This potentially led to a disregard, in the moment, of the wider political and historical context of race and the varied forms that institutionalized racism takes.

Because of the intense sensitivities that surround the politics of race, including anxiety about unwittingly perpetuating racist attitudes, to critique a lecturer 'doing her best' feels like an incredibly emotive position to take, yet it feels necessary to engage with the problem. I feel compelled to remind the reader that I too have been in situations where I did not act to challenge problematic views. The earlier example in Chapter 1, drawn from a mental health setting, elucidates the point, as does the 'feeling angel' example discussed earlier. As readers and facilitators potentially engaging in challenging settings, 'doing our best' and finding a genuine compassion for the difficulty facilitators experience in moments like this, as part of reflection on action where on-the-spot decisions are made, is crucially important.

I would suggest that the lecturer's choice not to take a position within this discussion revealed a series of dilemmas arising from *discomfort* on a range of levels which impacted on her facilitatory and pedagogical choices (her reflection in action) at that time, and which in turn impacted on how a crucial issue such as addressing racism was handled. I am not suggesting, however, that the feeling of discomfort necessarily leads one to make a 'wrong' decision. In fact, the feeling of discomfort in itself heightens our sensitivity and alertness to the potency of a moment, which might be crucial in deciding where to go next. I do not believe that this choice was 'wrong' or particularly 'right', although I do believe there were problems emerging from this strategy. Ultimately, I do not feel that it is useful to engage in 'hand-wringing' regarding what 'should' (or should not) have been done in any particular situation, as this exacerbates the problem by playing into a blame culture, which serves to individualize the problems and thereby disregard the wider cultural contradictions and misunder-standings that inhibit discussion and on some level maintain racism. We are *all* affected by these discourses, and for the facilitator the way we understand these dynamics crucially affects the way we self-reflect and influences our future actions. It is crucial, therefore, that the impact of our decisions (such as to act or not to act) is understood in the wider cultural context. The tendency to moralize and individualize through self-blame can be reframed. This example demonstrates the importance of acknowledging the 'doing' (and our 'feeling' responses) to a crucial social and political issue and to note the regimes of emotion that are operating.

The layers of discomfort felt in a situation such as this may be due to several factors. First, there is the sensing of the potential discomfort of others and feeling a responsibility towards them. A participant's awkward articulation of a belief or of something they have observed may be an indicator of something being expressed for the first time. This person may be vulnerable, lack a wider socio-political understanding of their statement and may be reproducing a belief held within their household or community. This presents a dilemma for the educator/facilitator, who is committed to pedagogies that consciously resist silencing, and who works instead towards respecting and affirming people's views and being able to 'hold' different opinions within the group. Freedom of speech is held as a totem in modern liberal democ-racies and education is seen as an important space to allow expression by 'all'. We may also feel uncomfortable with our position of power and privilege as lecturer in imposing our ideas, having a more informed voice than others and risking silencing others as a result. We may also have had previous negative experiences of challenging students and encountered defensive, even hostile, resistance. We may also be aware that getting into conflict over views can generate a locked-in oppositional resistance by default ('I'm entitled to my opinion'), which reduces the possibility of any shifting of positions. We may feel personally offended by positions that are taken, and be struggling with the 'best' response at that time. We may be unsure of how our own identity as a black or white lecturer, and the position we are taking, is being perceived by the group. We may have had similar responses in the past and this alone can generate an understandable dilemma for the educator/facilitator encountering such tension on each new occasion, which might lead to an habitual avoidance of sensitive topics. All of these are valuable responses that are also emotionally influenced and that draw attention to the wider cultural, political and pedagogical dilemmas and serve to remind us of the relationship between our emotional responses, our own world-view and the choices we make.

We also perhaps need to make a distinction here between a *liberal* practice and a *critical* practice, noting as we do the ethical difference between these two approaches. Megan Boler reminds us that in the classroom not all speech is free, so the liberal position of fairness and parity and allowing space for all voices to be 'equally' present needs to be reappraised: 'Power inequities institutionalized through economies, gender roles, social class and corporate-owned media ensure that not all voices carry the same weight' (Boler, 2004: 3). In the light of the inequity of voices, Boler proposes an 'affirmative action pedagogy' that commits itself to critical engagement with 'any expression of racism, homophobia, anti-Semitism, sexism, ableism, classism' (ibid: 4). Such a pedagogy 'ensures that we bear witness to marginalized voices in our classrooms, even at the minor cost of limiting dominant voices' (ibid.). Her proposal is not to mount what she sees as the impossible: to sanitize or neutralize what is spoken or 'uttered' in the classroom, or even to prevent the inevitable 'hostility' that will emerge. In fact she argues that an affirmative action pedagogy requires 'more than rational dialogue':

[A] discussion on racism or homophobia cannot rely simply on rational exchange but must delve into the deeply emotional investments and associations that surround perceptions of difference and ideologies. One is potentially faced with allowing one's worldviews to be shattered, in itself, a profoundly emotionally charged experience. (ibid.)

For Boler, therefore, the moment described in the opening of this section is a highly 'teachable moment' (ibid.), as is the refusal brought about by the earlier feeling angel exercise, even if both strategies were initially misjudged.

The proposal for an affirmative action pedagogy that 'shatters' is challenging for the facilitator faced with the need to confront their own discomforts and to work creatively with the discomfort of others. However, as Boler notes, we have little option:

[T]he risky business of addressing emotions within our classrooms is a productive and necessary direction for the exploration of social justice and education … In order to name, imagine, and materialize a better world, we need an account of how Western discourses of emotion shape our scholarly work, as well as pedagogical recognition of how emotions shape our classroom interactions. (Boler, 1999: 77)

Helping students to understand how regimes of emotions impact on our views, opinions and understandings of the major issues that confront society offers the student a perspective through which to understand the politics of their own feeling responses. As Boler articulates, for the white person engaging with the spectre of racism, it is possible to engage in the discomforts of ambiguity via the precarious, relational construction of our identities without resorting to guilt (Boler, 1999).

For the facilitator, the feeling of discomfort is an inevitable and important *effect* of the dilemmatic space and a means through which to become aware of a range of pedagogical possibilities and political necessities for change that are present. Facilitating others (whether children, young people or adults) to tolerate discomfort by understanding our emotional investments as we engage with the unfamiliar and the potential 'shattering of world views' (Boler, 2004: 4) is a necessary part of critical facilitation.

A pedagogy of resilience

We have looked already at the multifaceted roles that are inevitably played by facilitators in their attempts to enable and build effective structures of working, where the quality of the relationship forged with participants, pedagogical or otherwise, is paramount. As cultural workers operating in complex and unpredictable contexts in the face of contemporary cultural drivers, imperatives and contradictory agendas, experiencing a lack of support and having to deal with one's own and others' difficult 'feeling' responses is part of the necessary cultural work involved. Awareness of the inevitability (along with the contradictions) of the emotional labour that is involved in working dilemmatic spaces is important, not only for the facilitator's well-being, but for an effective critical facilitative pedagogy. A pedagogy of facilitator resilience is conceptualized here, as is the need to support facilitators to harness the following capacities in themselves and each other.[6]

1. To be able to exist 'in the mess': to be able to acknowledge and work with uncertainty, ambiguity and complexity.
2. To 'listen' to what is happening and draw on a courage to enable us to act in the moment where there is no obvious 'right thing to do'.
3. To engage in a critical reflection on one's actions, motives and choices in a curious and non-judgemental way that can acknowledge strengths and weaknesses but that can also see these as part of a relational and cultural dynamic.
4. To be sensitive to one's own personal feelings that arise (such as shame, anger, resentment, hope, cynicism and passion), but also to listen with a cultural awareness that can connect one's own feelings with regimes of emotion.

5. To be able to draw on one's critical knowledge of the themes and discourses that are being played out.

Cultivating the personal resources to *feel*, *act* and *be* in the moment, especially during moments of difficulty and challenge, takes work and requires that the practitioner is able to see the dilemma's s/he is experiencing as part of a political whole of which the self is an important but not by any means the sole element. As Applied Theatre emerges, the key challenge for facilitation is supporting the development of intuitive skills, of sensitivity to the moment, being able to listen and read what is happening, sitting with discomfort, and then being able to respond creatively in the moment in a way that will move things on, through helping to develop the thoughts and ideas offered by participants.

Working *with* the material offered by the participants takes facilitation to the next level, moving beyond the task-based experience and guided by instrumental objectives, moving beyond the 'intentions' focus of a practice to genuinely dialogical, generative and creative processes. Developing intuitive facilitation is a challenge for the coaching of emerging practitioners, not least because it involves honing a practice of unconscious expertise that happens in the moment as the facilitator 'thinks on her feet' and 'knows' what to do, how to adapt and reshape what is happening. It is not something that can be pre-planned or rehearsed and demands a strong capacity for improvisation.

Some people are drawn more easily to responding to others and will find themselves in an organic way mirroring, echoing and summarizing what is being said to them: they seem to possess a 'natural' capacity to do this as they seek to be 'in tune' with those they are with. Such capacities can be aligned with the 'person-centred' approaches (drawn from Rogerian counselling) of practising genuineness and responsiveness through listening, summarizing and paraphrasing, and this will take some practice to become instinctual.

Judith Kennedy writes about strategies that help develop intuition in trainee teachers who are at the borders of being unsuccessful. She identifies that these struggling teachers had difficulty in calling on their intuitive skills. In the classroom context, she describes how these trainee teachers:

> ... showed little awareness or sense of classroom realities – they can be insensitive to learner reactions, showing little flexibility or ability to 'think on their feet', and little intuitive judgement at any stage. (Kennedy, 2002: 47)

With these trainee teachers a common theme was an over-concern and anxiety about one's self-performance, and this prevented them from being aware of what was happening in the room. Kennedy established that the following core conditions needed to be created in these teachers to enable the capacity for working intuitively:

1. To alleviate anxiety by reducing over-observation,
2. To increase confidence through planning, thus reducing the amount of 'new' potentially overwhelming material to be engaging with at any point.
3. To not over-plan, therefore creating 'relative freedom' to allow spontaneity.
4. To enable focusing on the situation (or the participants) rather than the self. (Kennedy 2002)

Drawing on the Rogerian notion of person-centredness and these findings leads us towards a form of mindfulness that centres on observing and noticing, and being in the here and now (see Kabat-Zinn, 1994; Williams and Penman, 2011). Practising a mindfulness-influenced approach can engender a resilience to the stress brought about by the dilemmas of facilitation and an ability to *move towards* the challenges that are being faced:

1. Encouraging the teacher/facilitator *to notice* and to prioritize what is going on around her is a first step.
2. Developing awareness of one's tendencies to distraction (such as anxiety, which can take the form of over-concern with ourselves and our own performance) is the second step.

3. Noticing how this anxiety presents itself in our bodies and in the bodies of others is key.

4. Finally, being aware that our *plan* (what we had previously decided we were going to do) can take us away from what is happening in the present is important, but so is constantly thinking through how our values are shaping our approach with the participants.

The distinction made by Argyris and Schön (1992) and Schwarz (1994) between *espoused theory* and *theory in use* enables us to make the connection between the facilitators' values, one's aesthetic ideals and one's practice in use. This is helpful for an understanding of facilitator dilemmas brought about when our intuitive impulse is in conflict with our values, for example when what we do/say is not what we intended. Espoused theory reflects our values and beliefs about what we *say* we would do in a given situation (Schwarz, 1994). Theory in use is what we actually *do* – 'the theory you actually employ to design and act out your behaviour' (ibid.: 70). Schwarz explains that theory in use is very powerful because of the speed, skill and effortlessness that can be employed via the process of acting or responding intuitively. However, one is often 'typically unaware of what your theory-in-use is or how you are using it to design your behavior … If you had to think about it [it] would slow you down considerably and, at least, temporarily, make you less skilled' (Schwarz, 1994: 70).

Schwarz is locating the intuitive processes that facilitators (and anyone) employ, and for this to be effectively *applied* requires a strong sense of intention and consistent values to underpin them. Developing clarity around one's espoused theory is important, but the practice-based moments of action in context will also begin to inform one's espoused theory. Therefore, enabling facilitators to be really clear on their values and intentions, as well as having opportunities to practise in a real context, will enable the development of facilitator confidence and alignment with one's values in the moment of practice.

Van Manen discusses the phenomenology of pedagogical tact as a quality of knowing that occurs in the moment of practice, as in knowing when to say something and when to wait;[7] an active confidence that emerges from a deep sensitivity to the situation:

> A phenomenology of tactful action may reveal several styles of intuitive practice: from acting in a largely self-forgetful manner to a kind of running inner speech that the interior eye of the ego maintains with the self. This split awareness of self manifests itself as a kind of natural schizophrenia whereby one part of the self somehow dialogues with the other part. Teachers often say things such as: 'part of me wanted to complete the lesson and another part of me knew that I should stop and deal with the concern that had arisen'. (Van Manen, 2008: 13).

Van Manen discusses moments where *contemporaneous reflection* can occur that allows for a 'stop and think' in the moment. The opening three chapters of the book have identified a range of examples in which the facilitator steps back from the flow of the moment and makes a choice about where to go next. Reflection on action after the event may or may not tell us whether or not this was the 'right thing to do' at the time, but a reflection in action can help us to make choices in the moment.

Summary

Engagement and acknowledgement of critical facilitation as *practice* requires a conceptual understanding of politics, context and intention, but also needs the facilitator to operate a flexible, multifaceted approach that can embody and respond sensitively to the tacit, unspoken feelings and actions that are present when working with people. These are sensibilities that can act as a kind of barometer for the facilitator. Being able to 'read the room' includes listening to our own feeling responses as well as listening to others; what they say and don't say, and what they do and don't do – all these factors provide vital sources of information for the facilitator.

A resilient and mindful approach aligned with a critical facilitation practice can provide us with the capacity to notice and engage with what is happening in the room. Having the capacity to engage, even flourish, with discomfort, and the courage to harness an intuitive sense of where to go next is crucial when working in the dilemmatic space, but of equal importance is an insight into the broader social and cultural themes that lie beneath the surface of people and contexts with which we seek to engage.

Part Two

Case Studies: Pedagogies, Practices and Contexts

4

Send in the Clowns

Paul Murray

The fidget

I have always been a fidget. I've always moved around a lot. I had lived in eight different cities in three different countries with a mother, a sister and two different fathers by the time I was eight. Moving around in between strange and different cities and countries when I was young meant I was left with a strong desire to 'fit in', not to appear different; to be accepted as being like everyone else; to appear normal. To this end I became a keen observer and listener, picking up local characteristics, habits and traditions with which to perform my new identities.

On the simplest level I often felt most uncomfortable *sounding* different to everyone else, so I soon learnt how to change my accent. I saw no value in being different; on the contrary, the consequences of being thought of as such (in the playground) could have been dire. As I got older I developed a second and more sophisticated line of defence, that was (unlike a specific accent) applicable to any environment. I began to study how people behaved together: for example, how they made groups, where the power was, who were the leaders, who were the followers and how they played their status games. My last line of defence was to practise subservience: 'Don't bite me I am not worth biting.'

I honed these performance techniques over time. I was good enough at them that, although I went to nine different schools in eleven years, I was never picked on or bullied. I learned the benefits for survival of being a good performer; of being inauthentic; of performing other than myself and learning the rules of the game.

Despite appearances to the contrary, however, I was living in a state of constant flux and fear, always feeling like an outsider but trying not to show it. I was never relaxed. The only authenticity I felt was as a faker: someone who looked like they fitted in and was quite relaxed but didn't feel like it. I was a liar, a rogue, a scared one: '[He] … has the characteristic of the Brechtian rogue: cowardice. Or at any rate courage insufficient to the occasion … A passive sort of fellow (Azdak) acts less than he *reacts* …' (Bentley, 2008: 208).

The actor

It should be clear to you by now what my attraction is to the theatre. The self-confessed inauthenticity of the theatre makes me feel 'at home'. The theatre values extremely highly my abilities to explore the possibilities of being other than who I think I might be: my abilities to play, perform and transform. In fact who I think I might be is of no concern to the theatre; it gives me the chance to be who I am by performing who I am not.

It is in the theatre where I have always felt safe to *act*, to be honest about my inauthenticity (or inauthentic about my honesty). It is the one place I have always been completely free from any fear about my identity crises/experiments. It is where I am at peace, however chaotic the process may look to an outsider. In *my* theatre fidgets are welcomed as skilled improvisers or players. Here the re-actors are the actors.

I discovered the theatre space to be a safe place to play, to finally feel myself, but I didn't just want to keep my discovery locked in a 'safe' playhouse. I wanted to try acting/playing with the outside world rather than merely (as I had been up to now) reacting to it.

Although discovered and honed in purpose-built spaces, the theatre space I found most hospitable and safe was not any particular building; it was a state of mind, a way of seeing, a gaze, through which anything, anyone, anywhere could be reimagined. This gaze offered me a completely different view about my own feelings of inauthenticity. In the theatre space (the mental playground that I now carried between my ears) *nothing* is authentic, *nothing* is immovable, *nothing* is fixed; even the most solid looking people and structures have play to be found within them: everything is fragile.

Acting out: The street performer

It was not enough to keep this discovery within theatre buildings, where people came ready to disbelieve. I sought to test myself as a player on the street, where, by and large, people just wanted to get on with their normal lives. I wanted to be seen. I wanted to transform the streets by performing in them and transform people by encountering them through performance: to somehow playfully disrupt the course of their day to a point where our game took precedence (even for a short time) over what they considered to be important before they came into contact with me (e.g. buying potatoes or going to work). 'People going about their ordinary business are hard to divert from their tasks and … will only take much notice [of theatre] if they are mystified or if they feel they might miss something unique and special' (Mason', 1992: 92). It's not an easy job, but someone's got to do it!

Our performing group's simple aim was to get people, anyone, to stop and play, to improvise with us as we sang songs in made-up languages, improvised magic rituals and failed miserably with attempts at breakdancing and 'escapology'. Over a period of three years we kept going onto the street to find people to play with. I think this is why people played with us: because they perhaps felt mystified by the fact that the game couldn't happen without them. Suddenly you're playing with complete strangers; you've 'got them'. You can always tell when people are playing with you, when they have entered the theatre with you.

The years we spent street performing taught me three important lessons:

1. Not everyone wanted me to blend in, to be 'normal'. Many seemed to want someone to play with, and valued that I offered them the chance.
2. When I imagined everyone on the street being people who are trying to fit in and act normally, be serious, but would much rather just be playing, then it was easier to get them to play with me.
3. I was somehow being subversive. Even though the content of our performances could not be identified as being political in any way, we felt we were somehow undermining a dominant mood or way of seeing, even for a minute or two, and that this was significant. I became intrigued by this feeling and wanted to have the guts to pursue this type of playful subversion.

The theatre director

On the back of one of our street performances I was asked whether I could run some theatre workshops with a group of people with a history or diagnosis of mental health problems. Having no experience in this area of work but needing the money, I agreed to meet with the group. I was scared. I had never to my knowledge met mental patients before. What was I supposed to do with them? Are they properly crazy? Do they know I am not a psychologist?

I began to look for advice that could help me to work with *mentally ill people*. I turned to the literature on drama therapy, forum theatre, play therapy and so on, but although much of it made sense to me, I could not see myself using any of the methods suggested. They all seemed so serious!

In my panic I quickly recalled the lessons learned from our street work and did the exact opposite:

1. These people want to be 'normal', they don't want someone to play with and would be offended if I tried to play with them.
2. These people are clearly abnormal, crazy and would much rather

not be. They would much rather be serious. So it would be very hard for me to get them to play with me even if I wanted them to.

3. I felt that any playing I would instigate (using non-approved therapeutic methods) might be seen as being too subversive and upset the funders. I didn't really want to upset anyone.

Following these three simple prejudicial thoughts, my actions (or rather, my reactions) reverted back to my childish patterns of trying to fit in with the status quo; trying to disappear. Pretending to be authentic I was nervously trying to talk with the group, trying to embellish what little experiences I had with mental health to impress them with our equality. I spent the first few 'theatre' sessions drinking tea, smoking cigarettes and talking about mental health.

I was scared, blinded with prejudice, but pretending not to be. At school I was the one trying to avoid being perceived as different and now I was treating these people in exactly that way. Because of my prejudice I was treating them completely differently from how I was treating everyone else, even strangers on the street, about whom I knew nothing!

Eventually one woman in the group asked me when we were going to start the drama. I told her I had no idea what to do with them. She asked me why not? She had heard that I was some kind of theatre director and that is why I had been asked to go there. They said I should do with them whatever I would do with anyone else. They wanted to make theatre with me.

Having been given permission to put into use my theatre gaze, the people in front of me were immediately transformed into people to play with and the space into a playground. In this mode I can act. Using this method my fear disappears and I know exactly what to do: first to look again at what and who is in front of you.

> Man [sic] can be seen as a person or a thing. Now even the same thing, seen from different points of view, gives rise to ... entirely different descriptions, and the descriptions give rise to ... entirely different theories, and the theories result in ... entirely different sets of action

… To look and to listen to a patient and to see 'signs' of 'disease', and to
look and to listen to him [sic] simply as a human being, are to see and
hear in radically different ways. (Laing, 1959: 20; adapted)

We spent the time in the remaining sessions (one two-hour session
per week for two years) playing and making theatre as I played with
everyone else, and at the end of the process and despite two of the
participants being diagnosed as 'agoraphobic' we had done a twenty-
five-gig tour of England with an original show. The cast had had a
stand-up public row with Augusto Boal about the inappropriateness
of forum theatre for the treating of people with a diagnosis of mental
illness and the funders had extended our budget. It was quite a ride and
a huge learning experience for all of us.

By dismissing my prejudice about people diagnosed with mental
illness and instead seeing them as actors, I gave these people the chance
that was offered me in my first drama classes and the chance we offered
people on the street: the chance to play and to develop who you are by
playing at who you were not.

At the end of the process one of the participants came up to me
and said that she had been under medication, in and out of psychiatric
hospitals and under medical care for over twenty years, all of which was
designed to make her want to get out of bed in the morning. She said that
every day we worked on our show she wanted to get out of bed. So did I.

I didn't set out to have this effect on anyone, which I think is part
of the reason it happened. What we had inadvertently done was
create a culture that recognized theatre rather than mental illness (or
diagnosis) as a gaze through which to view each other and our actions,
and in doing so we made theatre. Becoming the type of person who
wants to get out of bed (even once a week) destabilizes one's identity as
someone who doesn't want to. '[E]ven the most general psychological
laws are relative to a "phase of mankind" … mental illness has its reality
and its value qua illness only within a culture that recognises it as such'
(Foucault, 1976: 60).

What I recognize as being valuable for making theatre is what
defines my character. Both my character and especially what I consider

valuable material for making theatre has changed over the past twenty years, as have some of my theatre-making methods, but my methodology, *my theatre gaze*, has remained identical with every group and within every environment in which I have ever worked. For it is only with this gaze that I have confidence to facilitate action.

This chapter represents the first time that I have attempted to define the precise nature of this *gaze* to a wider audience. It is the first time I have tried to articulate something about the character of this guy who holds this gaze 100 per cent of the time; my *alter ego*, who is both me and not me. The guy who gets things done, who asks first and asks questions later ... if ever: my clown.

The clown

When a workshop is about to begin I get into clown mode. Although we share many of the same views, I am not always in this mode. It is a role I step into when needs must. In the traditional theatre sense, it is like getting into character, but it is more like getting ready to play. It is a performance mode. Not all clowns are the same. Even as a seminal theatrical figure the clown character has different features which depend on the actor playing him/her.

What follows is a description of what I consider to be the features/ elements and philosophies of *my* clown, and following that will be a description from a recent workshop I/he facilitated in Serbia, as told by the clown.

What the clown does is best understood by what he does, his actions. But his actions are determined by what he sees. The following is a list of the clown's facilitation methods, which are actions based on his view of the world:

1. He comes to life through playing.
   a He starts the game. He creates the shared experience.
   b He uses all means and methods at his disposal to get people to play. Nothing is off-limits.

2. He sees everyone as a fellow clown.

   a He sees everyone in the room as a clown, even if they do not, or especially if they do not.

   b There is no identity, no prejudice attached to the people in the room who the clown encounters. No barriers to play.

3. He doesn't know what he is going to do.

   a At the beginning of the workshop there is no telling what is going to happen. It is all new. New space, new group, new process. The clown does not know what is going to happen. He is primed, heightened, alert, aware, in the mode, looking around for things to play with, for stimulus.

   b There is no content preordained. The form/the game is trusted.

   c He does not know the result before the start of the process.

   d He will attempt to stay in the place of not knowing.

   e He avoids patterns, predicted models of practice.

4. He sees laughter as the best way to engage people.

   a He finds a way of using the situation, the stimuli, the given circumstances, his own knowledge of games, what is going on in the room, to get people laughing.

   b He finds humour. He does what it takes to make people laugh, to get them on his side.

   c His aim is to get people to laugh at him and to laugh at themselves (as individuals and as a group) – at our absurdity.

5. He sees people as playing with him.

   a He wants to be liked by everyone. He wants everyone to play with him. He has to engage everyone in the playing.

   b All in the room are in his game even if they are unaware of it.

6. He lives in the *here and now*.

   a The clown plays with what is in front of him. His skill is finding the game, finding the space. He is the ultimate improviser, the subservient subversive. From the space that he sees as the playground, to his fellow players, he accepts all. Even if the accepting is a means of manipulation.

   b There is no judgement. The space is sacred.

c   There is nothing outside the room. There is no truth referential analysis of what takes place within the game.

d   The content of the play is immaterial.

e   There is no greater aim than playing in the moment.

7. He sees nothing as fixed.

a   He finds the play (the movement in everything). He uses chairs as boats, coins as balloons, tables as islands. Anything at hand he plays with.

b   He looks for fixed things to play with in order to test his abilities or the extent of his imagination.

8. He is the guardian/conductor/director.

a   Despite his playful nature and his desire to engage others in his game, the game is *his*. He can be challenged; he can give away power temporarily, but only within a frame that he agrees to. The responsibility for the game is his and he takes it very seriously.

b   He plays on his terms. He chooses the game.

c   He guards the equal rights of everyone to play and be played with.

9. Playing is temporary.

a   When the playing stops, the clown disappears.

b   His authenticity as player lasts only as long as the workshop/performance.

Case study: Serbia

I feel the 'team' looking nervously at me, looking for guidance. One of them asks me if I know what I am going to do. It was the moment that I had been waiting for. I smiled and said 'I have no idea.' The clown had arrived. I smiled at her, she laughed heartily. The other team members laugh nervously. I walked into the hall.

The group notices us come in. I am recognized by a few of them from a previous workshop in another space. I recognize them. Others

I do not know. It is loud. I say hello in Serbian. Those that know me
reply; others laugh. I say it again. More attention as all laugh. We are
playing. I ask the translator not to translate: that would stop the game.
I continue to speak my bad Serbian as I get fifty participants to stand
in one big circle. The energy is good, I feel we are playing together, but
some are not.

One girl in a yellow shirt is dancing next to some people in the
circle. She is having fun with them, but they push her roughly away
(there is too much going on to deal with her now). Four people in the
room are nervously standing near a wall. I playfully signal for them
to come over to the circle, and ask them in Serbian. The group laughs
again. The four people smile. We have tension, friendly tension. We
have another game. The four people come over and join the circle.

All in the circle now, an interesting-looking group. They look at
me and each other. The laughter is dying down. We are waiting …
what next? I don't want to lose this energy. I suddenly want to explain
who I am and why I am here. I try in Serbian. I lose confidence as the
shuffling begins. I look at the translator. She does as she was instructed
and smiles back. I have little choice but to continue … is this the game?
In Serbian I say 'I am Paul. I am English. I am an actor. I have lived in
Belgrade for five years. I do not speak Serbian very well; sorry. I would
like to make a performance with you today but I have no idea what it
will be.'

The joke of me speaking bad Serbian is still working but is wearing
a bit thin. I ask for their names … I really don't know what else to
do. There is so much going on, I cannot imagine being able to engage
everyone here for two hours. The name circle will buy me two minutes
to think of something to do next.

The first person says nervously in English 'My name is Marija.'
Unexpected. The group almost die laughing at her, but they do not as
strongly as she. Her game is taken up by the next person. She repeats
'My name is' in English. The next person says something in a language
I do not recognize. More laughter … the game is on, accepting each
contribution, and each person at least repeating something they heard

and some adding more languages: I recognize maybe five. The sight of their friends speaking foreign languages continues to bring the group into hysterics.

These clowns are not afraid to flop. They are the first to laugh at themselves and invite others to do so to a point where the game becomes ridiculous, more extreme as it goes around the circle, people seeking to out-flop each other. It is ridiculous, raucous, playful, new. Only the girl in the yellow shirt continues to be excluded from the game. She wishes to start her own game with another one of the group but again is roughly pushed away.

As the last few people speak there seems nowhere further to go with this language game. It is rare to see a group extend an idea to exaggeration. It is what I generally encourage people to do, but it rarely happens. It has been a while. Where next for the game? Look for clues, inspiration: what is emerging? What is in front of us? Narratives? Images? What can be developed? Look carefully away from the obvious. Then I see it. As the next person speaks in 'German', they first take up a German pose. Others around instinctively mirror this physicality. It is infectious. The same thing happens with the last few people in the circle and others mirror their physicality of English, French and Japanese.

There is something here … to what end? I point to the actions and encourage the mimicking. It is picked up. By the images and reactions to them I presume that these are known stereotypes, but they do not resonate with me in the same way. The English, for example, did not seem very recognizably 'English' to me, or funny. Only the reaction of the others, all copying and smiling, tickled me. I am intrigued by the difference in our mimetic as well as verbal language. In Serbian I say, 'Walk around like a German, eat like as Japanese, jump like a Serb, watch TV like an Englishwoman. Read a newspaper like the French.'

Following the breaking of the circle, about fifteen participants slowly stopped playing and went to sit in groups around the edge of the space. Others in the space continued showing each other their creations, and tiny narratives began to emerge as their reading Frenchmen read together or the Englishwoman became German while eating with the Japanese.

I was interested in the physical nature of the work, the mimetic languages that were being displayed and explored, the cultural differences in the physical signs of representation, as well as the emergence of a narrative between those still engaged in the game I had introduced.

I looked around the whole room. What is going on now? Some people sitting around in small groups; others still playing the game, narratives within the game and the room emerging, and me – I wanted to further play with foreign mimed languages …

Combining these aspects of what was going on in order to try to get everyone playing again, I split the group into smaller groups of about five or six people and asked them to sit around the space. The fifteen recent non-players were already doing this and the others who were playing joined them. We were all playing the same game again, except for me who stood in the middle of the empty space.

Without announcing the game, I began to mime a Serbian nursery rhyme very slowly, trying to engage the group in a new game which brought together the things I thought we were all interested in (including taking a break). The only Serbian rhyme I know is *Eci peci pec, Ti si mali zec, A ja mala prepelica, Eci peci pec*, which translates into English as Etsi, Petsi Pets (no meaning), 'You are a small rabbit, and I am a small quail', Etsi, Petsi Pets (no meaning).

Could I communicate in a foreign mimed language the simplest narrative that (apart from perhaps one or two people) I knew they would all know?

As I stood, the room was quiet (apart from the girl in the yellow shirt who took her chance to try to sit with her 'friends' – she failed). Other than this there was engagement in the game. I was amused that the poem I had chosen to mime had two lines which didn't mean anything. I began. For the first line I just tip-toed in an exaggerated way for three steps. For the second line I pointed to someone and showed my thumb and index finger close together to indicate 'small'. By this time the group had started saying the rhyme as I was miming it. They knew by the middle of the second line what I was doing and which rhyme I was miming, and as I carried on to the end, their recognition of my mime and their spontaneous speaking of its words made me feel that for the first time in five years I was actually speaking Serbian: not as a foreigner, not with an accent, not being looked at as foreign, not feeling foreign, not being laughed at, not with any other thought. It was just as though I was speaking (or miming) in English, but it was in Serbian, because I was thinking in Serbian and the audience were speaking my actions in Serbian: they were speaking for me.

At the end of the rhyme one boy from the audience came to the floor and asked to do a mime of his own. I indicated (in spoken Serbian) that I wanted each of the groups in the room to think of a rhyme of theirs to mime to see if they could communicate it to the rest of the groups. I didn't want these to be individual performances (I knew that we couldn't achieve this task individually owing to lack of time), so I refused the boy his request. I said that each group now had ten minutes to make this group mime and as I looked at the time and watched them begin to talk about the task, the boy whom I had turned down left the room with two others.

I hate it when people leave the group. It means I have failed to engage them. I am not offended, just disappointed with my lack of ability to get people to play with me. The rest of the group began working with various levels of enthusiasm at the task at hand. The two-year-old was now sitting on the knee of another, older girl. I asked the older girl if they could try to include the young girl in their performance … I didn't understand what she said but it was clearly not an idea she thought had any value.

Every group responded to the instruction I had given them and each went about creating their own performance. I was satisfied that I had been able to develop a game that those left in the room were willing to play and seemed (in some cases) to relish. The atmosphere was again energized. In contrast to the atmosphere in the room, my eye was drawn outside towards the three boys who had left the play. They were standing next to a tree looking towards where we were still engaged.

They were outside, I was inside. My urge was to go outside to try to play with them, bring them back in. I didn't leave the room.

Eventually those left in the room told me they had finished and were ready to perform. I asked them to perform the mimes twice, the first in silence, the second with the words of the rhyme they had chosen to dramatize narrated by the audience. As they performed the first version the audience couldn't help themselves from beginning to say the words as soon as they recognized the rhyme. I tried to *not* understand anything of what the audience was saying. (This is an amusing thing to do, which probably has further dramatic potential. Try not to understand a language that you only understand 30 per cent of in the first place.) I wanted to judge the communication of meaning through the actions alone and on the second playing I asked my translator what the audience were saying.

Each performance followed the same pattern. For the first few seconds (to a maximum of 15) the audience were studying intensely the mimed actions, looking for clues as to what the rhyme might be, but once they had figured it out, they almost ignored what was happening on stage and raucously recited the rest of the poem in unison. It was not even important whether their language coordinated with the mime any more. This surprised me but didn't seem to affect the playfulness of the performers. Only I and another person in the room kept our focus on the action as we struggled to keep ourselves in the place of ignorance, working out the story from the mimes alone. This action separated us from the feeling of the rest of the group. I felt foreign again.

The clock was showing that we were approaching the end of the session and I was about to ask the group if there was anything they wanted to say in terms of what they liked or otherwise about the session, when the three boys who were watching us from outside the window re-entered. They said they had made a mime they wanted to show, but it was not based on some existing rhyme. The rhyme should be made by me in English and another person in Serbian, a rhyme that would fit the narrative that they had created. They wanted their mime to be verbalized. They wanted an English and Serbian version and they didn't want them to be the same. They also didn't want to hear a translation of the English. Their actions were to lead the formation of my words, the meaning of which was unimportant to them.

This inversion of the game, whether intentional or accidental, added dimensions that enriched the outcome of this game immensely. The boys were not acting as spoilsports before. They had just chosen to leave, but they remained inspired to play outside and felt a need to share their game with us, which they did in a modest and joyful manner. The only thing more satisfying than people returning to a class they left is doing so in a playful manner, which enhances rather than disrupts the room they return to. As requested, I made up a rhyme for their actions which no one apart from me fully understood – which was a shame because is was great (trust me! very funny).

As the Serbian version of the boys' drama was completed, we were entering creative realms that demanded further exploration, but the time allocated to the workshop had come to an end. It was time for the game to stop. For a symbolic sense of closure, I beckoned everyone back into the circle and we each mimed and said a goodbye in a language of our choice. We then looked at each other. From outside the circle our eyes were drawn to the girl with the yellow shirt who had remained in the room throughout the workshop. She had been deemed by all to be too boring to join in our games and had failed to get anyone to play with hers. She was now dancing quietly on her own in a corner, free, away from anyone's concern – so I believe she thought.

Immediately there was a tension in the group between us and her. We were all looking. We all slowly turned to make an audience. Her back still to us, her dance came to a stop. I led the applause. She turned, shocked, seemed to think for a second, smiled, bowed and walked calmly out of the door. It was a satisfying way for the playing to come to an end.

Conclusion

When I first started experimenting with looking at the world outside of the theatre through the clown's gaze, I did so in order to be less fearful of it. If I regarded everything as play, I could go anywhere and find/ facilitate playing. In the first few years I would often choose to enter, or find myself in, situations of which I was most fearful, just to test the power of this gaze.

I soon realized that just through the power of my imagination I could temporarily remove my fear of things, people and places and, free of that fear, begin to understand how I got to be fearful of such things in the first place. I pursued my curiosity to discover that what usually made things appear serious to me was some kind of overhanging threat of physical, psychological or material suffering of not doing so (such as the Emperor's new clothes). It wasn't the thing itself that was serious. Seriousness is a power game. Of course, recognizing that something is *only a game* does not make the consequences of it any less severe, if you are seen to be not playing properly or are losing, and the person or people controlling the game are more powerful than you. Nonetheless, knowing that it is a power game allows one to subvert the power of the powerful, at least in one's mind.

I then came to the realization that there is no need to waste any more energy *imagining* things to be games. I could just take it for granted that they were. Even if nobody else thought so, why should it matter to me? Why not just invert the *up to now* status quo and let people whose serious lives were threatened by my playfulness waste *their* energy on subverting *me* rather than the other way around?

I am not sure when I started doing this exactly, but since I started doing it I have been liberated from the time wasted worrying about not being serious, and as a result I have been able to get on with facilitating more and more theatre with more and more people. Since then I have set up a theatre school for children and adults in Belgrade and now teach at least thirty hours of practical theatre a week to over 100 people aged six and up.

I do come across many 'serious' people who try to subvert my playfulness in various ways and for various reasons, but they are part and parcel of the game. As inevitable as it is that the actor cannot avoid playing with/within the confines of her own body, so the facilitator must play with/within the confines of the places where she plays and who he plays with. They are part of the game. This is the facilitator's (as opposed to the actor's) paradox and is part of an ongoing and welcome dialectic. Occasionally I am asked to work in 'serious' places and even more occasionally in 'very serious' ones, which allows me to test the power of my playful gaze in response to 'serious' opposition, and discern whether seriousness has got any more alluring. It hasn't yet.

As stated earlier, all of the principles of my work are the same as when I was a twenty-two-year-old graduate of theatre, setting out to play with the world. The only difference now is I spend more time acting as a clown and seeing where it takes me than worrying about feeling strange because I think like one. My personal search is to keep following this professional methodology and see where it takes me and my fellows; to see what we make and what others make us. I have no idea where this may be or what it may look like but I do believe that 'By considering the whole sphere of … culture as a play sphere we pave the way to a more direct and more general understanding of its peculiarities than any meticulous psychological or sociological analysis would allow' (Huizinga, 1950: 25). The fun for me comes from applying theatre to real life rather than real life to theatre and as long as it remains fun and people want to play with me I will keep doing it.

All Our Stress Goes in the River:
The Drama Workshop as a (Playful)
Space for Reconciliation

Sarah Woodland

Introduction

In the first part of this book, Sheila Preston makes the case for *critical* facilitation, wherein we might understand the 'macro-discourses' within which we are working, and the impact that these have on our practices. Within this, there is an acknowledgement that the drama workshop is a 'cultural space' that is layered with multiple meanings that emerge out of this wider political and social context. This chapter represents an attempt to grapple with these ideas in the context of a drama workshop programme that I facilitated with a group of indigenous Australian prisoners. Issues around critical facilitation, along with some of the personal and professional dilemmas that I experienced, form the backdrop to this discussion.

Many would be aware of Australia's deeply troubling treatment of its Aboriginal and Torres Strait Islander citizens, which stretches back in a shameful story of institutionalized abuse and neglect from colonization up to the present moment. The apology delivered in Parliament by Prime Minister Kevin Rudd in February 2008 was a highly significant symbolic gesture that moved the country towards a collective acknowledgement of past wrongs, yet health, employment and living standards for the majority of Aboriginal and Torres Strait Islander Australians remain far below the rest of the population, prompting damning reports by the

United Nations in recent years (Aston, 2010; Sharp and Arup, 2009). Since colonization, Australia's first peoples have experienced various forms of institutional confinement on a staggering scale: removed as children to be locked in residential schools, orphanages and Christian missions; locked into unpaid slavery and low-paid servitude by white employers (see Robinson, 2008); and more recently becoming overrepresented in the penal system. At the time of writing, Aboriginal and Torres Strait Islander peoples represent 27 per cent of the total prisoner population in Australia, despite representing only 2.5 per cent of the total population in 2011 (Australian Bureau of Statistics, 2012, 2014). The 1987 Royal Commission into Aboriginal Deaths in Custody shone a light on this disparity, the high incidence of Aboriginal deaths whilst in custody, a lack of care taken by authorities for those imprisoned and a lack of thoroughness and transparency in investigating and reporting on those deaths (Johnston, 1991). The Productivity Commission reports that in the past fifteen years, there has been a 57 per cent rise in the rates of imprisonment for indigenous people (Kidd, 2014).

As an educated white facilitator entering the correctional context to work with Aboriginal participants, this story bore a heavy weight. In entering this space, I was undertaking a 'border crossing' (Prentki and Preston, 2009), where there was significant potential for misstep. I was coming from the privileged halls of a university in the city to work in a remote rural location. This was my first ever workshop in an exclusively Aboriginal context, and I perhaps naively felt that if I went in with good intentions and an open heart, what could possibly go wrong? However, the 'gatekeepers' (Balfour, 2004: 16) who initially approved my programme were the (largely white) administrators of Corrective Services in New South Wales, to whom I articulated the work in such a way as to meet their criteria for the rehabilitation of offenders in general (not specifically Aboriginal men and women); nor did my programme proposal explicitly address our cultural positioning. The space I was entering was complex and, given these circumstances, there was a high risk of perpetuating the colonizing practices of my forbears. I was at risk of becoming a 'cultural missionary' (McDonald, 2005 cited in Balfour, 2009), offering the problematic 'gift' (Nicholson, 2005) of Western drama traditions and approaches to the group.

A number of scholars have noted that it is not useful to conceive the players in such spaces in binary relationships such as self–other, oppressor–oppressed or colonizer–colonized, and that the sites in which they meet are not fixed, but rather spaces whose physical, emotional and ideological significance are in constant movement and renegotiation (see Browne, Smye and Varcoe, 2005; Nicholson, 2005; Daboo, 2007; Hunter, 2008; Wilkinson and Kitzinger, 2009; Chinyowa, 2013). This echoes Preston's reference to Giroux (1992) in conceptualizing critical pedagogy in this book. She cites Giroux's notion that 'culture' is not seen as 'monolithic', but that it moves and shifts in constant renegotiation within existing power structures. Reflecting on my work now, I follow Greenwood (2001) in considering how the drama workshops might have become what Bhabha (1990 cited in Greenwood) describes as a 'third space' – a site of convergence not only between the two cultures of white and Aboriginal Australia, but also the range of Aboriginal language groups represented, and the various influences of contemporary post-contact Australian culture. An Aboriginal elder at my university has since urged me to find an orientation within the work and my relationships with the participants that might allow this third space to become a small site for reconciliation. If we are planning to deal with our difficult history, she said, my role as a facilitator is to work alongside the participants to 'bless it, release it, and move on'. Through the following case study, I will explore my practice as a facilitator, how I attempted to follow Fine's suggestion to 'work the hyphen' between self–other (1994 cited in Wilkinson and Kitzinger) and what were the unique qualities of this third space that emerged from the process. Initially wishing to devise performance with the group, I realized how much more important it was for them to play and laugh together after a stressful day. Early on, this created moments of tension, misunderstanding and even failure on my part, highlighting the bewildering dance of success and failure that we as facilitators must learn and relearn with every new song.

Background

The project took place in 2010–11 in Balund-a (pronounced Baloonda), a residential programme designed to divert Aboriginal people from custody. The residents live at Balund-a for six months, working on the farm and undertaking vocational education and intensive rehabilitation programmes to address issues such as offending behaviour, substance abuse and anger management. The property is located in Bundjalung country in rural northern New South Wales on the banks of the Clarence River, and its Bundjalung name, *Bugilmah Burube Wullinje Balund-a*, roughly translates as 'Be good now you have a second chance down by the river'. This community-based model was established as a kind of experiment in response to the Royal Commission into Aboriginal Deaths in Custody (see Johnston, 1991) and aims to combine traditional culturally sensitive intervention with contemporary approaches to offender rehabilitation. Residents are aged roughly between 18 and 40 and are sentenced to the programme for six months. Drugs and alcohol are strictly prohibited, yet there are no locked doors or gates. If someone decides to leave, they can; however, this is difficult given the isolation of the property and the attendant consequences of breaching their sentence, which operates in a similar way to a probation order. The kinds of offences for which the residents are commonly convicted include domestic violence, assault, driving offences and drug possession; and there are common underlying issues of drug and alcohol abuse and low educational attainment – very few of the participants I worked with had made it past year eight or nine. Aside from the farming, vocational and criminogenic programmes, residents participate in cultural programmes that are led by elders from nearby communities and sometimes engage in recreational sport.

At the time of my project the Balund-a programme was home to approximately 25 men and five women out of its total capacity of fifty residents; of these, approximately three were Anglo-Australian. As part of a practice-based doctoral research project, I stayed on site in the staff quarters at Balund-a for three separate four-day blocks one month apart and delivered drama workshops in the evenings. My approach as a facilitator was a hybrid practice that drew heavily on my previous work with the Geese Theatre Company, UK, using games and structures influenced by Theatre of the Oppressed and Theatre in Education in order to address offending behaviour (see Baim, Brookes and Mountford, 2002). Yet I was also beginning to explore how I might use improvisation and devised drama in a less explicitly rehabilitative way. Having recently worked on a testimonial performance with adult survivors of institutional childhood abuse, I was also interested in using drama as a way to represent personal narratives (Woodland, 2009), but I still felt I was finding my feet within the practice, trying to find my own ways of working within criminal justice contexts that were not limited by a direct alignment with institutional versions of offender rehabilitation. Having been invited to pitch a programme to the centre by the New South Wales corrections' locum psychologist, the only space available to me in the tightly packed daily schedule at Balund-a was between seven and nine at night, after dinner. This immediately changed how I could approach the project, as I will explore in more detail below. It was not being programmed as a core activity within the centre, but a recreational activity that would have to compete with the residents' usual pursuits of relaxing, watching television, chatting and playing cards. After delivering a taster workshop a few weeks prior, I designed the three four-night blocks that I ran at Balund-a to follow a fairly simple progression:

- Block One: basic drama games, group building exercises and image theatre.
- Block Two: more complex improvisation, image work and scene building; identification of key themes.
- Block Three: possible devising of a short performance showing for the fifth day based around the key themes.

We began the first block with thirteen participants. This fluctuated over the course of the three blocks, but averaged at around six to eight.

The cultural space

Balund-a is built on Bundjalung land dominated by the mighty
Berrinbah (now Clarence) River and home of the turtle divers. The
local elders who work on the programme encourage residents to
maintain their connections to culture and country, working not only
with their own people, but also welcoming whites and Kooris (New
South Wales Aboriginals) from other language groups onto their
land for this 'second chance'. The connection to land is a key aspect of
culture that underpins all Aboriginal tribes and language groups; the
natural environment exists as the foundation to everything else that is
layered on top of it, and as a facilitator entering this land, I needed to
recognize that I was adding to these layers. The orderly patchwork of
post-contact white civilization – roads, pastures, fences, buildings – had
been thrown blanket-like over the much longer history of this place; it
was subsequently woven with stories of settlers, bushrangers, soldiers
and stockmen. When I was there in the height of summer, the river was
high, and the sky, the animals, the land were all heavy with moisture.
Turtles, frogs, black snakes, kangaroo rats, lizards, cows, rabbits and
owls all crossed my path as I drove to and from the property. At
dusk, I had to shut all the doors and windows to keep out the tide of
mosquitoes, flies and other flying insects that I did not recognize. And
in the midst of this sat the Balund-a property, where traditional forms
of restorative justice and community intervention were knitted roughly
together with mainstream textbook-based correctional programming,
institutional versions of discipline and order, and the farming practices
of rural Australia: a complexly layered space marked by fire pits,
dirt tracks, classrooms, dormitories, sheds, stockyards and offices,
20 kilometres by unsealed road from the nearest tiny town. Taking
a drama workshop there was new to me, and new to the people who
stayed and worked there; I had to find a place within this culture that
was at once familiar and entirely foreign to me.

Through the three blocks of the programme, I had participants
ranging between 20 and 38 years old, mostly men but with two to three

women involved at different times as well. The Koori language groups represented were Bundjalung, Dungatti, Gumbaynggirr, Kamilaroi and Anaiwan, as well as two Anglo-Australian participants who had close ties to the Aboriginal community. Despite my fears to the contrary, a sizeable group turned up regularly each evening – and they remained for the most part enthusiastic, committed, excitable and involved, responding particularly well to the more energetic games and improvisation exercises. To the surprise of the elders, the participants seldom seemed to experience the usual 'shame' associated with being exposed in front of the group or making fools of themselves – the concept of shame in Aboriginal culture being quite common, and linked to embarrassment and vulnerability rather than guilt or remorse (see Harkins, 1990; Sharifian, 2005; Eades, 2013: 103). The drama games and exercises quickly began to teach me about the space of cultural intersection that we now inhabited.

During our creation of an embodied postcard of 'the bush', one young Kamilaroi participant stood with his arm pointing skyward. 'I'm a blackboy', he said without irony, using the old white colonial term for grass tree. During a round of the game Liar (detailed descriptions of games and exercises are included in the glossary at the end of the chapter), another participant instructed me in the centre of the circle to enact 'Billy Ray Cyrus singing a rap song', to which I responded by doing my best boot-scooting dance while singing 'Drop it like it's hot' by Snoop Dogg. Images were created that depicted the local pub, the dole office, drink driving, growing cannabis and *Sex in the City*, as well as diving for turtles, baking traditional bread and sitting by a campfire. This layering of culture put me on the path of embracing Bhabha's idea of a 'third space', a new space that Greenwood (2001: 194) suggests, '[e]merges through cultural encounters and … cannot be defined in advance'. In our new space, there was potential for a unique convergence of Aboriginal, white, Koori, urban, rural, popular and traditional that was made manifest in our representations of image and story in the drama. This brought to mind the approach adopted by acclaimed Australian arts organization Big hART, whose Yijala Yala Project 'seeks to highlight cultural heritage as living, continually evolving and in the here and now, rather than of the past' (Big hART, 2014). This approach supports Bhabha's assertion that:

> The representation of difference must not be hastily read as the reflection of pre-given ethnic or cultural traits set in the fixed tablet of tradition. The social articulation of difference, from the minority perspective, is a complex, on-going negotiation that seeks to authorize cultural hybridities that emerge in moments of historical transformation. (1994: 2)

Another layer operating in our case was the correctional culture of Balund-a, where participants moved through levels of privilege based on behaviour, had regular urine tests for drugs and undertook specialist programmes that addressed their offending, addiction and life choices. All of these aspects of the culture had a strong impact on the mood and participation of the group, as did the pull of the 20-kilometre road out of Balund-a, with participants sometimes voicing their struggle over whether to stay or whether to 'walk off' the programme. The power relations implicit within this space were marked, not only by our troubling post-contact history, but also by the mechanisms of control within the correctional context. As a critical facilitator, I also had to recognize the power that I potentially held here too: another white woman in a 'teacher' role, who was invited in by the department and spent the evening issuing invitations (and instructions) to participate in the drama.

The river became a strong symbol for me in understanding how the different cultural currents flowed through this space, and subsequently how I responded to the group's rhythms as a facilitator. When I returned to Balund-a for Block Two, we had just experienced the worst floods in nearly forty years, the impact reaching right across Queensland and New South Wales, from my home in Brisbane all the way to Bundjalung country. The Balund-a residents had been involved in the clean-up in neighbouring communities, and some of the elders' homes had been affected. Alongside this, some of the most striking images of day-to-day life that the group created together centred on the river: barbecues, family, friends, fishing, swimming, water sports. Regardless of language group and culture, this region of northern New South Wales is known for its network of creeks and rivers, and the majority of participants made a connection to this idea. I proposed that we devise our performance showing around the theme of the river, and it was only when we began a discussion around this theme that I began to see even more clearly the cultural layers that were operating in the space. The conversation ranged from general reactions about the river being a place of quiet and relaxation, to the idea of baptism (some of the participants were Baptists) and then to the traditional rules and rites around the river: 'It's not just fishing, swimming and having a good time, but with black fellas' ways and that, our ways, there's women's and men's business.' A participant I will call 'Davey' said this. But another, 'Mark', said 'I respect the culture and everything, but realistically, I go to the river and fish and eat and all that.' He later added, 'I would never go down to the river without a carton [case of beer] ... When I was a kid, it was just fun, you know, going down to the river with my uncles and they'd throw you in and we'd swing off a rope and it was a good laugh. But as you get older, you just go down there to drink.'

The conversation also turned to the Aboriginal creation myth of the Rainbow Serpent and all of the tribal totems from the region, as well as the different lands represented in the room: the participant 'Jane' was a 'salt water woman' and 'Paul' (who was white) was told by Davey that he was a 'cold country man' based on his origin in Lismore, a town higher in altitude than the river valley town Tabulam where Balund-a was situated. Davey suggested we make a traditional scene where women would be gathering berries and grubs and the men would be hunting. Mark laughed and pointed at Paul: 'We can all be down the river bank, and he can come along and shoot us all.' Everyone, including Paul, laughed at this light-hearted but potent reminder of our troubling colonial heritage, an aspect of our history that we never explored or discussed beyond this brief moment. Despite the fact that we never fully realized a performance about the river, this discussion was perhaps the richest moment in establishing our third space, where there was not only a layering of cultures and of the traditional and the contemporary, but also the potential to explore our 'troubled knowledge' (Chinyowa, 2013) around issues such as colonization and alcohol abuse. With the benefit of hindsight, I may have picked up on this opportunity and used it as the basis for further discussion and dramatic work, but as I will explore below, this may not have been appropriate or welcomed in our particular case.

The space to play

From the beginning of the programme, I was experiencing mixed feelings about whether or not to use the drama as a vehicle to directly deal with participants' life choices. On the one hand, the psychologist who invited me was familiar with and excited about the work of the Geese Theatre Company, but having been squeezed into the down time of the evenings, I thought it was only fair to be responsive and see where the participants themselves wanted to lead the work. From early on, the group threw themselves wholeheartedly and energetically into games such as Name Ball, The Wind Takes Away and Zip Zap Bop. There was a buzz in the room and regular explosions of laughter and playfulness. In reflecting later, participants said that they enjoyed the fact that they could 'have a laugh', 'come back down to earth' and 'blow off steam' at the end of a long day. 'Diane' put it rather beautifully when she said 'When we come here, all our stress leaves us. It goes in the river.' It soon became apparent that this was important for all of the participants, but particularly those who were undertaking intensive offending behaviour programmes during the day, such as Think First (McGuire, 2005). For some, these programmes were extremely difficult. Not only did they force people to 'face their demons' as one staff member put it, but they were also delivered using a textbook in a traditional classroom set-up with desks and a whiteboard. As another staff member observed, this recreated the very same negative dynamic and pressure to perform as many of the participants had experienced in their schooling. Indeed, twice when I brought out flip-chart paper during the workshop or went to write on the whiteboard, Davey, now in his early thirties, screwed up his face and said 'This is like classes now.'

I soon began to wonder how effective was the approach of knitting together mainstream correctional programming with more culturally infused, experiential and collaborative learning that was also offered at Balund-a. As one Aboriginal staff member described, he often found it difficult to navigate the 'grey area' between 'knowing how his own people worked' and having to implement decisions from Corrections. Here he was reflecting one of the many dilemmas of the cultural worker as described earlier in this book. Yet several of the drama group members noted that drama was an embodied reminder that they could have fun without drugs and alcohol. Paul observed that whereas the other programmes *told* participants that it was possible through textbooks, the drama programme *showed* them.

In Block One I kept the workshops fairly loose and exploratory, using the same methods I had learned from Geese to find out more about the group and what they felt comfortable discussing. After playing a few games just for fun and group building, I began to use them as springboards for discussion, inviting the group to make connections between the game and real life (see Baim et al., 2002). After the Boal (2002) game Columbian Hypnosis, where one participant must follow another's hand, Diane said it reminded her of the hold that drugs and alcohol had over her. After the game Wink Chair, I invited the group to talk about goals and obstacles. 'Tiana' said a goal for her was 'to be seen and heard … in your community, by other people, even on television or something'. When I asked what could hold her back from that goal, she said 'friends, your bloke, alcohol'. When 'Eric' said that women held him back from his goals, an in-depth conversation about relationships followed. Although they were more subdued during these conversations than they had been during the games themselves, the participants still seemed engaged and willing to talk about the life issues that they were facing. I would suggest that the overarching culture of Balund-a as a place for dealing with issues of crime and substance abuse, combined with the use of play to stimulate discussion, made the participants feel comfortable to share these insights with me early on. In her exploration of how 'safe space' is conceived in applied theatre, Hunter (2008: 5) describes it as a place of tension and 'messy negotiations'. She cites Nicholson, who suggests that 'Transforming highly regulated spaces into creative performance and workshop spaces is not just an interesting artistic challenge. It involves reconstructing how space is conceived, temporarily overlaying its codes with alternative spatial practices' (2005: 15). It seemed that the participants were using the playful practices of drama to negotiate this grey area for themselves, describing our new space in terms that responded to the correctional culture operating at Balund-a.

Our early creation of images and scenes showed just how immediate was the struggle with drugs and alcohol. When I asked the group to create an image entitled 'Life is Good', one group made an image of people in a car heading to a party, the driver smoking a joint, the front passenger passed out and the back passenger drinking. Diane narrated events for this group concluding with 'This is the road that got us all here to Balund-a.' When I asked the group to make images of 'Something You are Proud of', Davey represented himself receiving a football trophy, while 'Jeremiah's' showed him harvesting a sizeable cannabis crop. When I asked the group to create a scene entitled 'First Day back from Balund-a', 'Tiana' immediately said with glee 'I'm gonna get charged up! [drunk/high].' Her group then showed a scene where the protagonist first went straight to the pub to drink, then played the poker machines and then went to a job interview. These images and scenes pointed to the strong sense of ambivalence within the group, between recognizing the destructive nature of addiction and embracing it with enthusiasm. My intention at this early stage was not to encourage the triggering of participants' desires for drugs and alcohol, but to take the temperature of the group and make space for people to participate without censorship. A few evenings in, I decided to bring to the group my observation that there was a lot of drama being created that focused on drugs and alcohol. 'Sharon' said 'That's because it's our reality' and Davey agreed, 'If you put us on the spot, then that's what will come to our brain straight away.' Mark added, 'We get caught up in the moment, making people laugh.'

These images and scenes further reinforced the presence of drugs and alcohol in the participants' lives and communities – a significant cultural current that was at play in the flow of our experience together.

I also shared my observation with participants that I was beginning to notice more stark changes in energy between when we were just playing and when I tried to facilitate discussion, like I was pulling the plug out and deflating everything. I explained that this reminded me of the drug and alcohol buzz: the buoyancy that makes you laugh, carry on and forget the reality of life, but when something brings you back down to earth, the buzz is killed. I asked the group if they wanted to continue looking at real life issues and perhaps start challenging them through the drama, or would this kill the buzz. I got a mixed response, but the majority of the group seemed to want a bit of both. Mark said that there was not much point in the drama if it did not touch on real life sometimes, and Paul said 'It's like with the drugs, you know? If you get high, you have to come down sooner or later and face reality.' I therefore found it helpful to have this conversation openly with the group early on, rather than trying to guess, or even presuming to know, what was the best approach for them. This was crucial in trying to find the right balance as a facilitator in our unique space.

I commenced Block Two a month later, and found the energy and atmosphere somewhat different. A couple of the participants had been kicked off the programme for using drugs. There seemed to be a bit more stress around for the participants, and when I asked why, Davey said it was because a few of them had started Think First, to which Eric wryly replied 'Yeah and they don't want to think.' Based on the feedback from the previous block, I started off by more openly exploring some of the real life issues with the group to see if it would yield any performance material. I invited the participants to create a scene entitled 'The Drug and Alcohol Free Buzz'. They created a scene by the river, a barbecue with friends and water sports. At the end of the session, I gathered everyone together and asked what they thought of the material. 'Adrian' said 'It was good because it made us think of things we can do instead of drugs and alcohol.' Tiana said 'It gives us ideas of what we can do when we get out. If we can do it acting, then we can do it for real', and she laughed. I felt I had been given permission by the group to explore this territory after the previous block, but the participants' responses felt a little hollow – like they were telling me what I, and the textbook-based rehabilitation programmes, wanted to hear. The obvious way I approached it made it look like I was trying to hammer home some kind of moral message, rather than responding to the emerging themes. It was at this point that I suggested the river as a theme for performance, having seen how pivotal it was to this place and its people, having experienced the recent floods and reasoning that it might act as a unifying thread that ran through this environment and the stories that lived within it. Buoyed by the success of the scenes they had created in this session, the group were agreeable with this idea and I left at the end of the block with a solid idea of how to approach the work a month later as we moved towards a performance showing.

Block Three was characterized by the ebb and flow of confidence in doing a final performance showing, and it seemed that participants were being affected by a combination of different factors both inside and outside the workshop space. There had been drugs discovered on site early in the week, and my guess was that several of the group members were under the influence on the first night of the drama workshops. By the third day, three participants had been taken for testing and then walked off the property. Alongside this, the drama space was changing. We were now devising scenes for the final showing, and those who were in the room were having mixed responses. 'Tim' and Paul, two of our most enthusiastic young group members, withdrew after the first night, and only occasionally popped their heads in after that to see what was happening. When I spoke to them later, they said that they enjoyed playing the games more than devising the final performance; Tim said he didn't like making the river scenes because 'There wasn't a laugh in it.' At times, the devising seemed to go well, for example when I brought out a large piece of blue flowing fabric to use as our river, and Davey very convincingly dived into the 'water' and began swimming and waterskiing while others fished and sang songs by a campfire. But when we attempted to create a soundscape of the river, the group quickly lost interest and focus. People drifted out of the room to have a cigarette until there were only two left. Davey's spontaneous improvisation had made the scene funny, alive and energetic. Perhaps the soundscape was, in contrast, abstract and confusing.

By the third night, there were only four participants in the room, and it seemed they were being affected by our dwindling numbers, combined with the pressure of having to do the showing, and the lack of fun, connection, spontaneity and success that they felt towards some of the devising as opposed to what they had experienced in our early games and improvisations. Adrian was one of the participants who had been taken and tested positive for drugs, and he dropped by the drama workshop one last time before walking off the property. He stood in the doorway and laughed as we attempted to create a scene about the local floods. When I asked him to join us, he said 'I don't know if I can come in. This is different now.' After this, Davey and Diane's confidence immediately collapsed. Davey said 'This is not working' and Diane agreed, 'This is not going to work … they're all going to just laugh at us, I'll be shame [sic].' After Adrian's appearance in the doorway, and Davey and Diane's crisis of confidence, Davey asked if we could just play the improvisation game Holiday Snaps. He suggested that we play the game for the audience, instead of doing the devised work: 'We can't do all that other stuff. There's nobody here.' I went to the whiteboard where our running order for the final presentation was written. 'That's fine,' I said, 'we can just show what we already have plus some of the games we've played.' I then went about rubbing the flood and final scenes off the whiteboard, to show that it was easy, we could be adaptable, we didn't have to feel the pressure of coming up with new material. As I did this, Diane said 'Well that's it then, it's all gone.' I asked her what she meant. She said 'The play is all gone. We don't have anything now. There's nobody here.' She finished with 'Let's just get rid of the river.'

This felt like a particularly low point and the mood was disappointed and confused. We decided to take a break and have a discussion over a cigarette. We knew that other residents at Balund-a, as well as some of the community elders, had been invited to come and see our showing on the Friday night over a barbecue. We spent some time discussing how to tackle the showing. At one point Mark became annoyed at the other participants who were absent, saying 'They should just fire up!' Jane sat with her head in her hands and said, 'It's all just confusing.' Davey then said 'I'll get up and make a fool of myself, I don't care.' And Diane finally said 'Well why don't we just see who turns up tomorrow. If they come, then we can do the play, and if they don't, well we'll just show them what we can.' She then started running through the river scenes and saying what the four of those present would be able still to do without the others. Davey then enthusiastically said that the group members could just get up and explain a few things and basically improvise on the spot depending on who was there. Mark agreed, 'That's it, fire up!' After that, Davey said 'Let's play a game to get the mood back up!' As we were walking back into the room Diane said 'Where's the ball?' Davey said 'How about all the little balls?' So I got the juggling balls out and we had a round of Group Juggle that was very high focus and high energy. By the end of the session the mood had completely changed, and the group once again seemed happy and uplifted. While the first part of the session and the discussion that followed were quite fraught for me as a facilitator, I can see now that it was an important moment in our functioning as a group. We negotiated our way through a crisis and began to recognize our strengths, our limitations and what we needed in order to move forward with confidence. When things became particularly fraught, Davey twice returned us to the safe ground of the drama games, perhaps recognizing that these were not only easy but also spontaneous and full of joy.

During the fourth day, I was invited to the Balund-a community meeting to explain how our final performance showing had changed and try to entice those who had left the group back for our final session before Friday's barbecue. I explained that we would just be demonstrating some of the games and exercises we had done in the drama, and that it would be great to have the rest of the residents there to support the group. I also invited people to join us for the final evening to have some fun and get some demonstration games ready for the barbecue. Both Paul and Tim showed up on that fourth evening and we had a great session of general drama and improvisation games. The barbecue was a light, relaxed evening, with most of the Balund-a residents in attendance, plus some staff, one of the elders and a couple of visitors from the community, including Diane's mother. When it came to our demonstration of improvisation games, there was much hilarity and support from the audience, and the participants demonstrated greater focus and physical discipline than they had done throughout the programme. At one point, two teams of three participants were tasked with creating freeze frames on the spot in response to titles that I was calling out: 'the moon landing', 'the kids' birthday party'. When I called out 'Balund-a', Diane quickly became the director, bringing the two teams together and instructing them to create an image of the Think First programme class. She told Jane to be the teacher, and then the rest of the group stood in a line at the other end of the room, Paul giving the finger, Davey struggling with his paper, saying 'I can't do this', and general looks of boredom and disdain on everyone's faces. I was a bit worried about encouraging this kind of rebellion in front of the staff and elders, but this moment clearly illustrated the polarity between the evening drama programme and the daytime classroom work. And more than anything up to that point, it brought into focus the need for these participants to blow off steam from the intensity of the other daytime programmes.

Conclusion: A third space

The first three sessions in Block Three were exhausting for me. Returning to the metaphor of the river, I sometimes felt like I was being swept along and trying to grab at bits of grass on the way past (when we started late, when the energy was scattered, when there was conflict outside the workshop, when the participants lost confidence or momentum). Or else I was riding the tide – a boat tugging the group through their doubts one minute, and then surfing with their ideas and victories another. At all times I was keenly aware of the power that outside influences were having on the group, combined with their lack of connection with certain forms of performance that I was bringing to the table. Yet I am certain that this was not so much about a binary post-colonial conception of culture, where the ideas I brought from Western drama were inaccessible to the performance sensibilities of an Aboriginal group.

I have since worked with Aboriginal participants in prison using some of the same devising strategies and forms I have described here, with high levels of engagement and extremely rewarding performance outcomes for all involved.[1] I believe that this was a reflection of the unique, layered space that we were working in, where I had pushed the group as far as I could and had to concede that *play* was far more achievable, important and valuable to them than *performance*.

Working in the context of a criminogenic rehabilitation programme, this raised questions for me in terms of how play might be viewed by the elders, staff and administrators at Balund-a. I wondered whether this could be viewed as a cop-out; that I might be letting the group off the hook and giving way to their more impulsive and sometimes destructive tendencies to chase the 'buzz'. But what had taken place over the course of the three blocks was more complex than this. We had established a useful rhythm between the buzz of the games and improvisations and the more self-reflective conversations that surrounded them. At the end of the evening, one of the elders approached me and said that they were planning to speak to management about having more drama on the programme: 'I think it's really good for them. So much laughter and joyfulness, I haven't seen them like this for ages.' Or as Davey eloquently put it, 'You need to have a laugh or you just do your time hard.'

As an outsider I had immersed myself in Balund-a's complex cultural and environmental rhythms and worked alongside the group to try to bring something new into its flow. I felt both vulnerable and exhilarated – sometimes treading on the eggshells of politically correct cross-cultural practice, but also finding that my role enabled me to playfully explore new possibilities for ethical engagement and human connection. In most correctional environments, where success is measured in terms of good behaviour and reduced recidivism, the importance of stress management through laughter and play could easily become marginalized, but at Balund-a I was heartened that this was welcomed and valued.

The project's ultimate emphasis on play, laughter and joy, set within the Bundjalung culture and natural environment, had a profound effect on my practice, leading me towards new ways of understanding how I work with Aboriginal participants in correctional contexts. The most significant learning point for me was to conceive the drama workshop space as a 'site for reconciliation' where I should remain critically reflexive about the implications of my own cultural positioning, but not to the point of paralysis. I now see that each new site becomes its own third space, where multiple layers of culture operate that move far beyond a 'fixed tablet of tradition' (Bhabha, 1994: 2) or binaries such as colonizer and colonized. In these spaces, our shared knowledge, troubled or not, can be approached as much with humour as it can with gravity.

Glossary of games and exercises

Columbian Hypnosis

In pairs, Person A (the hypnotist) holds their palm about 20–30 cm away from the face of Person B – palm facing out, fingers upright. Person B must follow the hypnotist's hand as if they are indeed hypnotized. They must keep their face in alignment with the palm of the hypnotist's hand. The hypnotist can take their player on a gentle journey around the room, playing with levels, tilting of the head – encourage them to be adventurous, but not to the point of impossibility. After a few minutes, the roles swap. Additional variations include both partners simultaneously hypnotising each other; pairs joining onto other pairs; or a hypnosis 'machine' being created in which one person in the centre holds out both palms, two people attach themselves to those palms and hold out their palms, more people attach and so on (source: Boal, 2002: 51).

Group Juggle

You will need a number of juggling balls, rolled up socks or similar. The group stands in a circle. The facilitator introduces one ball that is thrown around from person to person. The pattern needs to be remembered and repeated, so when each person has had the ball, they throw to someone else and fold their arms. This way, they do not receive the ball more than once. Once the pattern has been established, and the group knows to whom they are throwing, the facilitator gradually introduces additional balls. The group must stay focused, remembering the pattern, despite the increasing number of balls being introduced. If a ball is dropped, players must retrieve it and bring it back into the game as quickly as possible. Once the rhythm is going well, the facilitator may introduce new challenges: reverse the order of the pattern; invite the group to break the circle and move around the space, still maintaining the pattern; recite tongue twisters, and so on (source: Baim et al., 2002: 82).

Holiday Snaps

In this improvisation game, one person tells the story of her holiday to the audience, and clicks through an imaginary slide show of exciting pictures from their trip. For each slide, a team of three players must use their bodies to create the corresponding image from the story as quickly as possible.

Liar

The group stands in a circle. Person A stands in the centre and mimes an action – it can be an everyday action, for example brushing teeth or sweeping the floor. Person B enters the circle and asks 'What are you doing?' Person A replies, but says something *other* than what they are actually miming. For example, they may be brushing their teeth, but they reply 'I am taking my dog for a walk.' Person B then says 'Liar!' and then takes the place of Person A in the centre of the circle, doing the mime for what Person A has said – in this case, taking the dog for a walk. Others join in at random, or the game can move around the circle until everyone has had a few turns in the centre. Encourage the group to progressively make the mimes more interesting/imaginative.

Name Ball Game

The group stands in a circle. They pass a ball around from person to person, each saying their name loudly and clearly when they receive the ball from their neighbour, and then passing it on. The ball is then passed the other way, with the same instructions but louder – with more energy. Now the ball is passed *across* the circle. Each person says their own name and the name of the person to whom they are throwing the ball. This carries on for a while. Next, players throw the ball and only say the name of the person to whom they are throwing. Try to establish a swift, regular rhythm. Next, the facilitator introduces penalties: for missing a catch, for a bad throw, for a hesitation, for saying the wrong name. First penalty – go down on one knee. Second penalty – put one arm behind the back. Third penalty – close one eye. Keep playing until only a few are left standing.

The Wind Takes Away

The group sits in a circle of chairs, with one facilitator in the centre. There are only enough chairs for those who are seated (no spares). The facilitator explains that her goal is to get a chair, and the way to get a chair is to find out what she has in common with those seated. She must use the phrase, 'The wind takes away anyone who ...' and then say something that is true for her. For example, 'The wind takes away anyone who has curly hair.' At this point, everyone who has curly hair must leave their chair and find a new one. The facilitator rushes for a chair, leaving someone new in the centre. When explaining the game, the facilitator can introduce additional rules: no moving to the chair next to you; no physical contact/tackling/dragging people out of their chairs; no returning to the chair from which you just came. Only say things that are true for yourself. If you find yourself in the centre and can't think of anything to say, then say 'All change!' and all must move to a new chair. The game is played until everyone has had at least one turn in the centre.

Zip, Zap, Bop

This is a classic drama game, which has many versions and variations. The group stands in a circle, and the facilitator explains that they will be passing signals from person to person around the circle. The first is a *Zip* in which you put your palms together, and turn to the next person, saying 'Zip!' as you pass the energy to them in a sweeping motion. The group try this a few times. The energy must move swiftly around the circle. The next signal is a *Bop*, which you can use if you want to refuse the *Zip* and make it change direction. For this signal, when someone sends you a *Zip* you put both hands out in front of you towards them saying 'Bop!' clearly. This means the person who *Zipped* you must turn and *Zip* the other way. Once the group has practised these for a few rounds, the facilitator introduces the third signal – the *Zap* – which is sent across the circle. If someone sends you a *Bop* or a *Zip*, you may make eye contact with someone across the circle, place your palms together and point towards them saying, 'Zap!' clearly. The person who receives a *Zap* can either *Zip* in either direction, or *Zap* someone else in the circle (but not the person who sent them the *Zap* in the first place). Also, you cannot *Bop* and *Zap*! Encourage the group to use full body commitment, voice and energy. Many variations exist and you may introduce new signals and challenges (Baim et al., 2002: 73).

Repositioning the Learning-Disabled Performing Arts Student as Critical Facilitator

Liselle Terret

This chapter articulates and problematizes the position and status of the performing arts student with a learning disability[1] within higher education. It will be argued that in order to make any sustained impact upon the current discriminatory structures prevailing, facilitation choices need to be carefully re-examined and critiqued by performing arts teachers so that students with learning disabilities are enabled to critically and explicitly explore the politics of their 'location' within and beyond such institutions. To highlight some of the challenges and consequences experienced by the student with a learning disability, where positions of leadership within the performing arts and training/education are still denied, the positioning of these students, *as* performance maker *and* facilitator, will be critiqued through the application of an emancipatory research structure (Oliver, 1992) and performance ethnography (Denzin, 2003).

The chapter will provide examples of two workshops on a course that aimed to explore the poetics of disability arts and disability politics through satire, parody and solo-performance art in order to shift the position of the student with a learning disability. Parody was utilized as a performative tool: to confront the stereotyped myths projected onto people with learning disabilities within the media and society at large, to examine the power dynamics played out in educational institutions, and importantly to challenge perceptions on who can do the leading.

These workshops are critiqued in the framework of performance ethnography as a means of politicizing the position of the learning-disabled student as subject and, crucially, as agent. Denzin discusses how performance ethnography is used to reveal 'struggle, as intervention, as breaking and remaking, as kinesis, as a sociopolitical act' (Denzin, 2003: 4). This analysis of the two workshops will be followed by an articulation of how an emancipatory research-model formed the basis of an ongoing reflexive and evaluative strategy occurring alongside the course. The emancipatory model is an approach in which the 'participants are involved in a process designed specifically to heighten political awareness and to lead to radical social change' (Walmsley and Johnson, 2003: 28).

In the vein of emancipatory research, the students, positioned as co-researchers and as co-facilitators, identified a number of questions that acted to interrogate and scrutinize the trajectory of the course, the tutor's pedagogical approaches in terms of relevancy and inclusivity, and the institution where the course is situated. A core group of seven learning-disabled students were co-opted to take on the dual role of co-researchers/facilitators as well as continuing as performing arts students on the course. Their role was to establish key questions for critiquing, evaluating and articulating the experiences, outcomes and politics of the course and so shifting the often assumed passive position of the student with learning disabilities to one as expert and decision-maker. It will be argued that an emancipatory research approach offers an opportunity for the power dynamic of the tutor–student relationship to shift and become more fluid. Data has taken the form of interviews, video recordings and workshop analysis in partnership and consultation with the students and tutors on the course.

Historically, learning-disabled people have been excluded from engaging in higher education, with this exclusion often being rationalized and justified as a way of protecting them from failure. The idea of exclusion based on pity re-enforces the medical model of disability where the person is seen as responsible for their own limitations and failings, rather than addressing the arguably inaccessible higher education system. This exclusion therefore assumes a narrow and also historically influenced stereotyped definition of learning disability that assumes that people with learning disabilities lack the cognitive ability to engage in higher education. The contradiction is that higher education is arguably all about critiquing, responding to and challenging structuralist approaches to knowledge and dominant notions of intelligence, but by excluding people with learning disabilities in the structural processes the cycle of exclusion and lack of opportunity continues. Kafer (2013) explains how prejudice is expressed through feelings of benevolence, with Schweik (2009) saying that disability-based discrimination and prejudice are often condemned not as markers of structural inequality but of cruelty or insensitivity. This kind of rhetoric 'sidesteps the reality of social injustice, reducing it to a question of compassion and charitable feelings' (Schweik quoted in Kafer, 2013: 10). The inevitable impact of an institutionalized depoliticalization of learning disability on 'grounds of compassion and charitable feelings' is dangerously simplistic as it returns to structuralist binaries of able/disabled and normal/subnormal. This chapter will therefore argue that a performing arts course for students with learning disabilities situated within higher education needs to embed reflexive, critically facilitative and emancipatory research into its working structures in order to shift and ultimately transform the politics and power dynamics surrounding learning disability.

The Performance Making diploma

The Performance Making course, designed for adults with learning disabilities, was created in 2013 by Access All Areas (a theatre company for adults and young people with learning disabilities based in east London)[2] in partnership with the Royal Central School of Speech and Drama,[3] and funded by the Leverhulme Trust. In 2015 the course won the Guardian University Award for Student Diversity and Widening Participation and is now entering into its third year with an intake of fifteen students.

The course was created in response to the exclusion of adults with learning disabilities from current professional higher education performance-related training courses within the conservatoire and theatre industry. The course philosophy espouses that disability is a cultural and minority identity, a social category, and is therefore purposely aligned with Siebers (2008), who explains that the experiences faced by those labelled with learning disabilities creates an affinity of exclusion with other marginalized identities (Siebers, 2008: 4).

The course therefore draws on learning disability culture, disability arts and disability aesthetics[4] and reaffirms the performer as co-creator in authoring devised solo and ensemble performances. The diploma is committed to developing and supporting new aesthetic performance forms and pedagogical practices that enable students to shift away from the current power dynamics that often still exist between student and teacher. The course focuses on devising within a post-dramatic frame, which is experimental, non-linear and often site-specific, with a focus on subverting and challenging hegemonic values and assumptions experienced by people with learning disabilities. Professional theatre companies and performance art practitioners who have taught on the course include Mat Fraser, Katherine Araniello, Graeae Theatre, Frantic Assembly and Punchdrunk.[5]

Key units within the course, 'Re-Representing Me' and 'The Politics of Performance', enable students to engage in critical self-reflection as disabled artists with agency, and in their relationship to the wider society. Nick Llewellyn, director of the course, explains the importance of this critical reflection as 'strong voices emerge as the students reflect upon their positions as learning disabled members of society' (Nick Llewellyn, 24 April 2015). The unit embraces autobiography and performance art, 'encouraging the students to use any kind of aesthetic they feel drawn to, and make choices about what they want to say' (ibid.). The course is committed to integrating politics implicitly and explicitly so that students can use the performing arts to respond to the institutionalized and social prejudices they experience on a day-to-day basis. The ethos of the course is about supporting each student with an individual means of communicating, expressing and engaging in this world, while confirming, affirming and valuing their contribution to society. Every student's participation on the course is taken seriously as they engage in performance as a form of politicized expression, influenced by the notable and important (and often unacknowledged) field of disability arts. As discussed by Hargrave (2015), 'Disability arts is an arts practice that addresses the oppression of the disabled person; a mechanism for self-advocacy and self-governance; the cultural vanguard of the social model of disability; a cultural weapon to be wielded against the twin oppressions of mainstream culture and therapeutically aligned art' (2015: 27). Disability art becomes a hybrid of performance art, offering a way in for the artist with a learning disability (in this case the non-actor-trained student/performer, who has not had the opportunity to gain any conventional actor training) to claim performance and performance-making in order to offer social and political comment. Performance art has always been at the core, if not the driving force, of the course, as it offers a tool for the students to negotiate and explore the idea of performativity with their own individual identities as learning-disabled artists.

Before we proceed, it is important here to acknowledge the politics surrounding the power dynamics between students (with learning disabilities) and tutor. Hargrave (ibid.) refers to Kathy Boxall's articulation of this dynamic experienced by people with learning disabilities who 'always exist under the shadow of exploitation' (Sheldon et al., 2007: 228 in Hargrave, 2015: 31). This 'shadow' is often, if not always, the elephant in the room when working with people with learning disabilities and dangerously undermines opportunities for the student with a learning disability to challenge the status quo. Boxall (2007) highlights the importance of any course for people with learning disabilities having the processes of the student–tutor dynamic made transparent and scrutinized by the students themselves so as to move beyond and challenge the status quo. The next section will articulate and critique two examples of workshops that occurred within the course and which embraced both disability art and performance art as a tool to move beyond Boxall's 'shadow of exploitation'.

Performance art

The first workshop to be discussed was facilitated by Katherine Araniello, also known as SickBitchCrips (SBC),[6] a performance and video artist who uses subversive humour to expose hypocrisy in response to disability and social awkwardness.[7] The workshop[8] used performing arts to re-examine the use of media and specifically television commercials in order to challenge the representation of disability in society. Araniello encouraged the students to create a type of anti-commercial that satirized the label of disability. She is interested in using performance to leave an impression, a mark on the viewer as a way of challenging narrow readings about disability. Throughout the workshop, Araniello emphasized that 'we should all be respected ... every disabled person I know is a lot smarter than a lot of people give credit for'. Araniello was interested in establishing how the students responded to how they are 'read' by the public as disabled people. She asked the students if they could recognize where types of representation or misrepresentation could be seen in the media, including films, television programmes and commercials. A number of students responded as follows:

> Student A: ... Edward Scissorhands is about someone who is somewhat different from other people but he goes out into society and people are scared of him and this is about disability ... it's about an unfinished invention.
> Student B: ... through my life I got bullied ... get stared at.
> Katherine: That's quite negative ... that's the idea of satire, we can play (with that stare). (ibid.)

Both students related to how Edward Scissorhands is perceived by his community and the fear that is generated when he is scapegoated in response to his Otherness. His 'scissorhands' are used against him; he is an easy target to point the finger at and he is mythologized as dangerous due to his different physical and cultural differences when he fails to comply with expectations placed on him. Student A's response to Araniello's question demonstrates his awareness of the social construction projected upon Scissorhand and he is able to interpret this instigated public fear as 'an unfinished invention'. Student B has a different response to the symbolism of Edward Scissorhands, as she shares her experiences of being bullied. Katherine responds quickly to Student B, encouraging her to shift away from the position of victimhood into one of reclamation of identity. She suggests that the student try to 'hold onto that stare you received' and to use this as an opportunity to disable the gaze that debilitated her. This session offered an important process for the students to reclaim their agency and develop critically reflective skills so as to use the performing arts to make personal and ultimately political responses and statements to these institutionalized stereotyped myths surrounding learning disability.

Katherine facilitated an exercise where the students were asked to create commercials that satirized and subverted the media's promotion and discriminatory representation of disability. One group created an advertisement for 'Together Forever Wristbands' that strapped the person with a learning disability to two (perceived) non-disabled people on either side. The students had created an advert that parodied the paranoia and fear that surrounds disability and so exposed how 'disability' is 'done' and to whom. This is reiterated by Morris (1991), who argues that people's fear of disability is socially produced as it represents something to be feared. This idea of fear is then used to justify the exclusion of the disabled 'from common humanity, treated as fundamentally different and alien … [hiding] their fear and discomfort by turning us into objects of pity' (Morris, 1991: 192). The very act of creating these parodied commercials as part of the course content became a political act of protest in itself, where these marginalized students were given a rightful space and place to speak of their own oppression.

The second workshop to be discussed explored autobiography, parody and live performance, and was led by Mat Fraser[9] who describes himself as 'A radically different actor entertaining with his radical difference.'[10] Mat began his workshop[11] by offering the students an insight into how he uses live performance to challenge misperceptions of disability through his own sexuality and anger: two emotions often disconnected from disability. Mat shared a video of one of his live performances with the students, which was followed by one student commenting that 'it was like taking the moment out of being disabled and so it turned the focus around' (Student C, 20 May 2014). This student could relate to Mat's work as someone frustrated at society's constant projecting of negative labels onto him as un-able. Mat contextualized the history of this exploitation and marginalization of disabled people and how this is perpetuated through a lack of opportunities for self-representation and denial of genuine citizenship. Mat asked the students to create autobiographical, live performances that challenged perceptions of learning disability within society and so repositioning the subject as agent. This process of using autobiographical performance to re-examine and politicize how disability is read in society can be viewed as a type of performance ethnography as the process of authoring, reframing and performing their stories enabled the students to use performance as a political act that revealed agency. The students created autobiographical solo performances, revealing an agency, authority and status with regard to their lived and embodied experiences. As Denzin articulates, 'the writer-as-performer is self-consciously present, morally and politically self-aware' (2003: 14–15), and so the students' actions in Mat's task became more than just 'having a voice' or a space for a moment in time. Instead, the course became potentially a vehicle that supported and nurtured these students as they exercised their rights as creative and politicized citizens. In another example, Student C performed his rap in response to the autobiographical performance-art task. The performance was about the constant challenge and resilience required to beat the daily experience of discrimination.

You see me walking everywhere,
People stop and stare.
I have to calm down, find the situation in the humiliation,
I have strong determination to fight it, to get out of the intention,
It's a big dose of communication.
I'm high up in the sky, trying to reach up,
Come on, don't tear me down,
Use that to rise up.
Don't tear me down. You are a part, inside of me.
It's like fight it, fight it, fight it. Don't go crazy.
Everybody is in it together.
And then there is peace and harmony. (Student C, 25 May 2014)

In this moment, Student C utilizes the performing arts to express and articulate the battle he experiences every time he walks down the street. Through his authored rap he shares his survival mechanism and expresses a profound empathy towards those who oppress him, saying, 'Everybody is in it together'; he forgives, and then there is 'peace and harmony'. Mat praises this student's ability to create an upbeat yet horrifying and real story performed as a poetic dance rap. This rap impacts upon its audience and, as Denzin notes, the 'performance authorises itself ... through its ability to evoke and invoke shared emotional experience and understanding between performer and audience' (Denzin, 2003: 13). The immediate reaction in the workshop by the other students was powerful and inspiring, with supportive gestures and comments including 'yes, that's it; but it's so hard to do' (25 May 2014). In contrast, another student's autobiographical performance began very differently; she presented a story of victimhood during which Mat intervened and facilitated a reframing of her experience:

Student D: My disability makes me feel uncomfortable. I have no life without being disabled. I feel left out ... my life is ruined ... cause of my disability.
[Here, the students gets upset and Mat steps in.]
Mat: You nearly had a mini-moment in that, but you took a breath

and you carried on. That's emotional stuff; we are dealing with the heart. You delivered it, you had your moment, you breathed it off. Very professional, so funny isn't always appropriate. Now your statement, I have no life is pretty strong. You're not allowed to get emotional, we are professionals. Take a deep breath. But if I'm watching someone dancing, with a damn life, and when you have a contradiction like that, that's very political as well. What do I think? Do I agree with what I'm seeing or hearing? It becomes a comment. The dance becomes the opposite. The dance says, 'damn, I have a life!' Once you learn it then it's just learnt words, then you stop being so emotional about it, but one thing dance does, it communicates what words can't do.

This is a crucial moment, where Mat demonstrates how the student can shift her position, in this case an emotional response to discrimination that has been internalized, and so gain agency by using performance. The process here seems therapeutic but only as a means to an end. The dance-poetry becomes performance art as the student performs a self-effacing parody through dance, thus shifting the parameters as to how she is 'read'. The student finds her own aesthetic, which becomes a tool for responding to the discrimination that she experiences.

Students as co-researchers and facilitators

The co-researchers (as described earlier on in this chapter) identified a number of questions as a way into interrogating and scrutinizing the trajectory of the course, the tutor's pedagogical approaches in terms of relevancy and inclusivity, and the institution itself where the course was situated.

Each year a number of the students took on the role of co-researcher/co-facilitator, meeting every few weeks to critically reflect upon the course and practice interview and facilitation techniques. These students became proactive investigators, evaluators, interviewers, facilitators and decision-makers, raising questions about the explicit and implicit learning opportunities within the course. The impact of this has led to the research model shifting from being an additional opportunity to becoming an integral and core part of the course, thus informing its ethos and philosophy.

These students took turns co-facilitating critically reflective discussions within the co-researchers' group and with the other students on the course, as well as interviewing the tutors. The journey that the co-researchers engaged in involved a process of re-positioning themselves as critical co-facilitators who questioned and interrogated the effectiveness, inclusiveness and relevance of the course. The co-researchers appeared to become more confident in articulating their reflections about their experiences of the course and what it raised for them. My reading of these conversations reminded me of Siebers' (2011) 'ideology of ability', and how he argues that this ideology has become the 'baseline by which humanness is determined, setting the measure of body and mind that gives or denies human status to individual persons' (Siebers, 2011: 8). These students appeared to be taking back what is rightfully theirs, and were moving into a position of clarity, self-advocacy and understanding of the potency of their own politicized performance and facilitation aesthetic. Rather than being passive receivers of yet another 'revolving-door project', students were defining how *they* wanted to use this course. The students *as* co-researchers and co-facilitators were able to decide upon the questions being asked in order to critique, inform and impact upon the course. But herein lies the contradiction: how was I to introduce the potential idea of the students as co-researchers and co-facilitators when they were sitting within the 'shadow of exploitation', as previously discussed?

Introducing the co-researcher through Mantle of the Expert

Early on in the course, and as an introduction to the role of the co-researchers, I facilitated a discussion with the group about their experiences as students with learning disabilities within a mainstream performing arts school,[12] with the intention of gauging if they were able to critically articulate, express and share their experience within this institution. However, my attempts to initiate discussion were met with silence, and I felt an uncomfortable tension and unease within myself and with how I had clumsily presented my questions to the group. Outside of the workshop-studio and in the grounds of this institution, I had observed the stares that the students had experienced, but I did not feel in a position to name these moments for them. A few students began responding to my question: 'it's great being here'; 'I feel so lucky to be here' (25 January 2014). This was followed by more silence and I uncomfortably felt that perhaps my question had created the silence and closed down any responses other than positive confirmation that the students perhaps felt they had to give me. As an advocate of Mantle of the Expert (MoE)[13] I felt it might be relevant to use this type of practice to create a dramatic frame where the students would be positioned as the experts in the room. I thought MoE might become a way for me to indirectly challenge the students' responses through role play in order to gain a more 'authentic' response. I explained the MoE technique and that I would re-enter the room in role as a visitor to the course, a potential new student.

I re-entered in role and quietly explained that I would like to join the group but was tentative at it being at a drama school. 'Do you have any advice for me? What is it like being on a course here?' I asked. Suddenly there was a buzz of activity, and the students offered their personal experiences, empathizing with my concern. Some of them spoke about meeting other students from other courses in the building:

> Student E: It's like they are in their own zone … You see other people doing their own stuff, and I'm like a window and I want to be like one of them … this is when I feel very nervous … will they actually like me?
> Student D: We need to prove to them that we have the experience, the courage, the understanding, we need to say to them, we may be a little bit different but we are so like you.

These comments led on to an enthusiastic discussion where most of the students shared examples of the challenges they experienced within an education environment that had been, historically, denied to them. The MoE role play ended and I was curious to return to Student E's comment, 'I'm like a window … will they actually like me?' In response to this stimulus, the students then worked in small groups to create short performances in response to their 'nervous' experiences. They worked speedily and independently, creating pieces with the consistent theme of 'don't be scared of us – we are like you'. My reading of the performances was that the students had re-represented themselves as gentle-outsiders/the Other, not to be feared, trying to persuade these other students that they would not hurt or damage anyone. I felt overwhelmed as I watched how these students with learning disabilities performed and embodied the very fear that was constantly projected onto them. The students then engaged in a critically evaluative discussion about the performances, making reference to the similarity of their experience, and that the fear and discrimination that they all experienced was something that they had to endure on a daily basis in their individual lives.

> Student F: I want to use performance to educate people about our learning difficulties and explain to them that although we are different, in many ways we are the same.
> Student G: There are many similarities between us and everyone else, [and] we are still capable of doing stuff that everyone else does. Society needs to realize that.

The performance task was one of reclaiming place, where experiences could be shared and respected, and where the students could perform their own responses to how they are perceived by other students at the drama school and beyond. Perhaps the very act of performing these to one another allowed for a solidarity of experience, moving the group into a stronger position as they did not become vulnerable to any outsider. The students articulated their awareness of the politics of their presence within a drama school, and reflected on how they wanted to further use performance to shift institutional attitudes about disability. Following this MoE session, a core group of self-elected students became the co-researchers who met regularly, engaging in many reflective discussions about the course including this short but poignant exchange:

> Student F: For me it's empowering because we have disabilities and people naturally put us into a box. But here there are normal people. So I feel empowered.
> Student G: Most people think only normal people will go to this college. You may think that of me but I can do this.
> Student H: It's giving them two fingers.
> Student G: With the showbiz industry you're more noticed if you come here.[14]

There is an obvious and explicit division articulated in the above dialogue, between 'able' and disabled, 'them and us', and the privilege of being part of such an institution and the expectations of 'getting noticed'. One of the students uses the phrase 'people naturally put us in a box … here there are normal people … So I feel empowered.' She demonstrates a sense of success in managing to exceed social discriminatory expectations and rules dictated to and placed upon her. Her choice of words to describe this is very visual, and she closes with a description of 'giving them two fingers', a slang and socially 'unacceptable' statement to those in authority. She is able to succinctly articulate her response to the imposed oppression that she has endured within the very place that historically and metaphorically has excluded her.

However, another question that perhaps needs to be considered is why this student places value on positioning herself within such institutions, and what is actually meant by this student's statement about 'being noticed'. This is indeed a common belief among many performing arts students and graduates: that as long as they can 'fit in' then one day they will be 'noticed' by the 'gate-keepers' and ultimately succeed. If this ambition of 'being noticed' is not challenged, critiqued and problematized, then these students will just continue to surrender any potential authority and autonomy. On the one hand this is troubling, but perhaps on the other hand, in order for these students to challenge the exclusion that they experience, they need to keep those 'gate-keepers' by their sides so that eventually they are able to reap the privileges denied to them.[15]

To apply this to the role of the co-researchers on the course, the students were interested in sharing their challenging experiences of being tutors and facilitators themselves, and wanted to explore why there were so few opportunities for such roles within the performing arts. The students felt that it was important to ensure that everyone understood the role and skills of such positions:

> Student J: A facilitator is in a position of leadership, someone who makes it possible for others to do things, like care workers.
> Student H: There are not many disabled teachers. I teach children with disabilities in the gym. If I ask to work with someone without disabilities, they say no. They see the wheelchair, not me.
> Student J: I was an LSA[16] in an SEN[17] primary school for 4 years; I wasn't diagnosed with Asperger's at this point and maybe wouldn't have got the job if I had told them.
> Student K: I teach people with disabilities to DJ. I like it when a facilitator breaks it down otherwise it's too much.
> Student G: It was the teachers who said I couldn't do things. (13 February 2015)

These students demonstrate an eclectic experience and understanding of facilitation in a range of settings, whether as support workers and facilitators themselves or as students being facilitated. The overriding similarity in their responses is that owing to experiences of how they are being 'read' as disabled people, they have received the message, directly or indirectly, that they cannot be part of mainstream society and that they should only work with other disabled people. Student G explained that if he had been labelled as learning-disabled before he gained his LSA position, he would not have been employed.

The only reason for these learning-disabled people coming together was their 'collective affinity' of experiences. Each of these individuals engages, articulates, creates, learns and facilitates in their own diverse way, which challenges any binary model of ability–disability. The idea of collective affinity is discussed and defined by Joan W. Scott:

> Collective Affinities as playing on identifications that have been attributed to individuals by their societies and that have served to exclude them or subordinate them … can be discussed in terms of disability politics, not because of any essential similarities among them, but because all have been labeled as disabled or sick and have faced discrimination as a result. (Scott in Kafer, 2013: 11)

The experience of discrimination, not the impairment, creates the collective affinity that brings these students together. Therefore, creating a space and a place for co-researchers to critique and share the impact of this discrimination enables an explicit sharing of this collective affinity. The act of doing this allows the student with learning disabilities to reposition herself or himself away from the institutionalized notion of *dis*ability which is based on a narrow binary of what she or he cannot do.

> Student K: Will I get the respect I need?
>
> Student L: I just want them to respect me as a facilitator and for the group to take part in all the activities. If they're talking and they are not paying attention, I'm worried what others might think of me or judge me.
>
> Student G: I worry that some will say I'm being stupid. [on reflecting about their discussion] I didn't contribute because I was waiting for a break at the right time. I need to wait for a gap because I've been told to be quiet for so long – because it's less important. When I facilitate I criticize myself a lot and always tell myself I should have been louder.
>
> Student R: Performing Arts is about playing to your strengths. If you have a weakness, turn it into strength.
>
> Student K: A good facilitator breaks it down. Confidence is slowly building up due to the skills that I'm learning and the friendships I'm building helps me to overcome my fears. The voice workshops have helped. I've been bullied before about my voice. (6 March 2015)

These fears may have little to do with impairment, and more to do with lack of confidence. For me, the course is not justifiable if it is only a performance-making course that does not address the issues of confidence and self-esteem. In order to end the exclusion of people with learning disabilities, there needs to be a commitment to the creation of opportunities for these people to be the ones who do the imparting as critical facilitators and teachers. For example, the students criticized and blamed themselves for what they felt they lacked, as a number of students shared their dislike of their own voices. Student G's response – 'I've been told to be quiet for so long' – indicates that she censors and edits herself so that she does not contribute. She also shared that her voice 'is too quiet to be heard anyway', which led to a discussion with the co-researchers about owning the space and adapting it in order to ensure that any 'difference' becomes a *quality* and an opportunity. The renowned drama educationalist Cecily O'Neill[18] often talks with a whisper when she is facilitating and indeed the benefit of this is that she gains full focus from the participants, and a sense of urgency and intention is created. Another co-researcher suggested using a microphone, which everyone agreed would be a great idea and indeed would enable other participants to explore different ways of being heard and seen. The co-researchers demonstrated immense support, empathy and encouragement for one another as they tried to reclaim a positive diverse identity and became the critical voices of the course, so that whatever was being explored or created during the workshops could then be considered and critiqued. As Denzin states, performance ethnography 'must be political, moving people to action, reflection, or both, revealing agency' (Denzin, 2013: 13), and so rather than giving someone a voice for a brief moment, the action is documented, 'moving people to action', 'revealing agency', enabling the students to become the self-advocates.

This chapter has offered an insight into a new performing arts course for adults with learning disabilities within a higher education institution, arguing that for change to happen the complex politics of learning disability needs to be made more explicit within such courses and placed in the hands of those historically excluded. Examples of participative performance practices that aim to shift perceptions of disability through a disability arts aesthetic for political and social comment have been presented. The discussion has also articulated the role of the students as co-researchers and co-facilitators, as crucial agents in enabling change, inclusion and an inclusive pedagogical practice that can inform dominant ideologies of ability still current within higher education. The experiences and articulation by the students in this chapter calls for a revisitation of *who* can access Performing Arts courses and equally who can lead and facilitate such courses. As a way into challenging the accepted norms and rules of facilitation and inclusion, it might be useful to end on Zola's 'Crip Time' as a response to those 'ablest barriers ... [that] involve an awareness that disabled people might need more time to accomplish something or to arrive somewhere' (Zola in Kafer, 2013: 26). Crip Time can perhaps be used to understand and embrace disability rather than using it as a justification for exclusion:

> It is this notion of *flexibility* ... that matters ... Crip time is flex time not just expanded but exploded; [it] requires reimagining our notions of what can and should happen in time or recognising how expectations of 'how long things take' are based on very particular minds and bodies ... [it is] a challenge to normative and normalizing expectations of pace and scheduling. (Kafer, 2013: 27)

Zola's Crip Time, placed at the centre of critical facilitation and participation, potentially offers a potent tool for challenging binary beliefs surrounding ability and disability. Rather than seeing disability as a barrier, Crip Time proposes an 'explosion' (ibid.) of stagnant values, and judgements that have been used to enshrine and justify the prevention of disabled people from gaining access to such skills and experiences. Instead, Crip Time insists on neuro-diversity, creativity and opportunity of engagement by those people with learning disabilities who have been silenced and excluded.

Acknowledgements

I would like to acknowledge the following graduates who completed the course and whose voices and experiences are documented in this chapter: Cian Binchy, Tyson Bushe, Thomas Fryer, Housni Hassan (DJ), Rhea Heath (Creative Partner), Terrie-Louise Huggett, Zara Jayne-Arnold, Bethan Kendrick, Lily Patterson, Chaz Carmon Salter and Gary Turner. I am also indebted to Ciara Rose Brennan, Patrick Collier, Alex Covell, Mairi Hayes, Nick Llewellyn, Sally Mackey, Catherine McNamara, Sheila Preston and Verna Rhodes, and finally Simon Wood, Zennie and Isabella for their love and support.

The Art of Facilitation: "Tain't What You Do (It's The Way That You Do It)'

Michael Balfour

Oh, 'tain't what you do, it's the way that you do it,
'Tain't what you do, it's the way that you do it,
'Tain't what you do, it's the way that you do it,
That's what gets results![1]

A few years ago there was a festival of theatre workshops for people interested in improving their facilitation skills. In one of the festival weeks there was a workshop by a psycho-dramatist, a forum theatre expert and a drama-therapist. What was fascinating was the inclusion of very similar (and in some cases the same) games and exercises that had very different impacts depending on who was facilitating the group. For the psycho-dramatist the emphasis was on demonstrating how exercises can surface emotions. For the forum practitioner the exercises were about freeing up spontaneity and creating a sequence to build to a piece of forum theatre, and for the drama-therapist it was about helping the group identify in one another the different ways in which group dynamics were operating. The way each facilitator calibrated the group's working environment for the day, his or her tone and pace, and even how the facilitator interacted with the group during the breaks had a strong impact on the group's working process.

In this chapter I want to concentrate on the interpersonal attributes of a facilitator. This is not to negate the importance of games and exercises and the need to design and plan workshops. However, it is also useful to ask what the intrinsic qualities of a facilitator are when they walk into a room and deliver the workshop.

The term 'facilitator' comes from the French word *facile*: to make easy; easy to do. As anyone who has facilitated a group knows, there is nothing easy about the process. A facilitator needs to manage complex social dynamics. Each group has a different energy: diffuse goals and agendas; different learning styles; varying attention spans; and an oscillating commitment to a process. The art of facilitation is about acknowledging the complexities of the social dynamics of a group while managing a process that supports the group to invest in itself or a common goal. Another term that has been used is 'animateur', someone who can enliven, encourage or promote aesthetic processes for groups. Animating a group process can be about encouraging groups to have courage, to be bold, to be safe, and to give spirit to a process.

This is not an argument for facilitators needing a big ego or having a high-status personality; rather the focus is on how the personal and interpersonal attributes of a facilitator have an important bearing on the group environment. There are plenty of examples of charismatic figures who over-perform high-status leadership of groups but who can miss the point entirely because the motive for facilitation is not the leader but the needs and capabilities of the group. As Preston mentions earlier in Part 1, Heathcote's register of teaching roles points to the different functions a facilitator plays in a workshop. The list includes provocateur, narrator, enthusiast, reflector, dogsbody, negotiator and someone who knows when to pull back. The role of the facilitator is derived from a conscious social performance that in some ways amplifies and accentuates certain personal traits. There are skills and techniques that add to these qualities, but what often shines through is a facilitator's willingness to bring their own identity into the process, not just a professional 'facilitator' identity but one that is reflective of their own approach, style and humanity. A facilitator, like a teacher, extends Hochschild's (2003) interest in emotional labour in which workers are increasingly expected to incorporate their feelings in accordance with institutionally defined rules and guidelines.

Hochschild's fascinating work focused on service jobs primarily, and the ways in which emotional labour was conceived of alongside stated duties (airline stewards, waiters, etc.). Similarly, theatre facilitation demands a very high emotional intelligence and attunement, coupled with a strong element of bringing one's one personhood into the space.

The emphasis in this chapter is on the *how* rather than the *what*. The potential of 'good' facilitation resides in two domains of interpersonal practice: the ability for a facilitator to draw on a *social* and an *aesthetic* instinct within the practice. The *social* instinct of the facilitator incorporates different aspects of social engagement and awareness. An experienced facilitator, it could be argued, is someone who can pick up, identify and work with all the various complexities that exist in a group in a way that is respectful, flexible and structured. For example, being able to set up contracts with a group, ensuring all group members feel involved in the process, managing the space, moderating exercises to suit the size of the group, active listening, building trust and being able to allay fears and anxieties, taking risks, establishing rapport and empathy, sorting out logistics and negotiating group norms and so on are all attributes of an experienced facilitator.

The *aesthetic* instinct is related to the ability to identify and introduce appropriate creative and imaginative propositions into a group process. Aesthetic work might include role plays, multi-arts, process drama, forum theatre, clowning, devising theatre based on real-life stories, comedy, poetry, puppetry or mask work (or countless other forms and styles). What makes Applied Theatre work so fascinating is the way it can incorporate the full scope of drama practices and ideas, adapting them to suit the needs and interests of a participant group. Intrinsic to Applied Theatre is the tenet of active participation and ownership in cultural production. The aesthetic instinct in a facilitator is about fostering the imagination of participants, not just in encouraging fictions but drawing on existing experiences and combining these with new perspectives or different ways of expression.

The combination of these instincts is key. Duffy (2015: 4), drawing on Dewey, discusses the distinction between procedural knowledge (group work planning, sequencing of learning activities) and artistic insight. Duffy (ibid.) reflects on his early mistakes and misadventures in his professional practice:

> An artist discerns, discovers, chooses and crafts. I merely executed. An artist sees multiple possibilities and outcomes. I steered lessons towards only one goal – regardless of what was unfolding before me within the drama. I saw the possibility of artistic practice within the work, but approached it like a technician.

The social and aesthetic instincts of facilitators need to coexist simultaneously but they offer different understandings of the process and define how the group work is shaped and developed.

The social instinct

The social instinct of a skilled facilitator can bring out the best qualities of individuals in a group. Their presence, confidence and innate understanding of social dynamics can set the tone and energy in the room. This calls for an attuned and vigilant social awareness (for more about attunement, see Hepplewhite's chapter in this book). Skilled facilitators need to pick up on what is happening within a group dynamic and be able to respond and react with sensitivity and respect. At certain times the way a facilitator designs a workshop shapes the behaviour of participants, while at other points the facilitator needs to adapt the design in order to respond to the group.

There is considerable work focused on group development theories (e.g. Tuckman, 1965; Kolb, 1984; Johnson and Johnson, 2009), and these studies explore the social aspects of how groups (of different sizes) behave and work. The research in this area identifies different repertoires of behavioural responses at different stages and phases of a group-work process. For example, Tuckman (1965: 386–7) defined the basic architecture of a group process as follows: forming, storming (resistance), norming (acceptance), performing (engagement) and adjourning. What the group development literature draws attention to are the micro- and macro-stages of how groups develop socially both in terms of individual sessions and over a period of time. At times the facilitator needs to set the pace; at others points they need to be responsive, or active listeners. Most Applied Theatre facilitators gain these insights over time, as the result of leading and co-leading workshops with different groups. What group development theories offer applied practitioners is a way to make explicit embodied and implicit ways of knowing born from extensive experience. Group-work patterns can highlight a dialogical flow between initial beginning stages of groups, through possible resistance or defensiveness, leading to stronger engagement and closure. As Hogan (2005) notes, facilitators need to recognize that it is natural for groups to work at varying paces and in different ways. Sometimes it is right to push through with a group and stick to a planned approach; at other times it is acceptable to go where the group takes the process, so experiences can be accommodated. The key thing here is creating a group process that is both organized and flexible. There is an abstract architecture to the form and structure of a group process a facilitator understands to varying degrees, and that is constantly subject to review and renewal.

Facilitators need to adapt to managing the different social needs of groups. Some groups may be very excitable and high energy, or very low and unmotivated. Some have short attention spans; others might require time to process ideas and exercises. The social context of the group informs and influences the mode and pace of the facilitator. The facilitator needs to draw on a range of response cues, sometimes proposing firm guidelines and clear rules (that are enforced), at other times responding with high energy, demonstrating high status, cajoling, offering and accepting ideas with enthusiasm. So the social context and dynamics of the group shape the way facilitators need to design and respond, as much as vice versa. What is important is that facilitators constantly take the temperature of the group and assess how to respond in the moment. Sometimes the social instinct is right; sometimes the workshop ends in humiliating defeat.

Postcard from practice, No. 1, Failure

I am facilitating a group in a probation centre in greater Manchester, UK. There are three men in the group and all in their mid- to late 40s. The programme is for men with a conviction for domestic violence. They have to be there. The group is being co-facilitated with a probation officer. We are sitting at the end of a windowless corridor, on lounge chairs that sink deep when you sit in them. I am feeling out of my depth. The men are a lot older than me and have no desire to do any drama. We talk. They trot out their story about domestic abuse. There is lots of denial and minimization. We talk about values and respect. It's superficial. We select one of the stories and create some images that reflect the lead-up to the moment of violence. They stand and go through the motions. They reluctantly hold an image for a millisecond and then drop the pose. This is image theatre by court order. We do a few more exercises but it is painful and joyless for everyone. I wish a hole in the ground would appear ...

On this occasion I failed. Although socially conscious of the group's torpor and antipathy towards being in the room, I had no idea about what to do about it, no idea about how to facilitate the group. Partially this was owing to inexperience and lack of confidence, but it was also to do with not having the social maturity to understand how to relate to the men. I'd run the programme several times before. It was well planned and constructed, so it was not a design issue. It was a facilitation issue intensified by the context of the group. Facilitators can easily lose control of a group; the group dynamic is a powerful collective force with strong undertows. And sometimes owing to external factors a facilitator may never win over a group. Learning about failing is an important element of the process, and discovering your own social blind spots and inadequacies is an important development in becoming a skilled facilitator. These are one of the ways that the social instinct of a facilitator develops and gets layered over time. In terms of group development theories, the example demonstrates that groups and facilitators can get stuck at different points.

In my case we got stuck at the stage of resistance and once the group realized I was stuck, there was little trust in moving as a group beyond this stage. For the remaining weeks we put up with one another but were frozen in stasis. A number of strategies would have helped to move the process forward. First, I was the sole facilitator, and there is a strong argument about the value and benefits of working (at the very least) in pairs. The co-responsibility of groups is shared, but equally there are additional benefits as co-facilitators can offer different modes or influences in a group. Second, while I was aware the group was stuck, I wasn't very good at articulating it either to myself or to the group. As a facilitator I kept on trying to use the same approach, and didn't reflect enough to consider what different strategies might be available to me. For example, as Hogan (2005) highlights, possible strategies might have been to create a more explicit structure for active listening, such as a life review (Westwood and Wilensky, 2005), continued norm setting and renegotiation, or self-disclosure (surfacing doubts in the groups). Groups can and do let facilitators struggle and flail and even enjoy the spectacle. However, if there is a surfacing of the issue, then there is a call to ownership. It takes a courageous facilitator to admit to failure in front of a group, but it is often this kind of response that resets the tone and level of engagement. Third, the context of the group was challenging, particularly for a drama facilitator. As is often the case in applied contexts, drama facilitators are brought in to enliven group processes, but in this instance the group were on a contracted probation order to do a group-based programme about domestic violence, and had no expectation of doing drama as part of the process. It was a surprise act and was resisted all the way. Therefore preparation and establishing expectations ahead of the process would have at least foreshadowed how the group was going to work. To some degree I think the group felt ambushed. Added to this was the complexity that the group was compulsory.

What I think this highlights is not just the individual attributes of a facilitator or a project, but the investment in time that goes into the infrastructure of a project. By that I mean how much planning, detailing, piloting and preparation go into the design and the development of a collaborative partnership and where and how the workshop is situated within the core business of the organization. The most efficacious of workshops I have seen are a direct result of long partnerships developed over time where everyone understands what is expected and how to support the arts project. As important is the way in which the facilitator is supported within the arts organization itself (if there is one). Most Applied Theatre companies who undertake facilitation tasks are characterized by low funding, ad hoc arrangements born out of passion, and mixed skills bases. Developmental support is often in short supply. Training, observing and working with other facilitators can help a facilitator hone their instincts. Key to this is having mechanisms for reflection and debriefing as an element of the automatic part of running a workshop. Some of the most powerful conversations I have had about the nature of facilitation have been on the bus home after a workshop! While that is rather flippant, what I mean to say is that the before and after of a workshop can be very powerful periods and it is important to respect and set up the right kind of time to reflect.

Recently I have been part of a team examining the practice of two Applied Theatre practitioners working with people who have dementia. The project involved two facilitators and two observers watching the sessions; one observer was an expert in drama, the other was a dementia researcher. It was striking that the reflections produced a rich and varied mosaic of impressions, observations, feelings and thoughts. Some seemed to cross-reference with each other, while others were striking insights from a particular perspective. What was interesting was that although it did inform the ways the practice developed, the process had an even greater impact on our ability to see the work from multiple perspectives and through the complex layers of social interaction. In other words it made us more attuned critical facilitators, because deep reflection was an essential part of the process. It was also fundamental that the practitioners were paid for this part of the process, an important political imperative, and often one that gets forgotten. If we are to take Applied Theatre facilitation seriously, then putting in place appropriate economic and professional strategies of support and development is key.

The point here is that facilitators learn through experience and reflection how to calibrate their practice and approach to each group. It is perfectly natural for resistance in some measure to be present in most groups. As Emunah (1985: 75) suggests in relation to drama therapy work:

> The skillful drama therapist takes into account the particular challenges this activity represents for the adolescent. Establishing a relationship with the client and engaging him or her in a constructive way is a gradual and delicate process. Both resistance and involvement take various forms during the course of a session or series of sessions, and the drama therapist must be prepared to respond to each sensitively and efficaciously.

Resistance can be part of a process in developing mutual, reflexive goals as well as an opportunity for facilitators to deepen their understanding of individual needs and perspectives. Dismissing resistance may lead to the problem festering and destabilizing the process or in individuals leaving the group. The facilitator needs to find ways to negotiate the resistance and be able to draw on a range of strategies and approaches. Preparation, professional reflection and an interest in understanding the resistance are important elements in defining the needs and finding/ testing out appropriate responses. Failure and reflection on failure are healthy aspects of work not confined to beginning practitioners. I'd like to believe that confronted with the same situation now, I'd have some possible options, but there are no guarantees. Failure and vulnerability are an important part of facilitation – because, if reflected on deeply enough, they add to a deepening attunement to the group context.

The aesthetic instinct

The aesthetic instinct is one that shapes and designs a group-work process focused on developing arts-based praxis. In Applied Theatre this can be a workshop in many different group contexts, such as in prisons, with young people or seniors, people from a refugee background and so on. What characterizes Applied Theatre work is working in contexts where theatre or drama can be an unfamiliar form. Some groups are established, while others come together because of the drama. If a facilitator has a drama background, it is not too difficult to lead games and exercises, as workshops are a fairly orthodox part of the training. However, the art of facilitation in Applied Theatre is how to design and select appropriate exercises for a specific group's needs and capabilities. And it is in this fusion of social and aesthetic imperatives that the possibilities and challenges can exist. In training undergraduate theatre students, the most significant area of development is aligning the skills they have as theatre makers to the distinctive, unwritten and implicit needs of the context in which they may be applying their skills. And it is in this constant adjustment and reframing of their experience that their facilitation expertise starts to grow and develop.

Aesthetics has been a useful introduction to the lexicon of Applied Theatre and drama education (see White, 2015), as it has enabled a discussion about the arts being more than self-expression and self-esteem building. The utilitarian value of Applied Theatre is linked so inextricably to its instrumental intention that the discussion of facilitation as an art form seems facile. Cohen, Varea and Walker (2011: 6) offer a clear definition of aesthetics in relation to its experiential value and what it facilitates:

> We use the term aesthetic to refer to the resonant interplay between expressive forms of all cultures and those who witness and/or participate in them. There are several defining features of 'aesthetic experience' – or aesthetic interaction with artfully composed expressive forms, such as songs, images, gestures and objects. First, aesthetic experiences involve people in forms that are bounded in space and time (e.g. by the frame around a picture, or the lights fading to black at the end of a play). Secondly, aesthetic experiences engage people on multiple levels at the same time – sensory, cognitive, emotive and often spiritual – so that all of these dimensions are involved simultaneously

in constructing meaning and framing questions. Thirdly, aesthetic experiences engage people with forms that are able to acknowledge and mediate certain tensions, including those between innovation and tradition, the individual and the collective. Because of these defining features, an aesthetic experience is one in which an enlivening sense of reciprocity arises between the perceivers/participants and the forms with which they are engaging.

A group process that also integrates an aesthetic dimension is therefore potentially building on the qualities of a social group process. The specific patterns identified with group development theories are both enhanced and disrupted by arts-based practice. The issue in Applied Theatre work is the nature of the group, understanding the needs and expectations of individual members and then designing, inventing and sharing processes and forms that might be appropriate. What makes the role of an Applied Theatre facilitator so challenging is that there is a living interplay between the social and aesthetic instincts. Switching, aligning and integrating the different responses is where the *art* of facilitation resides.

Postcard from practice, No. 2, Relationships of Trust

We are in a women's prison in Victoria, Australia, observing two facilitators from Somebody's Daughter theatre company, who have been visiting the same prison for twenty years. The drama space is a large area attached to the prison's leisure centre. Next door to us there are women working out in the gymnasium and a couple playing basketball. The drama area is composed of a long row of kitchen cabinets, a sink, tables and chairs scattered throughout the room. Karen, one of the facilitators, chats to the group. The mood is relaxed. This is the first time they have been together since staging a large-scale musical six weeks ago. Karen keeps getting up to try and get someone from one of the prison wings to come down for the group. There are multiple negotiations that need to occur simply to get the group together.

Justin, the other facilitator, suggests getting up to do some warm-ups.

Everyone gets up and comes into a circle. Justin runs through some basic physical and vocal warm-ups. The group becomes focused and attentive. A woman who is soon to be released is anxious and sits the exercises out, looking distracted, but is respectful of the group.

Justin suggests they sing some of the songs from the show they have done. This is partly for us as the observers, but it's also a good way to reconnect with the group. Instantly the women snap into their routines with the same discipline as when they did the show. The songs are written and composed by the women in the group in collaboration with Justin. Some of the songs are jokey; others are hard-edged raps or beautiful melancholic songs about difficult childhoods.

Observing this practice highlights the qualities of how as facilitators Justin and Karen weave together the aesthetic and social focus of the day. At times they act as prison negotiators (to get the women to the group), low-key listeners, organizers (they bring in the lunch), workshop leaders, composers, directors, informal arbitrators between the group and the support staff. After twenty years of coming to the prison, they are familiar, trusted, respected. In some ways this is a high-functioning social group that happen to devise shows and put on theatre performances once a year. The blur between the social and aesthetic imperative is organic and seamless. There are women in the group who have been with the project a long time and act as mentors and gatekeepers for the group. They support and encourage as well as act as guardians of the safety within the group.

This is a fairly rare example of a long-term group process and how the social and aesthetic can combine to construct a healthy group dynamic. The social and aesthetic seem symbiotic with each other. It seemed that the health of the group was determined sometimes by the facilitators emphasizing the drama and creative process, and at other times it was about having a cup of tea, chatting and listening. There are different ways in which groups can derive a common sense of trust and belonging through diverse forms of communing and being together. And for this group, in this context, with these facilitators, it seemed to create a strong and rich process.

Training

The challenge of training non-drama professionals in integrating theatre work highlights another issue. I used to do quite a bit of training with probation, prison and social workers on using drama-based techniques in workshops. There was considerable discussion about how best to do this. The problem was that the people being trained were highly skilled facilitators with a strong social instinct for the group they worked with but with little or no drama training. So getting a group to stand on their feet and do things was challenging. Creating an image or developing a scene could lead to all kinds of unexpected responses. There was a danger and risk associated with action-based processes. A couple of weeks after a training session a probation officer rang me with some degree of urgency in her voice. She was in the middle of a group attempting to implement some of the drama techniques and was stuck on what to do next. She had told the participants to freeze in a still image and had then given me a call. We talked through some ideas and she went back and tried them out. It was a bit like guiding a pilot on how to land a plane at 20,000 feet. The point is that a drama workshop is nothing without the drama. For a non-drama facilitator, while they may be familiar with icebreakers and so on, the nuances of developing story and characters, or developing the kind of aesthetic experience that Cohen, Varea and Walker (2011) outline, are profoundly new skills.

The anecdote about the trainer demonstrates that aesthetic knowledge and strategies need to be deep and not just a subset of group-work methodology. Without a breadth and depth of drama and arts techniques, workshops can be reductionist and anodyne. This is also true of those of us engaged in working with students in higher education contexts. For me, the ideal Applied Theatre facilitator is someone who has been exposed to a wide and deep knowledge of theatre practice and history, or even film, digital arts, sculpture or poetry. I'd much rather work with someone who has a grounding in multiple art forms but a strong conviction for social justice, than a well-trained theatre practitioner who only knows how to do image and forum theatre. The reason for this is that participants change, surprise us, are fascinated by digital worlds, adore poetry but call it rap, draw wild pictures in the back of their school books, but would never call this art. Do they still need a facilitator, a provocateur, a champion, someone to believe in them, someone to critique them? Sure they do. That's why this book is so important, to understand not just the *what* but the *how* of critical facilitation.

In the course of any drama workshop a facilitator is faced with myriad decisions based on a fine-tuned analysis of social cues and dynamics. The craft of facilitation is derived from the ability to negotiate the dynamics, to acknowledge and identify them, and to work with them towards a positive outcome or goal. The more informed and experienced the facilitator is with a group, the more precise the responses can be. For a drama facilitator these social impulses are entwined with the aesthetic instinct in which decisions about forms and approaches coexist with the social climate of the group. It is critical that these two instincts work with one another, and when they flow together, this can lead to groups experiencing processes that are alive and have genuine soul.

More than a Sum of Parts? Responsivity and Respond-ability in Applied Theatre Practitioner Expertise

Kay Hepplewhite

The qualities demanded of a facilitator in Applied Theatre are notoriously difficult to describe and can appear daunting to a novice practitioner. This chapter will introduce a concept of *responsivity* as a way to reveal the more enigmatic sensibilities of Applied Theatre facilitators, such as how they spontaneously respond to the creative contributions of the group. While the practicalities are perhaps more easily explained, responsive expertise in an experienced theatre artist in participatory settings is made up of a complex combination of skills and judgement which enable them to make good choices in the moment of practice. They build on their foundation of art-form knowledge, blending the ability to guide activity with participants and create performance outcomes with facilitation of positive engagement through interactive exchange, which, in turn, takes account of the aims and context. To manage these multiple demands, a good practitioner develops a holistic expertise *in response to* the work and primarily to the participants. But, as this research revealed, they also value their role as a theatre artist who is able to use their art-form knowledge with others in positive ways. Responsivity is a way of discussing how in-the-moment choices are made by Applied Theatre facilitators.

This chapter draws on observations and reflective dialogues with a range of experienced practitioners in community settings to focus on how they demonstrated responsive forms of performance and workshop practice in a sample of education, youth and health contexts. However they were labelled, all of the researched practitioners identified themselves as artists with theatre, drama and performance as the foundation of their practice. Tim Prentki and Sheila Preston discuss Applied Theatre, highlighting how the 'very form itself is responsive to the circumstances in which it is used' (2009: 10). The researched practitioners illustrated how they use skills to 'respond' to participants and contexts, as Prentki and Preston suggest, as well as how they responded to and were enriched by the work themselves. Sheila Preston notes, in Part 1 of this book, how practitioners develop a critical resilience in order to operate within dilemmatic locations of contemporary practice. A responsive approach details an artistry of facilitation that enables the work to thrive within such contexts.

The concept of *responsivity* was developed to describe a fundamental ethos that informed the artists' values and motivations for the work, and was evidenced through their expertise. Qualities that make up a responsive practitioner are labelled as *awareness* (of issues relating to context), *anticipation* and *adaptation* (being able both to plan and to respond well), *attunement* (having an empathetic and informed response to the practitioners) and *respond-ability* (where practitioners are able to grow and develop themselves through the work). These interlinked facets of a holistic quality of responsivity are not proposed as a universal catch-all list of 'how to do it', but as a way of illuminating some approaches to facilitation of those experienced in participatory drama, theatre and performance. The qualities of responsivity can contribute to an enriched experience of the art form for participants and practitioner. Each of these attributes will be further explained through the examples of practice discussed in the chapter.

Research with practitioners: Reflective dialogues

The extended research that generated the ideas of responsivity was undertaken in dialogue with a sample of practitioners in the North

East of England during 2013–14, chosen to represent a range of Applied Theatre practice which used participatory drama, including youth theatre, Theatre in Education (TIE), storytelling and a learning-disabled performance group. In alignment with Prentki and Preston's (2009: 10) definitions of Applied Theatre in which artist/facilitators work 'for' and 'with' communities, each project had an emphasis on change for the groups and individuals *beyond* the processes of the work itself. These practitioners were selected for the research because they effectively managed the creative theatre activities *as well as* the developmental interactive undertakings with the group, whether it was with older people, a youth group, refugees or those with disabilities. In the earlier stages of research, an initial series of conversations with theatre artists in participatory projects about skills and training (see Hepplewhite, 2013) had prompted the closer examination through a series of reflective dialogues using video (for a discussion of research method, see Hepplewhite, 2014). Each practitioner was filmed during an observation of activities (weekly session, group rehearsal, one-off workshop, participatory performance, etc.) and the videos were used to reflect, with the practitioners commenting on the rationale for their decisions made in action. The reflective dialogues took the form of re-viewing the action, debating practice choices with myself as researcher and discussions around practitioners' underpinning motivations and objectives.

The researched practitioners demonstrated sophisticated skills in performance, theatre-making, directing, storytelling, choreography or clown (for example), and this predicated their participatory practice. Knowledge of their art form was seen as an essential foundation for their successful operation as a practitioner and, for some, applied practice was only one part of their working life in theatre. (Correspondingly, facilitation as an art form itself is further explored by Michael Balfour in another chapter of this book.) However, the ability to focus on and *respond to* the experience of participants distinguished these projects and practitioners as Applied Theatre. Monica Prendergast and Julia Saxton (2013) highlight participant needs when outlining a series of desirable qualities for an applied drama facilitator. They conclude the list by profiling 'the kind of person who … is able to "de-centre"; in other words to see the work as about and coming from the participants rather than from him/herself' (2013: 5). For the particular artists discussed here, the chapter will explore examples of how this 'de-centred', responsive focus on participants is evident as qualities of expertise in practice.

Reflexive ethos and benefits for the artist: Respond-ability

Applied Theatre's responsiveness through form rightly implies that the interests of the participants are prioritized. However, the researched practitioners articulated that they also value the rewards of the work, and that the experience can enrich an artist's genuine connection and commitment to the practice. This cyclical quality of respond-ability forms an addendum to the widely accepted premise of Applied Theatre that participants are the ones who gain from the experience. The emphasis on dialogue and reflection (between facilitator, the work, the participants) as a source of change in the artists emerged as a key distinguishing feature of the researched practitioners. Helen Nicholson highlights the important pattern of constant revision within the field: 'Applied drama has a reflexive ethos, a tradition of creative and critical questioning, and the process of interpretation and re-interpretation is central to all its various practices' (Nicholson 2005: 166). This 'reflexive ethos' is a key factor informing the concept of responsivity, and reflective discussion also forms a vital part of this chapter, utilizing practitioners' own voices to express ideas. Significantly, it is a deliberate choice to place the practitioners' own articulations in verbatim form at the heart of this analysis. The practitioners in this research appeared open to a potential 'reinterpretation' of *themselves* through the work. The practitioners' words underlined Nicholson's 'reflexive ethos' not by presenting themselves as fixed, knowing experts, but by revealing themselves as open to Applied Theatre's philosophy of change. Discussion of this *respond-ability* is illustrated by the researched practitioners with *attunement*, following on from practical examples of *awareness*, *anticipation* and *adaptation*.

Planning and responsivity: Awareness, anticipation and adaptation

Key to the central theme of responsivity is a cycle of planning, revision and reaction, which underpin the features of *awareness*, *anticipation* and *adaptation*. In considering their session activities, practitioners debated the balance of planned structures and responding collaboratively in the moment. They spoke about developing an understanding of the specifics of context, emphasizing the need to understand issues relating to the participants and their social circumstances (awareness). This informed objectives for the work and ability to plan accordingly (anticipation). Whether designing new or revising tried-and-tested methods, planning is integral to an informed and effective perspective. This is coupled with an ability to read the room and listen to participants, think on their feet, adjust to the needs of individuals in the moment and change the structures that they had initially proposed (adaptation). In the reflective dialogues, these qualities of their expertise were always articulated as acquired skills which had grown over time. The following comments outline the different ways that planning (paradoxically) enabled the practitioners to be more responsive within their work and illustrates the concepts of awareness, anticipation and adaptation.

Annie Rigby ran a session at Cramlington Youth Centre, North Tyneside, as part of her wider long-term project 'Best in World'. I observed Annie in a day-long workshop with the group which was aimed at older teenagers. The group was made up of young people with disabilities and behavioural issues; for some, their communication was affected. Annie discussed her relationship to planning the work (practitioner initials are used after reflective dialogue comments and full details are given at the end of the chapter):

> I always have a written plan for a session. I always kind of write down what the exercises will be and what the steps are, and I quite rarely totally follow it. I quite often adjust it as I'm going. But I feel really stressed if I haven't got a plan, I feel really, really stressed if I haven't got anything kind of written down. AR

Annie's session was made up of group exercises, small groups devising scenes and presentations based on what *they* felt they did 'best'. This included stories about an experience on a zip wire and catching a fish and utilized a range of verbal and physical presentation styles. I observed how she responded to the ideas the groups came up with, changing the activities to suit the suggestions they offered, ensuring her plans worked for all their individual needs. Her awareness of the circumstances of the work allowed her to operate inclusively with the contributions the participants made and the diverse ways of communicating their ideas. Annie highlighted how she gained satisfaction from not locking down the processes, and allowing space for the individual interests, energy and creativity of the participants to shape the work:

> I am interested in sharing my skills but I'm interested in creating structures for other people to be creative and seeing what journeys they might go on through that. I suppose that informs my planning a lot in what I choose to do in a session. AR

Annie went on to discuss how her thorough planning allowed her to be more responsive within the circumstances. The preparation ironically allowed her to be able *not* to stick to the plan:

> I find it much easier to be in the moment if I know I've got quite a clear plan or a set of activities and sometimes it's slightly about buying myself headspace because of course you can completely rewrite a plan and take a totally different direction but I find I need to have built something, a little headspace to do that thinking. AR.

Annie's awareness of the context enabled her to adapt her planning to the particular nature of the group.

Catrina McHugh also discussed how planning was her way of remaining flexible to respond within the circumstances of the session. She was reflecting on a session with a Barnardo's group, Culture Exchange, in Byker, Newcastle, for women who were recent migrants to the city. The session included activities for the group to exchange, through a name-sharing activity for example. Many of the participants had not brought the story books preparation asked for in the previous session, so Catrina used an exercise where participants answered previously prepared questions in envelopes:

> I always – the type of worker I am, I can change my plan but I know what I am changing it to [laughter] ... how could I creatively support discussion? So I made the whole envelope questions up and can adjust and that would be my back-up plan. Because if they haven't done that, then what will we do? I'll have a plan but I will also have a back-up plan. It's not written down, but it's the one I know in my head so I understand what I'm going do and where it's going to go. And ... generally, I can respond to this situation but I still think that I think about it before it happens. CM

Catrina's additional plans illustrated an awareness of the nature of the group and that they may not all be able to prepare in the same way. I observed how her use of the questions in envelopes activity had acted as a safety net for a positive participant experience, evidenced her anticipation for the work and enhanced her ability to respond to the whole group within the session.

Artists can also use a deliberately open approach as a strategy that plans to be responsive in the moment. Pady O'Connor is artistic director of the Fool Ensemble, Gateshead, a long-running performance group for adults with learning disabilities based around clown training. Pady discussed how the improvisational strategies at the heart of clown techniques underpinned all his work with groups, whether they were professional actors or community performers. Pady spoke of how he had developed skills to trust in the openness of the approaches, and he was now able to allow space for the creativity of the group's contributions:

> I began with everything on a piece of paper and I'd go 'that hasn't worked so where should I go now?' Whereas now I'm in a fortunate position where I feel I could go in a thousand different ways. I think what's a really important thing as well is to not fear, not fear as a practitioner that you are also learning in that moment. That's the exciting thing to me ... when I don't know what's happening it's the most exciting point for me now as a director and practitioner. I go 'this is where something magic is going to happen, this is where something exciting is going to develop, we're on a journey, we're a bit in the dark here, this is brilliant!' PO

Pady's views underline the importance of his role as 'director and practitioner' to allow space for the unexpected when 'something magic is going to happen'. This participant-centred approach can benefit the creative product and the participant experience as well as reward the practitioner; as Pady said, 'you are also learning in that moment'. I observed how the Fool Ensemble were able to perform effectively and creatively around the task brief that Pady gave in the clown-based exercises. For Pady, there was no distinction between his facilitation expertise and his artistic method and role as a clown director. The improvisational approach of clown assigns a creative authorship to the individual characteristics of the performer, aligning well with the ethos of Applied Theatre, which values the diverse contributions of each individual participant.

Amy Golding was observed facilitating a session for an outreach youth theatre group, run by a large theatre but based in a community location. The group were devising a performance around the theme of favourite toys and games to present at a sharing with other youth groups at the theatre in a couple of weeks' time. In the reflective dialogue, Amy discussed how the session had blended activities that were prepared and other aspects that responded to the group's contributions:

I generally have it [a plan] in the back of my head. I know now – I plan a session less rigidly. When I first started facilitating, I probably thought about exactly what exercises we were going to do and how long each of them was going to take and now my plans are much more open. So I might still plan some exercises that we're going to do, but be very aware we might not get through that, or we might bring some of that back next week. I don't know how long that's going to take, so it'll be just there. Who knows what's going to happen? Or it might go off in a direction. In my planning, there's much more flexibility within the structure of a session, so I guess I am subconsciously planning for that flexibility of what might happen with the participants. AG

As with the practitioners above, Amy was paradoxically 'planning for that flexibility'. The ability to go with 'what might happen with the participants' meant Amy had to prepare to go off-plan, improvise in the moment and respond intuitively, as it was important to allow space to value each participant's creativity. Amy reflected on how detailed preparation used to be more important for her as a less experienced, or less confident, facilitator:

I feel confident about going in with a loose plan, whereas before I would've been like, 'uhh God! Like, I haven't spent ages and ages thinking about exactly what I'm going to do and exactly how I'm going to deliver this and will this be clear instructions and how long's that going to take and have I got enough material to fill a session?', and all those things. And I don't worry about all that any more. I trust myself a bit more. AG

Amy emphasized how she could see that her ability to respond in the moment was an indication of increased experience and enhanced expertise. Building a repertoire of activity and responses is key to identifying a senior practitioner, in applied performance as in many other skill areas. The process was complemented by Amy's confidence to 'go in with a loose plan' and her articulated ability to 'trust' in her response.

Amy went on to discuss how, with accumulated skills, an experienced facilitator becomes more intuitive within the work and less troubled by making the in-the-moment decisions. She used a metaphor of learning to drive to describe her developed 'instinct' – how the choices she used to consciously take had become embodied within the responses to the group:

> I feel like I follow my instincts and I'm not necessarily going 'I'm going to do this now because this is a technique that's going to work in this situation'. Often it just happens or I just do it, and I don't kind of think about it. It's like learning to drive I guess, you think about all of the manoeuvres and all of the things you need to do at a specific point and now I don't think about that very much, and I'm much freer with being more flexible and yeah, I just take those decisions as and when they come. I think I used to stick to a plan a lot more as well, and I've been able to throw that out of the window. AG

This illustrates how a conscious plan for the work is less important with senior expertise, where skills of decision-making have been absorbed and are therefore less visible; as Amy stated above, 'I just take those decisions as and when they come'. The use of instinct enabled her to improvise through what the individuals offered, still ensuring the group got to the next stage in the process of devising their performance.

The ability to operate well spontaneously in the moment is connected to a strong core of skills, as considered here in a discussion about improvisation in music:

> Spontaneity relies on a discipline of readiness and an awareness of one's environment. Hard work and commitment underlie the seemingly impulsive spontaneity of a performer's gestures. Consider improvisation as ebb and flow between internalized skills and extemporaneous utterances, a continuous probing of acquired knowledge to pursue an adapted, and adaptable, form of expression. (Arroyas, 2013: 1)

Frederique Arroyas here highlights the importance of the combination of 'internalized skills' and a spontaneous response of 'extemporaneous utterances'. Amy's abilities in responding had developed in conjunction with her ability to lead activity, make good directing choices and be sensitive to the individuals in the group. Her skills enabled her to be more fluid with her planning as she grew more experienced. Arroyas's 'adapted, and adaptable, form of expression' could also describe Amy's responsivity, which was developed to a level where she was able to 'trust myself a bit more'. Arroyas also emphasized the importance for an improviser of having 'an awareness of one's environment', confirming awareness to be a key component of responsivity. In Applied Theatre practice, this awareness also includes attunement: the ability to connect with the individual participants and respond appropriately, discussed later in the chapter.

Developing skills to respond in the moment

As illustrated by these facilitators, the acquisition of senior skill is brought about through implementing tried and tested methods, where response to a situation can draw on previously experienced circumstances to inform how well a practitioner can respond in the moment. Research revealed how the practitioners quoted above had a different relationship to planning than two less-experienced workshop leaders also involved in the research. Claire Hills and Laura Baxendale worked as early career practitioners with the Focus Group at Lawnmowers Independent Theatre Company, Gateshead, a project for adults with learning disabilities. The observed session explored the use of shadow and silhouette to make visual storytelling, drawing on significant landmark images from the region. The group worked in small groups to come up with their own sequences of shadow versions of famous buildings and locations around the city, processes which took some time to develop. Claire and Laura reflected that the ability to leave space for the participants themselves to respond to the drama processes was a valuable facilitatory tool:

> … it might be a sort of awkward sort of jarring moment in the room but to know that is just what's happening in the room, there's a thinking process going on. CH

They were reinterpreting their perception of the 'jarring moment' as a positive 'thinking process', illustrating how an increased attunement enabled them to respond to the participants' pace of work and engagement with the creative process. Reflecting on how they found it difficult to change the course of the planned work, even when they were aware it was not going well, suggested they were not able to improvise through a challenging situation. They did not yet have the bank of experience to enable them to draw out new plans in order to restructure the work mid-flow. However, Claire and Laura were increasingly recognizing the strength of allowing for the participants' journey within the tasks given and the value of leaving creative space for the contributions of the participants:

> LB: Yeah, have more of like a bat and ball kind of relationship so you throw something at them they throw something back rather than just going –
> CH: Deliver, deliver.
> LB: It's nicer that way as well 'cause they come up with little gems of ideas.

Through the metaphorical image (bat and ball) of their growing ability as facilitators, Claire and Laura articulated the benefits of an enriched dialogical relationship with participants. They had been clearly motivated by the group's ideas to be increasingly directive, and a more relaxed approach had in turn encouraged participants' creative contributions. Claire and Laura spoke about how one measure of their growing expertise was the relationship between planning and action: the more experienced they were, the less they were fixed to a plan and could improvise by responding to the individuals and what the group offered. Recognizing participants' significant contribution to the work ('little gems') supported an ethos of practice that valued each individual and, in turn, enabled richer work.

The ability to allow space and time to respond to the unknown/unplanned can be seen as a key characteristic of good facilitation in Applied Theatre contexts; it values the creative role of participants and shows a developed level of responsivity. Claire compared this 'additional', superior skill to a style of facilitation that is comprised solely of leading a set structure of activities:

> It keeps us thinking on our feet. If you were just to regurgitate, I'd switch off. I wouldn't be a practitioner, I'd just be an actor who was delivering something rather than a facilitator, 'cause I kind of see those two things very differently you know, an actor who's doing a game. CH

Claire's comments propose a model of a complex 'switched on' practitioner who is more than just adapting actors' games. She recognized how a facilitator should allow space for contributions that would deepen the collaboration. She noted the value of a responsive approach, marking a significant difference between 'an actor who's doing a game' and a facilitator.

Having considered the role of planning and responding for facilitators with examples of awareness, anticipation and adaptation, the chapter will now consider attunement as a further aspect of responsivity before going on to look at the notion of respond-ability and the developmental potential of facilitation for the practitioner.

Attunement

The ability to respond personally to participants as individuals and collaborators distinguishes good Applied Theatre facilitators. Attunement describes an empathetically heightened connection with the participants and the work; practitioners are tuned in to group and individual needs, aspirations and issues. Having good attunement means a facilitator can listen well, accommodate moods and the group atmosphere, and respond to individuals and the energies of the workshop or rehearsal whilst also tending to longer-term goals. This connection is important whether work is creatively led by the group, or the leader is running structured activity; a good facilitator will connect with participants in all modes of applied or participatory practice.

The research observed the way Amy Golding worked with individuals in the small cohort of her youth theatre group, allowing for the wide range of personalities and contributions. Amy described her role as '[c]reating a space that is safe and comfortable for them to be able to speak about things that are important for them, and taking that to other places' (AG). Her ability to be attuned was evident in the individualized interpersonal negotiations around creative processes of drama. I observed how she listened attentively to one person's idea for inclusion in the performance and found a way to ensure his voice was heard, even though it was a suggestion that was not realizable and a concept the rest of the group did not support. She gave him time to contribute, empathetically sensing the need to listen and support the individual's attempts to describe his ideas for the devising process, whilst enabling the rest of the group to be actively engaged. This balance reflected an ethos of valuing all contributions; she was well attuned to the group.

Amy also discussed the importance of accommodating positive processes with making a performance product: 'I have a responsibility to the young people that they look good on stage.' She was conscious of negotiating between her role as director and as facilitator, making choices in action that attended to building skills and confidence for all the individuals in the group and directorial choices for the final performance that would also form a positive outcome for participants.

Catrina McHugh demonstrated that she was attuned to the group in the context of an awareness of social aspects of the participants' lives, here located in a common experience through gender:

> There is something happens in that room where women are come together and they are then sharing their experiences, not in a victim way, in a life experience way of going, 'this is my experience'. But because we live in an unequal society and a gender-oppressive society in terms of women, there is that connection going. CM

Catrina was collectively seeking 'that connection' between, as well as with, the women participants, informed by her feminist belief that the personal is political. Alongside a social emphasis in her work, Catrina highly valued a personal connection with participants:

> [Y]ou can have lots of techniques and you can do that, but they've got to meet you and they've got to go 'I get you' and you've got to go 'no I get you' and we're all alright! CM

One workshop outcome was material for an installation about the women and it was possible to observe the development of personal connections between facilitator and members of the group. An empathetic approach underpinned Catrina's intuitive responses to individuals, which was informed by her emphasis on social and gender aspects of the work. Individual attunement to become sensitive to the women's needs and interest in the work was fed by an awareness of the underpinning social and economic circumstances. These combined to enable Catrina and participants to connect ('I get you') and build a relationship within the work.

Attunement articulates how responses to participants in the moment are influenced by an understanding of the objectives of the work, whether the focus is therapeutic, or concerned with community activism, social or political outcomes, for example. Attunement is a way of attending to the minutiae of practice, whilst ensuring it echoes the meta-objectives of the work. In this way, attunement connects closely with the priority of awareness, growing from an ethical focus on the participant as the principal factor informing wider practice choices within the given context. These concerns distinguish Applied Theatre as art-form participation; without awareness and attunement, the participatory aspects can become a trick or routine where drama and theatre work may be customized, but is not truly responsive. Through attunement, the ethical focus of the practice ensures that the facilitator in Applied Theatre is receptive to the participants' interests and needs above all else, even when balancing other (possibly conflicting) external factors.

Responsivity and respond-ability for facilitators

Change is a key theme for Applied Theatre as an objective for participants, but the research demonstrated how the facilitator's ability to
respond can build on attunement to affect change within the artists
themselves. Annie Rigby articulated a clear motivation for facilitating
participatory work:

> Actually the reason I've been doing it is because it feeds me, I feel a bit
> more connected to the world. AR

When practitioners are also fully engaged, it is possible to see their own
ability nurtured, challenged and grow within the work. The research
evidenced how expertise is composed not just of what the practitioner
does, but also by an ability to grow the work and grow within the work.
The artists facilitated practice that aimed to promote change for the
participants; they also valued the potential for change that enhanced
creativity and rewards for themselves, emphasizing an egalitarian,
collaborative approach.

Comments from the researched practitioners illustrate the particular
ways they experienced enhanced outcomes of participation in Applied
Theatre. Luke Dickson worked as an actor/facilitator with Theatre Blah
Blah Blah's performance in a secondary school in Leeds. He described
the rewards of making a connection with audiences through participatory aspects of the Theatre in Education (TIE) programme:

> The acting's great, the acting's wonderful, and to do it is very rewarding,
> but to do it when it's engaging! There isn't a more rewarding aspect
> to it than when you are working with somebody who is there to be
> worked with, and to offer what they can offer. Just those moments
> when you are gelling in the space, whoever you are, it might be a
> whole audience or it might be just one person you're working with,
> where you just have those clicks and you see them start to bounce off
> you. It's the golden nugget. LD

Luke put into words the moment when the relationship between facilitator and participant 'clicks' as a 'golden nugget'. He spoke of an

attunement with participants as 'gelling', highlighting how the ability to connect ('click') with a participant enables participants to 'bounce off you', which he valued as the 'golden nugget' of the work. This ability to be open to pleasures of the practice became part of the reward for the practitioner, enhancing his enjoyment of the work through respond-ability.

Kate Sweeney was observed using storytelling approaches with older people in a residential home, many of whom had memory problems. The process used the stimulus of a photograph to gather stories from the group which were all documented, no matter how they related or whether they connected with her own ideas. Kate described her work as a 'gentle process' because there is 'no need to get anything right'. She was open to all contributions and also in her attitude to the residents' attendance at the session:

> It's a subtle or gentle thing that they can control, a power that they can have, and a situation that they don't have that often. KS

Kate put the residents and their experience at the centre of the work, not wanting to pressure them to attend. She interpreted their actions as a performative act, describing their participation in the activity as a 'gentle' enactment of 'power' and giving a value to the work beyond the storytelling activity itself. Kate highlighted how she sees the role of visiting artist not as a giving to the participants, but as one where they are giving to her:

> So, sometimes I think that residents, or the people you work with, it's a small performance for them to find the energy to want to come – but also to be able to refuse. And then to be able to do you a favour, and they *are* doing me a favour; I can't do the sessions if they're not there. And it's nice to be able to let people *know that*. KS

Kate saw the attendance of the participants – 'they are doing me a favour' – as a gesture that contributed to a satisfying experience as an artist who is able to apply her skills in that context. She demonstrated a quality of respond-ability in the way she gained value even from the act of attendance and the contributions of the older people.

Asked to describe how she sees herself when operating within the context of the youth theatre sessions, Amy Golding spoke of an uplifting experience:

> Oh god, like a ball of energy! I become different in terms of my energy, as an energy ball, I am giving out energy. That's my style, I am a heightened version of myself [gesture], Ta dah! The way that I move and the way that I speak, I am performing a different version of myself and that is different whatever context I am in. A ball of energy, it adapts differently, has different energy. It's about how I present who I am, sometimes standing back is the right energy. AG

The 'energy' in facilitation here is not just concerned with a facilitator's responsibility to generate a dynamic for the group within the session, and for the satisfaction of others. The generation of power that Amy discusses reflects the energizing *she* experiences: the work satisfies her as a facilitator and artist, but without taking focus from the participants. Amy highlights that when responding, even 'standing back' is appropriate at times, noting the importance for a facilitator not to be centre-stage, and that the ability to listen and do little can be an appropriate response. This echoes Prendergast and Saxton's (2013) 'de-centring', discussed at the outset of the chapter. Amy highlighted the performative element of being a facilitator, using 'a different version of myself'. The opportunity to find satisfaction within all the roles consciously played in facilitation underscores these comments. Amy's emphasis on the 'ball of energy' being able to 'adapt differently' connects with a concept of attunement, where the facilitator must be sensitive to individual connections which may vary from one participant to another.

In many cases, prior personal experiences formed a blueprint or experiential model which operated as a guide for the practitioners' ability to give theatre a strong personal impact. They recalled an embodied sense of rich sensory and emotional journeys taken by making or performing theatre, and this frequently was a source that informed and motivated their work. Practitioners spoke of significant encounters within a group or being influenced by inspirational figures, which had the effect of heightening their sensibilities as a facilitator about how the work can create change in those involved, whether as participant or practitioner. Their positive prior experiences contributed to their respond-ability. Amy Golding illustrated the value of empathetic experience, citing the formative impact of her own encounters with facilitators during her time in youth theatre:

> [They were] really positive role models who allowed me to be in a place where I could be myself and they allowed me to be creative. They listened to me, they told me I was good at something and I wanted to be like that and that's why I do what I do, because I saw them and it was like, 'Wow!' AG

Pady O'Connor also discussed his personal engagement with the work as a motivating source, as a way to gain satisfaction and nourishment from what he did. He described his own experiences learning with a clown teacher and how that influenced his approaches to the Fool Ensemble. Pady highlighted that there was little difference between the approach to his work with community groups and the work he directed with professional performers. He specifically valued a lack of preconception about people's abilities as performers, and applied an egalitarian expectation that everyone had the possibility to perform well. An ethos of respect and equality for all within the practice underpinned his attitude to the work, which Pady recommended to other facilitators:

> I would always say an openness, just a complete clean slate. An openness that when you go into that room you sort of expect the unexpected and you're willing to go with that and play with that and have an openness to that. PO

The potential for the facilitator also to be enriched by the work was evident. Pady demonstrated his own respond-ability through his applied practice (as in all his performance work) and his ability to be open to new knowledge. Pady articulated how he is sustained as an artist/facilitator:

So I think to try and find a confidence in that environment yourself is a wonderful place to be in: 'Some things I know, a lot of things I don't', and that's it! And I have a very thin, you have a very thin infrastructure [circle gesture] that then allows the core of it to just go [explosion noises/gestures within circle] and start to live on its own. I think that's – for me – the most exciting thing about my kind of work and the people I work with. I think it keeps me alive, I think it keeps me excited. PO

Pady extended a view of the rewards of his work to nurturing in a wider sense: 'it keeps me alive'. His view of a 'thin infrastructure' and exploding core performatively demonstrated how he viewed being a practitioner as having a major personal impact. He articulated a sense of openness for the work to be controlled by the energy of the participants. His readiness to be affected by the experience of the work also pointed to the fact that he is open to change in himself.

This self-engaging aspect of responsivity seemed to be a common experience with other practitioners: when the work was well facilitated, both participants and practitioners were set to gain from the experience. Annie Rigby articulated a person-centred approach which underpins her participatory work, being guided by people's own interests rather than imposing activities on them. This respondability allows the participants to have a greater role in authoring the work:

I don't think it's useful for me to have a pre-existing sense of what's possible for people and what isn't – and what people will enjoy or not enjoy. I prefer much more to be in the kind of setting and meet those people and discover things *with* them, rather than to be in the role of a kind of informed expert … usually the best projects are the ones where those things really meet and there's a kind of shared interest in investigating something together. AR

Annie resisted the role of 'informed expert' to set the tone for a more egalitarian approach with participants; she wants to 'discover things *with* them'. Facilitation is more collaborative and less a process of getting a group to go through an imposed process. She highlighted how this is also more personally satisfying for her when operating as a facilitator:

> For me participation work is rewarding because it's interesting to be in another setting and it's interesting to meet people I don't normally meet. It's to me more rewarding to have an experience in that space where I feel that I've connected with somebody and I feel like I've heard what they've got to say about the world and who they are and what they're interested in, rather than I've got them to achieve something that I wanted them to achieve. Because that to me feels sometimes slightly unnecessary: 'So what? They did that exercise I wanted them to do'. AR

Annie's comments indicate that the work is most productive when both practitioner and participants are engaged and affected by, and can influence, the work. It is clear that for Annie, being a facilitator is about more than getting a group to do 'that exercise that I wanted them to do'; it is more important for her to 'feel that I've connected with somebody'. Although Applied Theatre aims to have an impact on the participants, one reward of facilitation arises from the real connection with the participants and allowing them to impact on the work, and on facilitators, through a respond-ability.

From an egalitarian perspective, artists articulated how they valued opportunities to positively engage with and be nurtured by the work. There appeared to be a potential for the dialogue between artist, participants and the performance practices to have a defining quality; the artist is also reviewed and refreshed within creative practice. Participatory artists invest in and are rewarded by the work: being alert, accessible and receptive to the collaborations enriches them in turn. The potential for their own learning and growth was cited as a key motivator for practitioners being drawn to Applied Theatre.

Responsivity: Adding to a view of facilitation

This research set off to find ways to describe qualities of Applied Theatre facilitators and proposes a concept of responsivity to make evident many aspects that may be hard to articulate. When working with a group, facilitators prepare tailor-made activities for experiences that also seek to be directed and co-authored through the role played by the participants themselves. Negotiating this balance is a key skill which can distinguish a senior practitioner, and this research was motivated by finding ways to make these approaches more visible through articulation of the concepts of responsivity.

Chris Johnston described a facilitator as one 'who looks after forms and structures enabling the group to generate content' (2005: 18). He also concedes that this 'methodology is subordinated to the reality of what is possible in the circumstances' (ibid.: 20). In all workshop situations, participants' contributions mean plans may have to be adapted. The facilitator is required to be an improviser, making decisions 'on the hoof', whilst still balancing the objectives of the session with the wider aims of the project, reading the dynamics of the group, the individual personalities and moods of the moment. Rather than being a compromise, as Johnston's comments above could suggest, prioritizing the influence of context and participant authorship can be an ethically-made choice within an empowering ethos of practice that can lead to the richest quality of work, if factors are well handled by good facilitation. A notion of responsivity contradicts ideas of complacency and cosy practice.

This potential for a creative, improvisational and responsive medium is valued by those who practise or research the work. Helen Nicholson discussed how a label of 'Applied Theatre' could become associated with a fixed set of practices, which was reductive in understanding the wider potential for theatre in community and education contexts. A lack of creativity and diversity increased the potential for the work to be linked with sameness and poor practice traditions. As Nicholson suggests:

… there were 'applied theatre practitioners' who had acquired a battery of dramatic practices that fast became known as 'applied theatre'. My suggestion is that this shift in meaning risks limiting the field if it leads to one, homogeneous set of practices rather than an informed understanding of its pedagogies or principles. (Nicholson, 2010: 152)

A formulaic approach that is regimentally applied regardless of the conditions does not lead to work that is aesthetically and experientially valuable. Nicholson goes on to highlight an ability to respond as a key feature that distinguishes good practices:

Contemporary theatre practitioners who work in educational and community contexts are, at best, developing practices that are both responsive to the narratives and cultural memories of the participants with whom they are working and artistically imaginative. (Nicholson, 2010: 152)

Nicholson focuses on the nature of the participants and aesthetic priorities, advocating ways of engaging with participants that allow space for their stories to be framed with, or triggered by, the practitioner. A good practitioner can ensure that a participant-led agenda is satisfied whilst balancing a creative artistry.

These potentially opposing priorities of aesthetic or participatory choices do not necessarily suggest that being fully responsive can sometimes be a matter of compromise when facilitating in Applied Theatre settings. The practitioners in this research discussed the positive opportunities of responding to moments arising in practice with participants. Such collaborations and encounters were viewed as an excellent source of creative potential, and a resistance to following very fixed processes or satisfying predicted outcomes was seen as helping engender a strong creative product and positive experience for participants and facilitators.

Gareth White highlights the many layers of experience and a plurality of interpretation which contribute to shaping an aesthetic value for Applied Theatre, concluding 'there is art in participation that invites people to experience themselves differently, reflexively and self-consciously, and that is shaped both by facilitating artists and by participants themselves' (2015: 83). Acknowledging the prioritization of participant focus, I suggest, as does White, that a facilitator does not have to be a selfless or invisible part of the creative process. Indeed, omitting the role and motivations of the artist in the formula for practice risks losing much of the possible value to the work as a whole. Facilitators are situating themselves within the work in the same way they hope the participants also contract in. And the rewards for the practitioner can also lead to a greater enrichment of the participant experience. Respond-ability can promote valuable outcomes and ensure the practitioner's own full engagement within a responsive medium.

White emphasizes the function of the professional's role in discussion of aesthetics in relation to the processes of Applied Theatre, asserting that 'participants themselves, working in collaboration with directors, facilitators and other professionals, have personal experiences of beautiful moments throughout the creative process' (White, 2015: 66). Being responsive to the theatre experiences within the group is an ethically sited position for many facilitators which, as White outlines above, can also be a source of 'beautiful moments'. The facets of responsivity aim to develop the possibility for practitioners to recognize and build on the collaborative potential, enriching the experiences of both participants *and* practitioners.

Written from reflective dialogues with practitioners working at the following locations

Laura Baxendale and Claire Hills with the Focus Group at Lawnmowers Independent Theatre Company, Gateshead.
Luke Dickson with Theatre Blah Blah Blah in a Leeds secondary school.
Amy Golding with Live Theatre Youth Theatre outreach group, Newcastle.
Catrina McHugh with Open Clasp Theatre's workshop with women in Byker, Newcastle.
Pady O'Connor with Fool Ensemble, Gateshead.
Annie Rigby with Unfolding Theatre's workshop in Cramlington Youth Centre, North Tyneside.
Kate Sweeney with an Equal Arts project with older people in Gateshead.

The Artist as Questioner: Why We Do What We Do

Ananda Breed

This chapter will attempt to address some of the methodological and practical applications of applied performance practices within the context of conflict and post-conflict scenarios, primarily reflecting on my previous use of performance in the geographic and political context of Rwanda (2004–12) and Kyrgyzstan (2010–14), whilst recently delivering a workshop for participants training to be drama practitioners in India (2015). Applied performance is just that, an application of performance. Performance is laden with varied cultural forms that are commonly associated with ethnicity, regionalism, spirituality and religious beliefs. These forms contain a myriad of signifiers that often reflect what Clifford Geertz reads as 'text analogues' regarding 'how the inscription of action is brought about, what its vehicles are and how they work, and on what the fixation of meaning from the flow of events – history from what happened, thought from thinking, culture from behaviour – implies for sociological interpretation' (Geertz, 1980: 175). Victor Turner has evolved the notion of social dramas that arise out of conflict situations towards a kind of public reflexivity in redressive processes. I use the term 'applied performance' to extend the use of cultural forms towards public reflexivity in redressive processes, as the terms theatre and drama imply a Western notion of theatrical forms that may not extend to the often conflicting political, social and cultural negotiations taking place at times of conflict or post-conflict through wider forms of performance. I will analyse the role of the facilitator within these contexts through an auto-ethnographic approach based on my facilitation of a workshop from 22 to 28 June 2015 at Shriv Nadar University, New Delhi, India. The participants included a group of thirteen freelance practitioners, non-governmental organization (NGO) workers and drama school educators as part of the initial Theatre for Education and Social Transformation (TEST) workshops, one of the first Applied Performance programmes established in India (2015), directed by Maya Krishna Rao. I will use Liz Lerman's critical response process to interrogate the role of the facilitator as 'Artist as Questioner' towards public reflexivity in redressive processes, alongside adult education theories.

Lerman and Borstel (2003) pose a structure for feedback and evaluation of artistic models through the following four core steps: (a) statement of meaning, (b) *artist as questioner,* (c) neutral questions, and (d) opinion time. There are three primary roles included within Lerman's facilitated discussion process: artist, responder and facilitator. Following the presentation of a work in progress, the responders are asked to provide statements of meaning to the artists or creators who've developed the work, noting anything remarkable or meaningful that has emerged. Then the artist of the work in progress asks the responders questions that might help them develop their work further. The responders ask the artists neutral questions to further think through the work. Finally, the responders are able to give their opinions with permission from the artists. Throughout this chapter, I will unravel various paradoxes and contradictions within my own practice using Lerman's critical response process to interrogate the role of the facilitator as artist as questioner, alongside adult education theories. In relation to learning and adult education, Alan Rogers notes, '[t]here is a distinction to be drawn between the *type* of learning change desired (the development of new skills or the acquisition of new knowledge, for example) and the *processes* by which those learning changes are brought about' (Rogers, 1996: 94). Here, I will primarily be focusing on the processes of applying performance in the contexts of conflict, justice and reconciliation.

Applied performance has a unique form of engagement that intends to hone participants towards a shared communitas, or an unstructured spirit of community (Turner, 1969). But, what are the aesthetic *processes* through which one creates a shared communitas? *Why does a facilitator use one form over another? Should forms or methodologies be applied 'true to form' or adapted within the context of one's own work?* I address these questions, while going back and forth between the workshop that I was conducting for TEST and previous facilitation experiences in Rwanda and Kyrgyzstan. One reason for this is that I believe the facilitator is always positioning him- or herself within the present situation while negotiating past experiences and contexts. In this regard, Rogers states 'Analogical thinking and trial and error are used frequently in the adult learning episode' (Rogers, 1996: 95). Usually on the spur of the moment, the facilitator must decide upon a direction to take an exercise based on these experiences or assumptions, as one is engaging with new questions and challenges to former ways of knowing. It is this paradox between the knowing and the unknowing, and between probability and possibility, that I want to explore within the facilitation of the workshop itself.

Artist as questioner

Turner argues 'that every major socioeconomic formation has its dominant form of cultural-aesthetic "mirror" in which it achieves a certain degree of self-reflexivity' (Turner, 1990:8). The aesthetic is intimately connected to the use of varied cultural forms within workshops in the context of transformative processes of social and political engagement. Thus, how the facilitator works within the contexts of a socioeconomic context evolves into a kind of artistry. As Thomas F. Crum states:

> Nothing gives us a greater opportunity to break through to 'artistry' than conflict. It is precisely this understanding and our ability to capitalize on conflict that will enable us to accomplish all we desire and, in so doing, help us to appreciate and enhance the most precious moment of our life – this moment. (Crum, 1988: 26)

In what follows, moments are explored through the frame of artist as questioner, where questions are highlighted with italics for added emphasis. I will also often serve as the responder, primarily because I want to incorporate a dialogic negotiation within the material through my writing and I want the critical moments when the facilitator becomes artist as questioner to be transparent. Case studies or examples of practice will be indented within the text to examine reflexive processes towards applying performance as I traverse between workshops at Shriv Nadar University, India (2015), the Youth Theatre for Peace project, Kyrgyzstan (2011) and the Mashirika Creative and Performing Arts studio space, Rwanda (2004).

I begin in the workshop room.

> It is 23 June, the third day of the workshop at Shriv Nadar University in New Delhi, India. We have explored Boalian exercises to dynamize the senses (Boal, 1992). I explain that if we are to envision conflict scenarios from various perspectives, then we need to awaken our senses in order to have a heightened sense of awareness to touch, taste, smell, sight and sound. We move from Boal to Playback (Salas, 1993). I conduct exercises based on active listening and the creation of images to demonstrate active listening through non-verbal communication, playing back the story through movement and sound. We close the day with stories in preparation for the following day when the participants will create a Forum Theatre performance based on an experience when they had a goal but were blocked by a series of obstacles. We had practised active listening of the teller's story.

I use the term 'teller', borrowing from Playback Theatre, for the individual who shares his or her story with an audience. Interestingly, there is no identical term in Boal's Forum Theatre. The instructions for Forum Theatre in Boal's *Games for Actors and Non-Actors* state that 'The text must clearly delineate the nature of each character, it must identify them precisely, so that the spect-actors can easily recognize each one's ideology. The original solutions proposed by the protagonist must contain at the very least one political or social error, which will be analysed during the forum session' (Boal, 1992: 18–19). The original story and storyteller is almost secondary to the main goal of constructing Forum Theatre that relates to a common social or political problem, unlike Playback Theatre where the emphasis is based on listening and playing back the essence of the story as verified by the teller. While in Forum Theatre, the original story is collected and rehearsed prior to the actual public performance; Playback Theatre literally plays back the original story as an improvisation. However, I would contend that the focus on the teller's story is a vital component of understanding and problematizing situations and contexts of conflict and violence.

One participant asked, 'Can you replace the role of other members during Forum Theatre?' I replied, 'There are many different versions and adaptations of Forum Theatre. But, in the way that I conduct Forum Theatre, it is important to only replace the role of the protagonist.' *Why?* This stance aligns with Boal's original intentions for Forum Theatre that had originated in response to political conflict – although it has since been adapted to address many contemporary events and contexts.

Thus, the insistence on replacing the protagonist goes back to Geertz's 'text analogues' regarding 'how the inscription of action is brought about, what its vehicles are and how they work, and on what the fixation of meaning from the flow of events – history from what happened, thought from thinking, culture from behaviour – implies for sociological interpretation' (Geertz, 1980: 175). Basically, we are using performance as a way of thinking through how social dramas link to cultural performances and then back again to social dramas, and noting that one influences the other. The sociological interpretation of the conflict scenario allows for public reflexivity through active listening and problem-solving. I did a quick mental replay of the various workshops that I had taken; with Augusto Boal, and when I had adapted Boalian techniques in different contexts. In a microsecond, I analysed the numerous variations of form based on the different objectives of the workshops and the contexts in which they were employed.

I responded 'It's due to the teller. It's still the teller's story.' It occurred to me that it was vital that it be understood that the original story should be honoured. I continued 'That particular story, told by that particular teller, is already perfectly situated within a specific context that can be better understood by one's fellow Forum Theatre makers and audiences through the unpicking and rearticulation of that true-to-life situation.' I realized that my understanding of this had been formed from own experience as a company member of Big Apple Playback Theatre directed by Hannah Fox in New York City between 2000 and 2004. I was intimately aware of the conditions through which stories are often told, held and performed within a public forum. This was an ideological and practical praxis focused on active listening through which I was now training others. *Where had this thinking originated?*

Most of my practice has evolved from working in non-Western countries, encompassing song, dance, folklore, games and music within the workshop environment. I often seek to incorporate folklore into the workshop process in order to explore the varied dynamics of characterization, plot and storytelling. This will provide a link between understanding social and cultural issues through storytelling and extend that knowledge and understanding to methodologies like Image Theatre, Forum Theatre, Playback and other participatory practices.

For example, when serving as the lead consultant and facilitator of a project entitled Youth Theatre for Peace (YTP) in Kyrgyzstan (2010–14), we explored a folktale called Yssy-kul about a young girl who is kidnapped by a Khan and locked in his tower. When she refuses to marry him, the Khan attacks her and she throws herself out of a window and into the gorge below that has been filled by her tears. This legend is believed to tell the origins of the salty lake Yssy-kul. The folktale provided a vehicle for the young people to explore current social and political issues such as bride kidnapping and youth suicide, both of which are rife in Kyrgyzstan. *How does the facilitator ensure the incorporation of the stories, aesthetics and cultural practices of the community in which one is working?*

The YTP project included several exercises in which cultural forms like storytelling were performed, taught and adapted between regions and across ethnic identities. The exercise Regional Exchange provided an opportunity for participants to devise a workshop based on a story, song, dance or game from their region. Often, this would include participants facilitating the regional context of a game or exercise, alongside embodied representations of their region. By 'embodied', I use Edward S. Casey's terminology concerning how the body integrates itself within the environment though a kind of corporeality based on perception. Thus, the body becomes a locality, a place and space of knowledge. As Casey states:

> Given that we are never without perception, the existence of this dialectic means that we are never without emplaced experiences. It signifies as well that we are not only in places but of them. Human beings – along with entities on earth – are ineluctably place-bound. More even than earthlings, we are placelings, and our very perceptual apparatus, our sensing body, reflects the kinds of places we inhabit. The ongoing reliability and general veracity of perception (a reliability and veracity that countenance considerable experiential vicissitudes entail a continual attunement to place (also experienced in open-ended variation)). But if this is true, it suggests that place, rather than being a mere product or portion of space, is as primary as the perception that gives access to it. (Casey, 1996: 19)

In this way, perception and the body as place provides the knowledge to communicate and negotiate histories, geographies and topographies. YTP exercises contained regional specificity that included an evocation of place and space. In this way, 'we examine the relationship between the two modes of acting – "in real life" and "on stage" – as components of a dynamic system of interdependence between social dramas and cultural performances' (Turner, 1990: 16). Apricot orchards, mountains, lakes, rivers and the spirits associated with these places were personified through manas, poems, dances and songs. Exercises contained traditions, cultures, beliefs and stories to enable the sharing of geographic and political landscapes of their environs. Senses were evoked through the smell, touch and taste of food particular to each region. Poetry, music and the visual arts provided context in terms of the location of place relating to the participants' origins, creating for them a 'being-in-place'. These varied forms were used to explore contemporary conflict and post-conflict issues through cultural practices.

Yet, I believe there are times when one cannot and should not use participatory performance – as will be illustrated in an example of performance in the political and social context of post-genocide Rwanda. What I emphasize here is not so much the aesthetic or practice in and of itself, but the phase of redressive action within which applied performances practice or processes might take place. In the next example, I explore the correlation between 'telling' within a dramatic form and the national juridical processes that also call for 'telling' in the form of testimonial accounts of genocidal crimes.

> I'm in a rehearsal room with company members of the Mashirika Creative and Performing Arts in Rwanda. It's 2004, ten years after the 1994 Rwandan genocide against the Tutsi when over one million Tutsi and Hutu moderates were killed within a span of 100 days. I'm in the beginning year of my doctoral studies and I've come to Rwanda to explore whether I can conduct my research based on the use of theatre for reconciliation in post-genocide Rwanda. I had not yet discovered some of the complexities relating to how testimonies were rehearsed and pre-scripted for the juridical *gacaca* courts, or how performances of cultural forms could be used to resist or reinterpret state-driven narratives. We are playing theatre games and telling stories. I ask a simple question within the Playback role of conductor (similar to the Joker role in Forum Theatre, the conductor guides the discussion and action between the Playback actors and the audience): 'Does anyone have a story that they'd like to share?' *I'm thinking this general question will navigate around the fact that I don't necessarily want to evoke stories from the genocide.* Kenny begins his story with a situation when he successfully engineers a large drug bust. Several of the biggest drug lords are either killed or imprisoned. However, the drug cartel retaliate and Kenny's whole family is massacred. Kenny states that he was about to commit suicide and had a gun to his head when he remembered the words of his friend: 'You must continue living for the dead, to keep their memories alive.' At the prompt 'let's watch', the actors play back this story, but it ends with the massacre, with the bodies on the

ground. The actors are crying. The audience is crying. It's no longer just Kenny's story. The bodies are symbolic of other bodies, potentially linking to images and experiences from the genocide. I was the conductor. *What do I do now?*

I ask whether the teller would like to bring out any other aspect of the story. Kenny states that he wants to see the moment of hope. I ask for the actors to begin again, this time moving into the transformation of hope based on his later experiences. The teller notes that he feels relieved – that it was relieving to tell his story.

After this experience, and owing to the proximity in time of the actual genocide itself and the complexity of theatre in relation to justice and reconciliation connected to the *gacaca* courts, I decided not to use Playback Theatre in Rwanda. However, despite the intention not to use Playback Theatre, the very act of listening and witnessing can open up opportunities for individuals to share stories that they may want to tell. Within the social and political context of Rwanda's history, there's a dichotomy between the limitations of participatory theatre and the dangers of 'telling', when any story could be used as evidence, in contrast to the desire or need to tell and potentially to have one's story witnessed. Although Kenny's story was not directly related to the genocide, I was aware that Playback could evoke these stories and that perhaps a workshop room might not neutralize the risk of 'telling' if any such stories were then retold during *gacaca* court proceedings. The political and social imperatives associated with 'telling' from a microcosmic to macrocosmic scale, from the ontological to the epistemological, have to be considered. *How does one create a space for deep stories to be shared and listened to?*

We're back at Shriv Nadar University on 23 June 2015, during the last exercise of the day. Participants share personal experiences from their lives based on a time when they sought to achieve a goal, but faced obstacles that prevented them from achieving that goal. They were given this task the day before, so are prepared to offer their story as the potential starting point for the development of a Forum Theatre model. One female participant shares a story about visiting a friend and being sexually violated. There are other stories about exploitation of street children, of peer pressure, of gender-based discrimination, of mental illness. However, the group selects the story of sexual violation, noting that it reflects on a culture of violence. *How does one speak about something that's been culturally silenced?*

The participants go through a series of exercises to understand the story better. They use 'hot seating' to explore the context of relationships between the two friends, the relationship between family members, and the community in which they live. They seek to understand the sexual violation beyond the physical act itself. Following rehearsals, the Forum Theatre groups come back to present their five freeze frames and to receive feedback from the audience regarding whether or not their performance effectively communicated the information and meaning that they wanted to portray. The group presents metaphorical representations of violence and collages that don't necessarily embody characters or situations, but rather concepts. I intentionally use Lerman's critical response method to guide the discussion. Responders make statements of meaning, followed by the performers serving as artist as questioner. I ask, 'What did you see? Was there a clear antagonist and a protagonist?' The respondents state that 'It wasn't always clear from the freeze frames who the protagonist or main character of the story was, and it seemed that there was a series of antagonists or characters who prevented the protagonist from achieving his or her goal.' The discussion eventually moves to responder as questioner, when the audience is able to question the artists. *I question whether or not the intended audience will be able make interventions with metaphors.* After other questions from responders, we move to opinion time. I state 'I would suggest that you make a clear protagonist and antagonist so that the audience is encouraged to step into the shoes of the protagonist to make interventions.' Yet, another part of me wants to encourage them to explore the metaphorical and to take risks with the form. I am curious whether or not a non-theatre-going audience would make interventions using metaphors as opposed to people or characters, for example a concept like 'the burden' as opposed to the direct issue itself; the feasibility of representing sexual abuse through theatrical realism.

The final sharing on 27 June 2015 was performed in a basement workshop space for a small group of students, administrators and friends. Our 'shout out' exercise, daily agendas and creative tasks are visible on the surrounding walls and the space inherently evoked a sense of 'being in the middle', of what the students had experienced over the previous two weeks.[1] We begin the public sharing with a warm-up led by one of the participants in the exercise room in order to relax the audience members and encourage their participation, and then another participant uses a song to rouse the audience members into a chorus that travels to the next room where the Forum Theatre performances will be presented. The first Forum Theatre performance, entitled 'Raju's Story', explores the exploitation of street children, while the second Forum Theatre performance, entitled 'The Burden', explores sexual abuse. In 'The Burden', I focus on the moment when the audience is asked to participate, after the final scene when the Joker yells 'Freeze' to stop the action. The protagonist is at the highest point of crisis, the performance is staged without a resolution and the audience is asked to enter the stage as a spect-actor to make interventions towards eventual solutions to the staged problem. Performers from 'The Burden' had questioned this moment, whether or not people would voice or actually physically intervene in a situation that may be culturally silenced outside of the drama.

> 'The Burden' progresses to the final scene, a dinner scene. The main character turns to her best friend. All the characters freeze. She tells her about the day that she went to her house when she was sexually abused. She questions whether or not her best friend was abused. She states that she's worried about her. She pleads with her mother and her father that she doesn't know what to do. The two Jokers (one male and one female participant from the workshop) yell 'Freeze!' There is no movement. There is no sound. The audience is silent. The Jokers approach the audience in silence. Barley audible, one Joker whispers 'Okay. What did you see? If you could provide one word, what would it be?' There is no response. There are no words. *I feel uncomfortable and comfortable at the same time. I've never seen a Joker use silence*

as a tool to encourage dialogue. I felt comfortable with the ease that the Jokers projected with their silence but discomfort because I wasn't sure how the audience would respond. They were holding the space in a room that echoed emotions and stories from the Forum Theatre performance. After several seconds, one audience member said 'There is a culture of silence. No one wants to talk about it. The mother knows and is complicit.' With a gentle and soft voice, still barely audible, the Joker asks 'Why don't *we* talk about it?' The Joker is suddenly part of the complicity. The audience begins to discuss the need for parents and families to talk about different kinds of touch from a young age at home. They point out the fact that during one of the initial scenes, it is apparent that the maid has been violated and leaves the home abruptly. There is a discussion about whether or not she could approach the police to report the crime, owing to her social standing and illiteracy. The Joker asks whether she can move interventions to the next scene when the protagonist approaches her friend's house, when her friend's father accosts her. I become uncomfortable. This scene has been crafted metaphorically. The protagonist is facing the audience downstage centre. The father is upstage centre with his back turned. The protagonist is backing up towards the father as the father comments on whether or not she goes to the gym, moving into his lustful description of her body until it reaches the point of sexual abuse. There is no actual physical interaction between the characters on the stage. An audience member yells 'Stop!' It is a woman in her late 20s to early 30s dressed in a green and gold sari. She has been silent throughout the performance until this point. The Joker approaches her and almost apologetically asks 'Would you like to take the place of the protagonist? Could you do or say something different so that the situation or outcome could change?' The woman half nods, not completely confident and perhaps questioning whether or not she should have raised her hand and yelled stop. She looks around her for reassurance. The audience claps their encouragement. The Joker leads her to the stage and the woman in the green and gold sari gently 'taps out' the protagonist to take her role.

The woman replaces the protagonist. When the character of the father in the performance comments on her body, she yells for her friend 'Hey! Your father here is commenting on the gym and hard bodies! Does he ask you about the gym?!' The audience burst into laughter and the Joker prompts the audience into a discussion about how humour can be used as an intervention strategy to bring awareness to a situation, offering a different approach to a conflict situation

Following the performance, I ask myself *'How and why was silence used to initiate dialogue?* I reflect on the rich experience and knowledge of the facilitators, as the main Joker serves as an NGO worker with street children in India, and go back to my initial contemplation about the importance of witnessing and the active engagement with true-to-life situations. Additionally, I ponder whether our work using Playback has served to strengthen active listening, the ability to find the essence of a story, and the necessity for stillness. In order to listen, one must position oneself in a state of heightened awareness and active listening. That state of being, in and of itself, draws out stories. I ask one of the Jokers how and why he chose to use silence in the way he did and he states that it was because he saw the faces of audience members during the final freeze. He looked into the audience and saw that people were emotionally moved; he saw that the protagonist's story was also their story. Thus, he decided to allow time for them to feel, just to feel, and then take them out of that place a little with a gentle voice to remind them that we as Jokers, performers and audience members are there to listen to them. In that way, the direction of the action shifted to the audience. The Joker was no longer solely facilitating the audience towards the play, but rather to the recognition of their own stories. At last, it was a publicly reflexive and emotional space as opposed to one of active physical engagement.

Before I move to the next section, I want to consider an earlier comment about the aesthetic of performance. In the case of 'The Burden', there were several scenes that were staged metaphorically. In the end, the audience interventions worked fine, with a more metaphoric than naturalistic performance. Further, the metaphorical staging provided protection for the 'teller' and the interventionist through aesthetic strategies, in which the interventionist and the 'teller' did not need to address the situation from a realistic or naturalistic scene. In this way, they were given space – both physically and metaphorically – to enact their possible solutions. The use of metaphor was introduced earlier during the workshop through Playback exercises like 'three-image story', which encourages performers to create three metaphorical images based on the essence of a story. Additionally, the exercise 'fluid sculpture' plays back a story as a chorus, each performer listening and watching for subtleties within the story to create a kaleidoscope of sounds, movements and words to best illuminate the multiple dimensions of a story. In addition, Boal's arsenal of games, including the foci based on 'feeling what we touch', 'listening to what we hear' and 'dynamising several senses', provides the necessary training of the body and imagination to extend the practitioner into a metaphorical way of working.

Both Playback and Boalian methodologies require participants to call 'upon existing knowledge and experience and accumulated experience of each other in an attempt to see possible similarities that may indicate a solution' through the interaction between the artist facilitator and the participants within the workshop environment (Rogers, 1996: 95).

Responders

During one of our closing sessions, we created a 'necklace of appreciation'. Everyone was given a long piece of string and were asked to think of one thing that they could appreciate about themselves during their own personal and collective journey in the workshop. They were then asked to tie a knot to join the string as a 'necklace' and place the string around their necks. Next, they were given 13 short pieces of string and instructed to tie a piece of string around someone else's necklace while making a statement of appreciation about them. What I discovered from the feedback in this exercise is that participants expressed their appreciation of my ability to integrate them into the workshop.

In an earlier session, a participant asked 'How do you gather participants before a session begins or after a break?' I considered how I had observed their interactions during break. *How did they relax? What transitions were they making informally that could be introduced formally?* I had enjoyed their moments of singing when the coffee and tea room would erupt with music and laughter, so I'd suggested that for each transition we could call attention to the beginning of such sessions and regroup with song and music. The same participant continued to ask questions throughout the workshop. These questioning moments helped to guide me towards the unknowing, towards possibility versus probability, thus enhancing moments of learning between the student and the workshop leader focused on student-based learning from responders.

After a particularly physical morning, the same participant asked 'What are some relaxation exercises? We've had a particularly physically exertive [sic] morning and I wondered how we could also incorporate relaxation. Relaxation does not mean not working.' I thought about how I had structured the week-long workshop, and that there weren't too many moments of relaxation other than the incorporation of reflection exercises, and also how I often associated work with physical and mental activity. Based on his prompt, I transitioned into an exercise called 'I wish ...' and instructed the participants to lie on the ground with their heads at the centre of the circle and their bodies stretched out flat on the floor. I led them through a physical scanning exercise to release any tension (often associated with meditative practices of mindfulness). After deep breaths and full relaxation, I asked them to whisper the statement 'I wish ...' and then think about a wish or desire. Participants began to whisper their wishes and desires around the circle. I noticed that several members were emotionally moved and that everyone was deep in thought. Following the exercise, we had a discussion to reflect on how individuals experienced the exercise. One participant said 'It was a very challenging exercise. I realized that I had not even recognized my own wishes and desires.' Here, we move towards possibilities. Many of the participants had stated that they experienced something similar, that they were trying to come to terms with their own desires or wishes and that they were also affected by hearing the wishes and desires of others. I considered that the emotional and intellectual engagement of both Playback and Forum Theatre is often related to desire.

The art of questioning and the role of responders facilitates the learning process through the construction of meaning. As Rogers states:

> Adults often rely on the creation of *meaningful wholes* to master new material. These structured shapes and relationships summoned up by cues are employed to make the newly learned patterns of responses more permanent and enable the adult to incorporate the newly learned material into existing patterns of knowing and behaving. (Rogers, 1996: 95)

The art of questioning can also be related to the experiential learning cycle, when the responder is asked reflective questions that aim to construct patterns and relationships. Some of these questions might include the stages of experiencing, publishing, processing, generalizing and applying (Jones and Pfeiffer, 1985), as defined in the ASTD Trainer's Workshop Series (Chen, 2003: 25–7) publication, *Coaching Training*:

> Experiencing – is the activity phase of experiential learning. It involves learners engaging in a common learning activity that provides the basis for extrapolation to the 'real world'.

> Publishing – involves learners sharing what they experienced and observed during the learning activity, or Experiencing, phase. This sharing may consist of feelings, thoughts, and reactions to each other's behavior. This constitutes the 'raw data' from which learning can be abstracted through the next two steps of the cycle.

> Processing – is group discussion of the dynamics of the learning activity. The search here is for commonalities, trends, and other patterns within the data set flushed out by the Publishing step.

Generalizing – requires moving the group discussion from 'in here' to 'out there'. It means drawing 'truths' from the common learning experience.

Applying – is discussing what was learned and committing to putting it to work. The facilitator leads learners to respond to the general question 'Now what?'

For each stage of the experiential learning cycle, the responder develops new patterns and constructions of meaning that can be applied to one's own context and experiences. The artist facilitator generates questions to lead from one stage to the next. In this way, the questions create 'patterns of responses more permanent and enable the adult to incorporate the newly learned material into existing patterns of knowing and behaving' (Rogers, 1996: 95). I would argue that both the questioning and the responses are based on a navigation of self and other derived from an inner motivation for learning.[2]

In summary, I've identified key facilitation moments as critical incidents that emerged while facilitating a workshop based on applied performance techniques at Shriv Nadar University in New Delhi, India. These moments included the importance of the 'tellers' story in relation to contextualizing social and political issues and the use of metaphor and the role of silence within facilitation, alongside the focus of desire. *What drives our teaching and learning?*

Why we do what we do

My own positioning as artist as questioner relies on the 'adaptation of knowledge and experience gained in other spheres of activity to the current issue' and 'proceeds by being highly selective of the material felt to be relevant to the task in hand … by relating different elements to each other' (Rogers, 1996: 95). I end this chapter by asking the opposite question to the subtitle of this section, 'Why do we *not* do what we do?' At one point or another, the facilitator must ask herself or himself whether or not one can or should use interactive and participatory methods. I've given the example of a political and social phenomenon in Rwanda, when I decided not to use a particular form owing to the fact that any public storytelling could be used as evidence to incriminate within the *gacaca* courts. It is vital to understand the political contexts within which one works, and to envisage the potential consequences.

Involvement or intervention of any kind involves risk-taking and can change outcomes for better or for worse – but so equally can apathy and withdrawal from social or political situations. As a facilitator, I ask myself the following questions. *How can we create a third space as we strive towards either an imagined or real sense of community and understanding? Does it matter whether this form of communitas is real or imagined, or is it the very nature of reaching towards the other that shifts perspectives, environments and potentially the scenarios that create suffering and violence?* Turner uses the term 'liminality' to describe this third space, as we strive towards new forms and structures: 'Liminality can perhaps be described as a fructile chaos, a fertile nothingness, a storehouse of possibilities, not by any means a random assemblage but a striving after new forms and structure, a gestation process, a fetation of modes appropriate to and anticipating postliminal existence' (Turner, 1990: 12).

This chapter, using Liz Lerman's critical response process alongside adult education theories, has attempted to demonstrate the multiple layers, agendas and thoughts that often operate simultaneously to further analyse the role of the facilitator. I have sought to explore the ideological and pedagogical agendas that affect the way that I design and facilitate workshops, particularly in relation to conflict and post-conflict settings. Although the facilitator is often envisioned as a neutral or non-biased workshop leader who enables participants to create a dialogic space, neither the facilitator nor the workshop space are neutral. The art of facilitation requires further analysis concerning both public and personal reflexivity in redressive processes.

'Ain't you got a right to the tree of life?':[1] Facilitators' Intentions Towards Community, Integrity and Justice

Cynthia Cohen

What is it that we are actually trying to accomplish when we facilitate group processes? How do we understand the relationships among changes at the levels of the individual, the group and the society at large? How do we deal with power dynamics that inevitably arise in working with groups in conflict?

I, myself, am not a practitioner of Applied Theatre. But I learned that these questions are on the minds of many who work at the nexus of performance and social change because of the conversations I have been privileged to engage in while working on the project Acting Together on the World Stage.[2] My roles included working with artists while editing their chapters for a two-volume anthology, co-creating a film and toolkit for practitioners, and now leading workshops and trainings based on these resources.

My own practice has been as an anti-war and feminist activist, and as a community oral historian. For ten years I directed a multicultural, anti-racist community oral history centre in the Boston area that engaged people of different ethnic and racial communities in listening to each other's stories and working with artists to re-present personal and collective narratives through murals, songs, quilts, performance and photography exhibits. I have also worked as a facilitator of dialogues with people from the Middle East, Central America, Sri Lanka and the USA. I now find my theoretical and practical home in the broad field of arts and social transformation, leading action/ reflection projects, teaching and writing from my position as director of Peacebuilding and the Arts[3] at Brandeis University.

Throughout the many conversations that punctuated the Acting Together process and subsequent trainings, I have been surprised to learn that theatre artists, including some working in zones of violent conflict, have had almost no opportunities to learn core ideas from the field of conflict transformation. I have heard much important and productive discussion about the healing of individuals and small groups, but less conversation about how changes at these levels can be leveraged to contribute to transformation towards more justice and less violence in communities and societies. I have wished that my theatre colleagues had the opportunity to learn about these issues from two of my mentors, the Palestinian-Israeli facilitator Farhat Agbaria and African-American cultural worker Jane Wilburn Sapp.

Farhat Agbaria, a Palestinian-Israeli coexistence facilitator, has worked for decades leading dialogue groups for young people and adults primarily from Palestine and Israel. His work has been rooted in a belief that with support, individuals will choose to act with integrity, that is, to change what they say and do when they become fully aware that their actions are hurting others or colluding with hurtful societal dynamics. Currently, Farhat is focusing on creating empowering alliances among people from opposite sides of the Palestinian–Israeli conflict who are working to end the Occupation.

Farhat was born and lives in the village of Umm-el-Fahm, now in northern Israel. For many years, he directed Givat Haviva's programme Face-to-Face, a Jewish–Arab youth encounter programme at the Jewish Arab Center for Peace. He founded the coexistence programme at the Seeds of Peace International Camp, where he now co-directs a training programme for new facilitators and leads groups for parents in Haifa and Ramallah.

Jane Wilburn Sapp is an African-American musician, educator and cultural organizer whose practice involves building groups and strengthening communities through the sharing of narratives and music. She has worked within black and other disenfranchised communities in the USA, and also with multiracial groups that seek to build trust and capacity for joint action. Jane was born in Augusta, Georgia, and grew up under the system of segregation known as Jim Crow. She worked as a cultural activist during the Civil Rights movement, including leading the youth programme of the Free Southern Theater. Jane served as the Cultural Director of the highly respected Highlander Center in Tennessee. Her work has taken various forms, including leading choruses, supporting communities to build cultural institutions such as museums and festivals, and facilitating workshops that include singing and the collective creation of songs, dialogue and preparation for joint action.

Farhat and Jane are both committed to supporting and empowering people to build the awareness and the capacities necessary to create a more just, less violent world. Interestingly, the feel of the groups that they lead can be quite different. In Jane's groups, one is likely to feel the joy and expansiveness that accompanies being in a community that creates together and talks together about meaningful and difficult issues. In Farhat's groups, participants are often a bit on edge, wondering whether they might be challenged to acknowledge and question aspects of their own behaviour or beliefs. I see value in both their approaches and have incorporated elements from both into my own teaching[4] and work with groups.

Over the past twenty-five years, I have co-facilitated with each of them on multiple occasions and also written articles and reports with them as they reflect on their practice. I have witnessed them both working with artistry, subtlety, compassion and ethical clarity. What follows is a dialogue I have constructed between Farhat and Jane, drawing on transcripts of conversations and excerpts from works I have written with each of them. I have often asked myself how I could resonate so strongly with two approaches that feel so different. Writing this chapter has helped me answer that question.

Both Farhat and Jane have reviewed this chapter and feel comfortable with how their ideas are presented and juxtaposed.

*****

Cindy: How do you understand the role of the facilitator?

Farhat: As I understand it, the facilitator is supposed to help the participants to understand themselves better. In particular, I mean that we help people understand their beliefs and their thoughts, and what is behind them. I try to help people understand how much they really stand behind what they are saying and to become aware of things that they cannot typically see about themselves. For example, people express themselves partly through their body language. The facilitator can help people become aware of how relaxed they are, how much space they take up, how much they are using their hands. These are the kinds of things that a facilitator is supposed to reflect back to participants.

The facilitator is also supposed to help a group understand itself better, to reflect to the group as he sees it. Sometimes a group is judging a person, or people are judging each other. Sometimes a group doesn't have the courage to deal with certain issues. The group, as a group, has its own behaviour. So the facilitator must reflect that to the participants and encourage them to deal with it.

When people are not happy with the situation they are living in – whether they are in a community we would call oppressed or in the community we would call oppressors – often they need the help of a facilitator to realize the difference between how things are now and how they would like them to be. Whatever they need to do to be capable of making the changes they want to make in themselves and in the world, the facilitator should be there to help.

Jane: Although my approach to facilitation differs depending on the context, there are some things common to all of the facilitation that I do. The most important is to create a sense of community. It is important that people get to know each other and that there is space for stories to be shared. I believe that whenever people make something together – a life, a home, a marriage – the bond among them strengthens. In my working with groups, it's making music, composing a song together. It is up to the facilitator to create a space where participants know that whatever knowledge or gifts or special experiences they bring to the task and to the group they will all be welcomed, honoured and encouraged.

The point of creating a sense of community is to give everyone the sense that they can participate. It helps people to understand that they are a part of something. They aren't directing something, and they're not manipulating something. 'You are a part of this. You are one among twenty ... But you are not *the* one.'

An idea that I bring from the African-American culture is the importance of the circle. It's not about top-down; every voice matters. When I was a child, we did a lot of ring plays. I loved those ring plays because each person had the chance to step in the middle of the circle and do something unique with their gifts. The rings plays were fun, exciting and challenging because each person had to participate until the 'play' was complete. We didn't always know who would step in the circle or what they would do once there. However, we had all made a commitment to play. We had to trust that the fun and the laughter were not at our expense but about what would make the ring play interesting and sustain participation. For those moments, we were a community in a circle that held our imaginations, our uncertainties, our experiences, our trust, our missteps and our joy.[5]

I was practically raised in the black church, where communities are composed of a web of relationships between the minister, song-leader, choir and congregation. The voices are always connected, always aware of each other, always supporting each other. A space is created that is open enough to support individual expressions and to connect with and respond to the energy of the group, while building a sense of community that extends beyond the walls of the church. In my work as a cultural facilitator, I always think about how people are connected, and how they are honoured in their connection to each other.

Cindy: Can you give us some stories about processes you have facilitated that illustrate the nature of your work and the kinds of changes you hope to see?

Jane: I once facilitated a five-year process to support a group of 18 community leaders to prepare themselves to establish a new community foundation. I was invited as a cultural facilitator to help leaders of Southern, rural, community organizations think about how they could 'build a building that could stand the test of time'.

What an extraordinary group of people! They were organizers and leaders in their communities as well as grassroots educators. They were founders of organizations, leading voices in the fight for migrant and rural farmworkers, for women's and youth empowerment, for education reform, environmental and economic justice; for the rights of black workers and lesbian, gay, bisexual and transgender communities. I felt that if this group could re-examine their visions for change and reflect on who they were in the work for social change, something powerfully transformative might emerge. I started with the metaphor of the 'building': to stand the test of time, what would it look like? What and who would be inside of it? To feel connected, we sang and created ritual. Whenever we met, we made time to hear from every person, individually. At every meeting, people shared stories and updates on their work and lives. I asked 'Who is it that you bring with you, from your history, from your family? Whose thinking, whose values, whose spirit shapes your work?' People shared stories about grandmothers and other elders in their communities. Several members referenced other individuals whose examples they wanted to follow. They referenced their daily lives and the people and values that had become a part of the way they move and think in the world. They said 'I bring the courage of my community, the spirit of my ancestors, the love I have for my family and for you.' They wanted to look at the challenge of building a new foundation through the lens of their history, their values, their communities and their communities' struggles. I asked them to think of the group as a spice rack. If each person were a spice, what spice would they be? I wanted to help everyone recognize that each person brings something special to the table, to the mix, and that something special is seen and felt and heard by others.

As a cultural facilitator, I wanted to be sure this group could think as creatively and openly as possible. I frequently encouraged the group to use metaphors. When people think metaphorically, a more poetic voice emerges. That allows people to speak from within and think more deeply. I did not want them to repeat what had proven ineffective in creating change. I wanted to take away the routines to see what they would turn to if they didn't have the old props to depend on.

I wanted to prepare this group to own and understand the historical and cultural roots of their leadership and vision, rather than take on the culture of the philanthropic foundations with which they would interact, or lose themselves in the day-to-day bureaucratic routines of running an organization. The power of history and culture combined with their experiences would be a source of strength. They supported them to reach for their full voices and bring their full experiences to bear on our conversations.

The children of the Group of Eighteen were always invited. We sang and we danced together. There was storytelling; we shared a range of music: blues, gospel, Appalachian ballads; and we danced the salsa. There were prayers and testimonies about the work. We took that time to celebrate victories. They were great evenings with music, dance, stories, food, children and humour. We were able to witness the layers and wholeness of who we were and bring that critical awareness to our meetings.

If ever there is a time when trust is needed, it is when people are going to deal with issues involving money. The cultural exercises we did prepared the group for the difficult decisions they had to make about money, policies and structures. When anyone was uncomfortable, we wanted to make sure that everyone had a chance to understand why. Of course there were conflicts, but the group didn't run away from them. They didn't drop them. They went towards the conflicts and walked through the issues, staying close to who they were. People talked through every issue until there was a decision with which everyone was comfortable.

We met for a few days at a time, several times a year for five years. The group was ready to take on the exciting challenges that would follow, both for themselves and for their communities. The Southern Partners Fund was founded as a new kind of philanthropy, with a unique identity rooted in community organizing and the history, leadership and culture of the rural South.[6]

Farhat: In Israel, when we bring Jewish and Arab young people together, it is often the first time that they have come together to meet each other. And this already says a lot. Within Israel, generally speaking, people live in separate communities, five minutes by car from each other, and they don't dare to go to each other's communities to learn about the other culture. The kids, especially those from the majority community, come to our groups with a lack of knowledge about the other. They are filled with stereotypes, some based on the national conflict between Israelis and the Palestinians who want a state. So it is very complicated. The minority kids come with a lot of rage and anger, and a lot of curiosity to listen to the majority people to see what they think about the injustices within Israeli society. Also, I see that in many cases the minority is looking for some acceptance from the majority. It is a classic case.

In this situation, I do a lot of uni-national work, where I am looking to strengthen the minority, their belief in themselves, their sense of security in themselves and their self-esteem. I ask them 'Why do you need the majority to accept you? Can't you just live on your own, in your own community, with a separate educational system?' I know they somehow have a need to be accepted as equals. The first step for them is to seek to be accepted as human beings; then maybe the majority might think about the injustice and think that maybe Arabs should have full rights. These kids want to be accepted because they see their future is connected with their Jewish neighbours.

My goal for the majority is to bring them to a level where they can recognize the injustice and do something to change the situation. I don't want them to feel guilty or ashamed; I want them to do something to challenge the injustice. That might be a long-term goal. The short-term goal is to open their minds a little bit. I expect participants in our workshops to start asking themselves questions, to become more critical of the beliefs that they have about the other side, and about what is going on around them.

There are many techniques I can use in working towards these goals. I think it is very important to point out any positive contributions. When you see, for example, that an individual really has the courage to open up, it is important to compliment him or her by saying something like 'That kind of work really needs courage, and I appreciate what you are doing.' I also feel that it empowers the group when, as a facilitator, I recognize that, as a group, they are dealing with a difficult issue that many other groups don't have the courage to deal with.

And sometimes, of course, I challenge the individual or the group. You have to be very sensitive in this case. But somehow you can mention that you feel the group is avoiding a specific issue, or you can raise the issue of power dynamics in the group.

In general, I use a range of different strategies to *reflect* the group to itself, sometimes simply by making an observation. I might say 'I notice that David is always the first to speak' or 'I notice that members of the Palestinian delegation are struggling to have their own space.' Sometimes I reflect back to the group by asking a challenging question: 'What do you mean when you say you will give back the land?' Or, when someone describes or enacts a feeling of powerlessness, I might ask 'So, what kinds of power *do* you have?' Or I might ask members of one group 'Why do you feel that those from the other group have stopped talking?' Sometimes I paraphrase participants' comments to make the patterns more clear, both to the speaker and to other members of the group.

I also use a range of strategies to *intervene* in the group's process. For instance, I sometimes invite people who haven't spoken to take their space in the group, or encourage a member to share their feelings in response to the comments of another group member. Sometimes I might work with a particular individual about his or her own language or behaviour; this is partly to support growth for that one person, but the whole group learns from the experience.

When I want to challenge participants to think creatively and listen to each other, I use artistic forms in a variety of ways. For instance, in using a process known as *Photo L'engage*, I display a set of photographs around the room, perhaps thirty-five or forty images. Few if any relate to the conflict or even the region. Then I ask participants to choose an image that captures how they feel about the conflict. People's curiosity about how others interpret the images encourages attentive listening, and explaining how the photographs relate to their feelings encourages participants to think in new ways and to find new language to express their feelings.

Sometimes I prepare a set of cards, each one with a word or phrase that represents a cultural or political reference that is likely to have meaning for participants in the group. For instance, in facilitating a group of administrators at Brandeis University, we included words like *pluralism, truth unto its innermost parts* (the institution's motto), *flowering trees on campus, legacy of Louis Brandeis, social justice, The Rose Art Museum, #1 rising research institution, faculty commitment to students' learning,* and so on. Each person took five cards and was then challenged to 'let go' of them, one at a time. 'If you had to let go of something about Brandeis, what would you let go of first?' Then each participant explained their choice to the group. This continues until, in the end, they explain why they have held on to the final card that remains in their hand. In this process, people clarify their own values and learn a lot about the complexity of each other's sensibilities.

I've used a similar exercise with Palestinian and Israeli teenagers, sometimes starting out in uni-national groups, then bringing the groups together to share the last card that is held in each participant's hand.

Cindy: What about power inequalities? How do you support members of the group to acknowledge and change the dynamics of power, as they operate in themselves, in the group and in society at large?

Farhat: Sometimes I use a role-play exercise to help the more powerful group to walk in the shoes of the less powerful, or vice versa. For instance, first I ask a member of the subgroup to take on an identity of the other community. Let's say I ask a young Israeli settler to take on the identity of a Palestinian person. I might ask them to choose a name, to pick a city or town where they live, to think of a mother and a father telling them it's time to go to school in the morning. Once the identity is established, I then ask them how, in their role as a Palestinian teenager, they hear and understand the words previously spoken by an Israeli in the group. I ask them how they would like to respond. And then I would construct a parallel exercise for a Palestinian participant.

I believe that as a facilitator I should be committed to supporting the integrity of each person. I should help participants become aware of their own behaviours and attitudes, and make choices about how they want to relate to others in the group. I want these people to notice how their choices about language and behaviours affect themselves, and each other, and the group. All of the participants need to recognize that they have the capacity to make choices and that their choices can affect the trajectory not only of the group, but of the larger conflict. I believe that when I help participants see how the patterns they manifest in the group reflect the political reality of the region, and as they become more and more aware of their own actions in this light, they will choose to change the patterns of their behaviour that reinforce the conflict.

In this process, I find that participants become more understanding of the complexity of the conflict and of their relationships. They become less likely to rely on simplistic answers. My intention is that participants leave committed to learning more about the conflict and possible resolutions.[7]

Jane: Sometimes folks who are in positions of power know that when they speak, everyone else will stop and listen. If they start talking for too long in the group, sometimes I just tell them that they have to back off, that it is someone else's turn. I also ask the group 'What is going on here? What are you hearing? Who are you not hearing? Why do you think that is?'

I used to be the cultural director of The Highlander Center[8] and we often had black and white groups from the South together. When both groups came from poor communities, there were so many similarities between them. The white folks who came from Appalachia felt that they were always being put down as 'hillbillies', but when we brought in wealthier, liberal progressive groups of white people, they always assumed that they knew so much. But what they didn't realize is that they often didn't understand what it means to be in a community. I remember one meeting where a woman complained that there were so many children running around. In that case I needed to point out the cultural context: many of us grew up without any places to put our kids, so they came with us to meetings. In so many cases, these progressive but economically privileged people understand the issues and the historical analyses, but they have problems really living in the space of a community. People from European cultures can be very organized and systematic and that's a strength that works in some contexts, but not all. So when we're all together like this, we have to look at not only a sense of understanding the culture, but understanding whose way of looking at the world gets valued and how that plays out in the group that we're part of. I like to put that out on the table when I'm going to work with mixed groups: I generally start with the cultural context.

Sometimes when white people are present, African-American people do not want me to touch any subject that has to do with racism. They want me to act like everything is fine, everyone is happy, like there are no issues. Sometimes they just don't want to touch the subject because it is too painful. Or people will throw a comment back at me, saying 'You're trying to divide the races by talking about racism, or by talking about how we are different. Because when you talk about how we are different that just divides us more, rather than brings us together.'

Cindy: I think this is one of the biggest barriers in working towards racial justice in the USA: people don't want to touch the pain, and they're so invested in being polite and in keeping it all covered over. Perhaps they are scared of the rage that is underneath the politeness. And white people are often afraid of their guilt and the shame and of being on the receiving end of that rage. So we rarely get to a place where we build relationships that are real and truthful, and without speaking honestly, it is difficult to trust each other in deep ways. How do you create opportunities for people to deal with some of these harder issues?

Jane: I remember a workshop at Highlander where we had African-American kids from the South and white kids from Appalachia, and also some kids from the Northeast as well. And we were dealing with diversity, and one of the kids from the Northeast said 'I don't understand why we have to see these differences. Why can't we all just be the same?' So one of the black kids from South Carolina sits up and says 'Yeah, but same like who?' This was a breakthrough moment: you could just see them all thinking, 'Yeah, right. So if we were all the same, we'd have to choose whose image we have to become like.'

I remember another particular cultural workshop I led at Highlander, this time with adults, where there was an intense discussion about the Confederate flag. We had managed to create a safe space where both blacks and whites could bring their true thoughts and feelings. The African-American participants talked about the flag as an ugly cultural symbol, a symbol that immediately reminded them of the cruelty of slavery as it celebrated and dignified the culture that was responsible for so much suffering. But the white participants responded 'We just never thought about it that way. You know, my Mama had this flag, and my Daddy, but we never think about it in terms of the Civil War, but sort of like this symbol of Southern culture.' And one of the black participants responded 'Yeah, *white* Southern culture.'

So everybody felt like they could air their thoughts and feelings, like they could really say what they felt. No one got insulted or broke down, but it was an equal exchange and everyone was strong in what they had to say. And there was a moment when one of the white participants said 'I see what you are saying.' And then one of the very fiery and passionate black leaders said 'This is really part of your culture and that's how you see it. I'm going to have to think about this.' It was the moment when the group clicked; there was willingness from both groups to step over onto the other side and hear more closely what was underneath people's feelings. It was a real breakthrough.

Farhat: When working with people from an oppressed community, I think it is really important to support them to empower themselves. They need to understand that they can do it, they can make the change, they can make a difference in their own lives. Whether in the case of African-Americans or Palestinians, I think that the more they trust themselves, the more they are able to accept the other – the people who are in power, in these cases the white people and the Israelis. Otherwise, generally speaking, they will continue to blame the other side. They will say those others are wrong, the system is wrong, the system discriminates against us. All of that might be true, but it's not enough. It won't bring the change they are seeking. But I think it is very important to realize that all of the white people, or all of the Israelis, are not the same. They can't really judge the whole group and put them in one box. It is very important for Palestinians not to put all Israelis in the same box, to say that every Israeli is terrible and is oppressing us. I think it is important for Palestinians to recognize those people who are open minded and who are trying to help, and trying to make change.

Another thing is that there is a lot of work to do within Palestinian communities. I don't think you can oppress a part of your own people when you are asking for freedom. It's impossible to neglect these issues, to say 'Now is not the time for it.' For me, now *is* the time to fight against the occupation and to fight the oppressive dynamics within our own communities – for instance, in relation to gender. These groups must do a lot of work in parallel, at the same time.

I used to feel a dilemma about whether people living under occupation should be brought to groups where they are encouraged to empathize with their oppressors. I worried that if they let go of their anger, they would lose their energy to resist. More recently, I haven't been thinking about empathy that much. I think it is important for Palestinians to empower the Israelis who are on their side, who don't believe in the occupation, who are doing their best to end it. My priority is to build people's capacities to think strategically about who they want as their ally and to build coalitions with them to transform the root causes of our conflict.

*****

Conclusion

Both Farhat and Jane understand their facilitation in the context of struggles for social change. When they facilitate groups, they are interested in creating opportunities for people to strengthen their capacity – as individuals and as groups – to create a future that is more just and less violent. They support movement towards a world that, as a matter of justice, is more vibrant and more embracing of diverse cultures.

Both emphasize the importance of addressing the dynamics of power asymmetries *as these are expressed in the person, the group and the society.* Their repertoire of approaches allows each of them to recognize the shared humanity of participants in groups as well as to affirm and explore participants' distinct narratives and their very different relationships to the dynamics of power.

Jane and Farhat clearly value the individual, the group and the community as mutually reinforcing agents of change. But in this regard, their approaches are different. Jane works to build a community that embodies values of fairness and inclusion. With the support of that community, participants are encouraged to challenge their assumptions, affirm their culture and engage with their creativity, and to acknowledge and transform the dynamics of oppression they've internalized. Farhat, on the other hand, focuses on strengthening the awareness and integrity of each person, supporting them to see how they are complicit in maintaining a status quo that falls far short of the world they wish they could inhabit. With changes in awareness at the level of the individual, people can differentiate among those on 'the other side' and decide with whom they can create alliances for change.

As I have brought Farhat's and Jane's stories and reflections into relationship, I have discovered the common values that underlie their different approaches. While they of course support and challenge people on all sides of a conflict to listen well to each other's thoughts, feelings, stories and questions, and while they are steadfast in their commitment to the growth and integrity of all parties, they base their work on a clear sense of social justice and supporting people to be more effective in working to enhance it.

Jane Sapp has deepened my understanding about the importance of building a sense of community as a condition for the personal and collective growth required for social change. In the context of a supportive community, people become more courageous and creative. Community, courage and creativity are all requirements for effective work for social justice. I strive to create these conditions in my classes and in my work with groups.

Farhat Agbaria has helped me see how deeply the dynamics of a conflict reside within each of us, and how skilful facilitation can help people become aware of how they embody these dynamics. It can also support and challenge people to question their beliefs, narratives and values, even those they have held sacred. Practitioners who work in zones of violent conflict run the risk of doing harm if they have not engaged in this level of self-reflection and grappled with issues surrounding their own identity. I believe that, as a field, we must create the conditions for people to work at this level.

Every choice we make as facilitators reflects a complex interplay of our ethics, our politics and our beliefs about the capacity of human beings and how change occurs. I hope that readers of this chapter find Farhat's and Jane's reflections useful – not primarily because of their techniques, but because of the ethical and political commitments their stories reveal.

Afterword

At the heart of this book sits the need to explore the possibilities and confront the problematics of facilitation practices. This afterword offers closing thoughts on the challenges of facilitation around the themes of *pedagogies*, *practices* and *resilience*, stimulated by the individual contributions to Part 2. This discussion resists firm conclusions, but rather aims to inspire further, deeper interrogation into the challenges of critical facilitation in practice. The case studies in the preceding chapters, presented by a range of practitioners and scholars, emanate from a range of international contexts: Australia, Serbia, Kyrgyzstan, India, Israel/Palestine, Rwanda, the United Kingdom and North America. These seven chapters present a diverse range of cultural contexts in which facilitation occurs – often at the micro level – with groups whose complex histories and experiences have led them to be disenfranchised socially, culturally and/or economically. However, it would be misleading to suggest that diversity of practice is essentially characterized by geographical spread. The range of examples presented in this book also share a commonality in terms of the challenges of facilitating participatory practice from *within* community settings, wherever this occurs; whether a community centre, prison or school, or whether situated in East London, Belgrade or Palestine. As this book has sought to demonstrate, the negotiation of difference, contradiction and dilemma is apparent on many levels within all settings, with regard to the participants themselves, but also in relation to the choice of aesthetic practices that can be utilized and the sheer range of directions that any practice could take.

As an academic *and* practitioner (in common with each contributor in this book), the 'big' incongruences – between theory and practice and between the macro and micro – are only too present in my work, as are the smaller (but no less crucial), more nuanced contradictions that constantly emerge in the process of enabling genuinely participatory processes. A critical practice indicates (and this is *felt* wholeheartedly when one is a practitioner sitting 'in the mess' confronting a sense of failure) that there is often a mismatch between what is intended, or *said*, and what is *done* in the moment and afterwards. This mismatch is often invisible, obscured through subtle reportage of projects that focuses, selectively, on instrumental or aesthetic outcomes and impacts. Where pressure is felt to 'prove' that the stated objectives have been achieved, either to secure or justify funding or to satisfy the criteria of a research excellence framework, a challenge is presented to the ethics of practice (see O'Connor and Anderson, 2015). This book seeks to challenge the premise of ends-based, outcome-driven intentions, as often operated through an instrumental or technicist approach. If we are not careful, the instrumental outcomes of practice can reveal more about *our* declared intent rather than genuinely reflecting generative co-intentional processes. Argyris and Schön (1974, 1992) articulate the limitations of this kind of practice as 'single-loop' learning. Single-loop learning happens when one's self-protective responses and defensive reasoning close down the potential for openness to change, or rethinking of a plan or process. The rationale for this is confirmed through the selection of inferences that are made from one's observations, which function to confirm our existing thoughts and beliefs. This form of thinking has the potential to drastically reduce the realization of one's espoused values, expressed here as the pursuit of genuine participation and ownership. Instead, while small changes and adaptations are made to a plan, in response to and in order to pay lip-service to one's espoused values (such as an espoused intention 'I am open to change and I can be responsive'), the root of a problem, which may be structural or may involve risk and vulnerability to confrontation, will be ignored.[1]

This book has attempted to articulate a critical facilitation paradigm that moves towards, rather than shies away from, the contradictions of practice, by focusing on the pedagogies, practices and resilience of facilitation in the dilemmatic space. Part 1, 'Pedagogies', framed the idea of a critical facilitation practice by exploring the influence of critical pedagogy. In so doing, 'Pedagogies' has attempted to offer an espoused ethics of a critical practice, an honest framework that articulates the *intentions* of a thoughtful, values-based informed theory and practice committed to social justice, self-reliance and participatory processes. Contributors such as Cynthia Cohen follow this through by being up front about the standpoint of facilitators Farhat Agbaria and Jane Wilburn Sapp, noting the importance of clear values in underpinning their work as practitioners: 'they base their work on a clear sense of social justice and supporting people to be more effective in working to enhance it'. Similarly, Liselle Terret is very clear about the emancipatory intentions of a performance training programme with people with perceived learning difficulties. This openness of agenda, along with the overt investment in the participants role as co-researchers, enables the possibilities for one's espoused intentions of the pedagogy to be under constant critical renegotiation.

The focus on *practices* has offered an insight into how what we *do* might potentially become more aligned with our intentions if we move beyond a procedural and technicist 'ends-based' approach to practice and a procedural *application* of aesthetic forms. In this way, having an 'intention' doesn't necessarily require a preconceived map to an already fixed outcome. Sarah Woodland declares her intent to shift her practice from offender-rehabilitation models to an open participatory theatre process that works with personal narratives but articulates, in so doing, the challenges, even some contradictions of this shift, for her own practice, the participants and also for the correctional context where the work happens.

In confronting the challenge of uncovering what we *do* as opposed to concealing what we *actually did* in a selected rhetoric of espoused ideals, 'Practices' has articulated the possibility of furthering analysis of *doing* through drawing attention to the facilitator's action beyond the intended activity. A performative action analysis might thus enable us to get to the heart of acknowledging what we *actually do* rather than what *we say we do* when working in contexts, especially when working within the contradictions of neoliberal dilemmas. Signalling the facilitator as performer enables us to consider a complex duality of the moment beyond the task-based focus; of interaction and building relationships with others in context as a crucial part of the facilitation 'doing' process. Conceptualizing the facilitator as performer signals the need to try to capture this dimension. Several contributors have noted the range of performer modes and qualities that the facilitator plays. Paul Murray, having confessed to performing the social role of 'fitting in' for most of his earlier life, has found a freedom in the clown persona that becomes his *modus operandi* when working with groups. The clown performer offers Murray a particular performance quality that helps him to embody principles of *play* and the *here and now* and, importantly, the acceptability of *failure*. (See also Pady O'Connor, director of Fool Ensemble, in Hepplewhite's chapter in this book.) Balfour locates the facilitator as a 'conscious social performer', but importantly notes that this role carries an important personal authenticity: 'what often shines through is a facilitator's willingness to bring their own identity into her process not just a professional "facilitator" identity' (see Balfour's chapter). Balfour's point aligns with facilitator Amy Golding (quoted in Hepplewhite's chapter), referring to her persona as a facilitator being 'like a ball of energy! …That's my style, I am a heightened version of myself.' The personal, human persona, as a performed, heightened 'version' of self, reinforces an important need to 'keep it real' as articulated by Adam Annand, director of Speech Bubbles.[2] Although there *may* be a performed quality to the facilitator persona in a Speech Bubbles project, the project accommodates many facilitator styles, often working more effectively with a more natural and less 'performed' persona. Crucially, the work rests on the relationship established with children, so Adam Annand reminds those he is training of this priority, and of the crucial need for the participants to experience the adults as 'human' (see Preston, this volume).

The concept of *resilience* gets to the heart of the challenges for a strong, buoyant and flexible practitioner who can withstand and recover from the knocks and tests of the dilemmatic space. The facilitator seeks a tricky balance of 'keeping it real', allowing a level of openness that demands a level of vulnerability and sometimes a sense of emotional labour. Paul Murray's honest statement – 'I hate it when people leave the group, it means I've failed to engage them' – gives an insight into the challenge of remaining present in the *here and now*, but to do so means the accommodation of a level of discomfort. However, this response also reveals Murray's assumption, in that moment, that the participants' departure from his workshop was due to his own failure as a facilitator, which may not have been an accurate assessment. Murray admits later in his chapter that the young men's exodus from the workshop space wasn't necessarily to do with any failure on his part; in fact they were merely finding another space outside to engage with the task. Examples such as this remind us of the need to constantly 'reality-check' our assumptions, as our inferences can lead us in the wrong direction. For Paul, the persona of the clown becomes a resilient strategy that gives him permission to perform, engage with and even play with failure.

A consistent theme has been to extend the 'problem of facilitation' articulated above beyond an individual or pathological personal problem to be solved or overcome. Nonetheless there will be neurological impulses, habits and personal histories that influence our responses to situations in various contexts and it is important that we are able to listen to our feelings and triggers, by harnessing our 'emotional intelligence' to recognize and manage them. Managing the self is an important quality within personal resilience, and equally important, as has been discussed, is the capacity to enable one's humanity to be genuinely present in the room. However, for a critical facilitation paradigm, a resilient practice requires a cultural understanding of emotions that can in turn foster a deeper comprehension of social and political factors at work in all aspects of life. Such understanding is crucial for negotiating and facilitating in the dilemmatic space. Culturally produced regimes of emotion condition our feeling responses to events by feeding off our personal and individualized baggage, thus impacting on our ability or willingness to move towards discomfort or difficulty. Regimes of emotion will also affect how we feel, talk and write about our work, potentially impacting on our personal (and public) honesty about our values and work. Feeling a sense of personal shame about perceived failures of practice is understandable and very 'human', but the ways in which shame is conceptualized and understood limits our capacity to understand what is happening in the moment and its productive pedagogical possibilities. Understanding how the use of emotion in culture triggers personal responses – such as shame, guilt, pride, and notions of what it means to be 'successful' – are critical for a deeper awareness of the dilemmatic spaces, the facilitation process and reflective documentation and theorization of practice.

To this end, a critical facilitation practice requires the facilitator to practise deep honesty, humility, buoyancy and courage in difficult contexts. This book offers an insight into a proposed paradigm of critical facilitation which, if relevant to the reader, might offer an invitation to practitioners, facilitators and researchers to become more searching and honest (personally and culturally) about their intentions, with a view to generating a deeper awareness of the conditions and contradictions of context and the dynamics and challenges of process. A willingness to be open to different outcomes, resisting the temptation to 'win' (see Argyris and Schön, 1992), requires humility and the courage to be vulnerable. Moving towards discomfort requires a buoyancy of mind and body to 'stay afloat' in the moment, which is crucial if we are going to be able to respond to wherever this work take us, and as we move closer to alignment with an espoused, declared intention for social justice.

Notes

Chapter 1

1   I worked for two years in the mental health setting described,
developing drama projects with people who attended. I worked with
two groups: a 'mixed' drama group (by gender and age) and a women's
group (who attended on Mondays or 'Ladies day' when the centre
was closed to men). After working for several months with the two
groups, I picked up on the opportunity to address mental health issues
when it presented itself. Influenced by Paulo Freire, I was inspired by
the potential for enabling critical awareness of mental health and the
empowering importance of challenging stigma, perhaps as a way of
helping to allay some of the debilitating feelings brought about by lack
of self-acceptance. Since we had also been asked by the organizers of the
centre to create a performance for World Mental Health Day, there was
the potential for the participants to advocate to a wider audience about
the stigma of mental health. It seemed at the time like an opportunity
that had arisen out of a long, very open-ended process of devising and
exploring through drama, in which we had been searching for a central
idea to take us to the next stage of our work. I presented this idea to
the mixed drama group, who were then invited to decide whether they
wanted to pursue this; they agreed. As this performance possibility
had arisen from the context, and I was very much aware of the stigma
that the group often talked of (both in and out of the workshop), it
seemed a relevant way forward. I was keen to explore with the group
the potentially liberating possibilities of reclaiming the discourse of
mental health on their terms. By contrast, although many personal
issues were discussed in the women's group, the creative content did not
intentionally enter into mental health issues, although these issues did
arise in surrounding discussions. The 'work' with the women existed
at the level of using drama and storytelling as a recreational tool for
bonding and became a springboard for addressing the women's issues
that emerged. I tried, initially with little success, to get the women up

onto their feet to 'do drama', but we soon retreated into the comfort and
ease of storytelling from our seats (Preston, 2000).

Chapter 2

1   See Pearson Edexcel Level 1/Level 2 GCSE (9–1) in *Drama –
    Specification – Draft 1.0 – August 2015*, © Pearson Education Limited
    2015.

2   These elements of flow for creativity are drawn from Csikzentimihalyi
    (2013), 110–20.

3   Please see an example of this project in Prentki and Selman (2000).

4   For this example and the ones that follow I am indebted to the work of
    Sandra Heston, who has provided, through her PhD and the archive,
    a thorough documentation of the work of Dorothy Heathcote. From
    Sandra Heston's PhD, 'Dorothy Heathcote Archive', held by Manchester
    Metropolitan University, http://www.moeplanning.co.uk/wp-content/
    uploads/2008/05/heathcote-archive.pdf (accessed 3 June 2016).

5   Ibid.

6   This example has been taken directly from Sandra Heston's PhD,
    which can be downloaded from the Dorothy Heathcote archive held by
    Manchester Metropolitan University. Unfortunately, it is not possible to
    provide a date for the thesis. http://www.moeplanning.co.uk/wp-content/
    uploads/2008/05/heathcote-archive.pdf (accessed 3 June 2016).

Chapter 3

1   See 'The Power of Vulnerability', Brene Brown's TED (Technology,
    Entertainment and Design) talk, https://www.ted.com/talks/brene_
    brown_on_vulnerability?language=en (accessed 2 October 2015).

2   Speech bubbles is a national, drama-based intervention based in primary
    schools that works with children with social and communication
    difficulties, http://www.londonbubble.org.uk/projectpage/speech-
    bubbles/ (accessed 2 October 2015).

3   It should to be noted that there are plenty of other occasions when
     Lynette and I have both experienced students not necessarily taking such
     polarized and 'unsurprising' subject positions in terms of *who* speaks.
     It has also been common for black students to adopt contradictory
     positions that seem not to be in their interests, thus presenting another
     dilemma for the facilitator. However, what is a consistent theme in
     teaching around issues of race (and to an extent almost predictably so)
     is that the same competing range of discourses on the subject will be
     articulated (regardless of the ethnicity of the lecturer). This presents
     challenges in terms of how the matter will be addressed, and both
     Lynette, as a black lecturer, and myself, as a white lecturer, agree that
     we share a level of discomfort in how to address and challenge the
     predictable and contradictory subject positions that students may take.

4   I'd had a growing concern that issues of race (and class), having been
     brought to the forefront of one-off discussions such as this, needed a
     more consistent space to be unpicked, positioned and understood. In
     response to these observations I developed a module in 2012 called
     Difference, Representation & Critical Pedagogies. The ambitious aims of
     this module were to provide opportunities to make visible the students'
     'common sense' observations in society, as hegemonic discourses; to give
     minority students' permission to bring their identities into the room;
     and to give black, white and classed students a sense of awareness of the
     wider historical, social and political positioning of their identities. A key
     aim within this framework was to create a safe space for *all* students to
     speak and acknowledge their identities.

5   'An historicised ethics operates towards the idea of principles such
     as constitutional rights, but it also recognises the need to develop
     ethical principles that take into account that not all persons have equal
     protection under the law or equal access to resources' Boler, 2004: 4).

6   The following typology has been influenced by Hogget, Mayo and Miller
     (2009: 174), and their research with development workers and the
     ethical challenges of regeneration.

7   For example, he says that 'A teacher who is tactful has the sensitive
     ability to interpret inner thoughts, understanding, feelings, and desires
     of children from indirect clues such as gestures, demeanor, expression,
     and body language. Pedagogical tact involves the ability to immediately

see through motives or cause and effect relations' (Van Manen, 2008: 16).

Chapter 5

1   This work will be described in another volume in this series, *Applied Theatre: Women and Criminal Justice*, edited by Caoimhe McAvinchey and due for publication in 2017.

Chapter 6

1   The term learning disability is a contentious label. For an in-depth discussion on the complexity and politics of such a term, refer to Hargrave (2015), 21–7. However, the British Institute of Learning Disabilities states on their website (http://www.bild.org.uk/about-bild/aboutbild/) that 'The term learning disability is a label, and a label only ever describes one aspect of a person; a person with a learning disability is always a person first.'

2   http://www.accessallareastheatre.org/ (accessed 12 May 2015).

3   http://www.cssd.ac.uk/course/performance-making-diploma-learning-disabled-adults (accessed 8 January 2016).

4   As coined by Toby Siebers, 2008.

5   Please see S. Mackey and L. Terret (2015), 'Move Over There's Room Enough', *RiDE: The Journal of Applied Theatre and Performance* 20:4: 1–5

6   Katherine Araniello, http://www.araniello-art.com/Biog-Statement (accessed 8 October 2015).

7   Ibid.

8   The workshop took place on 8 May 2014 at the Royal Central School of Speech and Drama.

9   Mat Fraser, http://matfraser.co.uk/blogs/ (accessed 31 July 2015).

10   Ibid.

11   The workshop took place on 20 May 2014 at the Royal Central School of Speech and Drama.

12   The Royal Central School of Speech and Drama does offer students with
     disabilities support within its degree programmes through its Disability
     and Dyslexia Service, and as an HE institution it is important to
     acknowledge that it does welcome people with disabilities. http://www.
     cssd.ac.uk/content/disability-and-dyslexia.
13   Mantle of the Expert (MoE) is a 'system of teaching ... used in drama
     [where] the teacher assumes a fictional role which places the student in
     the position of being the expert'. D. Heathcote and P. Herbert (1985),
     'A Drama of Learning: Mantle of the Expert', *Theory into Practice* 24:3
     (Summer): 173–80.
14   This co-researcher's session took place at the Camden Arts Centre
     following a timetable session on 20 March 2015.
15   I would like to acknowledge that there has been consistent and
     sustainable strategies established to address the challenges described in
     this chapter, including the Creative Partners system (whereby students
     from other courses within the school meet up regularly with the
     Diploma students outside of curriculum time). There have also been
     opportunities for cross-course collaboration (with BA Drama, Applied
     Theatre, Education, MA Applied Theatre and the BA Performing Arts),
     placement and volunteering opportunities, as well as tutors from across
     the school teaching on the course as well.
16   Learning Support Assistant.
17   Special Educational Needs.
18   Observation of Cecily O'Neill at the Unicorn Theatre, London, in 2003.

Chapter 7

1   ''Tain't What You Do'. James 'Trummy' Young and Sy Oliver (1939). Ella
     Fitzgerald and ensemble with Chick Webb and his Orchestra, recorded
     17 February 1939, New York.

Chapter 9

1 The 'shout out' exercise refers to an activity in which participants are asked to write or draw their thoughts, feelings and ideas onto a large sheet of paper in relation to a question prompted by the facilitator.

2 Alan Rogers states: 'Motivation for learning comes from within; and the material on which the learning drive fastens is the whole of life, the cultural and interpersonal relationships that form the social context' (Rogers, 1996: 99). This view is based on humanist theories of education, versus cognitive or behavioural.

Chapter 10

1 This is the title of an African-American spiritual sung widely during the Civil Rights movement.

2 See http://www.brandeis.edu/ethics/peacebuildingarts/actingtogether/ (accessed September 2015).

3 See http://www.brandeis.edu/ethics/peacebuildingarts/ (accessed September 2015).

4 See http://www.brandeis.edu/programs/cast/ (accessed September 2015).

5 From The Group of Eighteen, http://www.brandeis.edu/ethics/ peacebuildingarts/pdfs/jsapp/JaneSapp_TheGroupOfEighteen.pdf (accessed September 2015), p. 5.

6 From The Group of Eighteen.

7 See 'Working with Groups in Conflict: The Impact of Power Relations on the Dynamics of the Group' by Farhat Agbaria and Cynthia Cohen, http://www.brandeis.edu/ethics/pdfs/publications/Working_Groups.pdf (accessed September 2015), for more on the topics discussed here.

8 Highlander serves as a catalyst for grassroots organizing and movement-building in Appalachia and the American South. We work with people fighting for *justice*, *equality* and *sustainability*, supporting their efforts to take collective action to shape their own destiny. See http:// highlandercenter.org (accessed September 2015).

Afterword

1   See Argyris and Schön (1972, 1992), who developed espoused theory and theory-in-use as two theories of action that are often contradictorily aligned in what we say and do.

2   Speech Bubbles is a nationwide, well-regarded intervention that works in schools with children referred with a range of speech, language and communication problems. Their approach is child-centred and based around the simple concept of story-drama. In 2016, Speech Bubbles worked in forty-two schools with 800 children, demonstrating its important social impact in terms of improving children's confidence, well-being and communication, leading to improved access to the curriculum. See http://www.londonbubble.org.uk/projectpage/speech-bubbles/ (accessed September 2015).

Bibliography

Introduction, Chapters 1–3

Archer, L., Hollingworth, S. and Mendick, H. (2010). *Urban Youth and Schooling*. Berkshire: Open University Press.

Argyris, C. and Schön, D. A. (1972, 1992). *Theory in Practice: Increasing Professional Effectiveness*. San Francisco: Jossey-Bass.

Baim, C, Brooke's, S and Mountford, A. (2002). *The Geese Theatre Handbook: Drama with Offendors and People at Risk*. UK, Waterside Press.

Boal, A (2002). *Games for Actors and Non-Actors*. London, Routledge.

Boler, M. (1999). *Feeling Power: Emotions and Education*. London: Routledge.

Boler, M. (2004). *Democratic Dialogue in Education: Troubling Speech, Disturbing Silence*. New York: Peter Lang.

Bolton, G. (1999). *Acting in Classroom Drama*. Portland, ME: Calendar Islands.

Brown, B. (2007). *I Thought it was Just Me: Women Reclaiming Power and Courage in a Culture of Shame*. London: Penguin.

Cohen, A. (1985). *The Symbolic Construction of Community*. London: Routledge.

Csikszentmihalyi, M. (1997). *Finding Flow: The Psychology of Engagement with Everyday Life*. New York: Basic Books.

Csikszentmihalyi, M. (2013). *Creativity: The Psychology of Discovery and Invention*. USA. Harper Perennial Press.

Darder, A., Baltodano, M. and Torres, R. (2008). *The Critical Pedagogy Reader*. 2nd edn. London: Routledge.

Davis, D. (2005). 'Edward Bond and Drama in Education'. In D. Davis, *Edward Bond and the Dramatic Child*. Stoke-on-Trent: Trentham Books.

Davis, D. (2014). *Imagining the Real: Towards a New Theory of Drama in Education*. London: Institute of Education Press.

Delanty, G. (2009). *Community*. 2nd edn. London: Routledge.

Duffy, P. (ed.) (2015). *A Reflective Practitioner's Guide to (mis)Adventures in Drama Education – or – What was I thinking?* Bristol: Intellect.

Faulkner, J. (ed.) (2012). *Disrupting Pedagogies in the Knowledge Society: Countering Conservative Norms with Creative Approaches*. Hershey, PA: Information Science Reference.

Giroux, H. (1992). *Border Crossings*. London and New York: Routledge.

Giroux, H. (2008). 'Critical Theory and Educational Practice'. In A. Darder, M. Baltodano and R. Torres, *The Critical Pedagogy Reader*. 2nd edn. London: Routledge.

Goffman, E. (1959, 1990). *The Presentation of Self in Everyday Life*. London: Penguin.

Goleman, D. (2006). *Social Intelligence: The New Science*. London: Hutchinson.

Goleman, D. (2011). *The Brain and Emotional Intelligence: New Insights*. Florence, MA: More than Sound.

Hargreaves, A. (1998). 'The Emotional Practice of Teaching' in Teaching and Teacher Education Journal Vol 14 no 8, pp. 835–54.

Heston, S. (1993). *The Heathcote Archive* (PHD thesis) http://www.moeplanning.co.uk/wp-content/uploads/2008/05/heathcote-archive.pdf (accessed 3 June, 2016).

Hochschild, A. (1998, 2003). *The Managed Heart – The Commercialization of Human Feeling*. London: University of California Press.

Hochschild, A. (2002). 'Emotion Management in an age of Global Terrorism' Special Edition on Emotional Labour, Soundings: a journal of politics and culture. Issue 11 Spring 1999, pp. 117–26

Hoggett P., Mayo, M. and Miller, C. (2009). *The Dilemmas of Development Work: Ethical Challenges in Regeneration*. Bristol: Policy Press.

Honig, B. (1996). 'Difference, Dilemmas and the Politics of Home'. In S. Benhabib (ed.), *Democracy and Difference: Contesting the Boundaries of the Political*. Princeton, NJ: Princeton University Press.

Johnston, C. (2005). *House of Games: Making Theatre from Everyday Life*. UK. Nick Hern Books.

Kabat-Zinn, J. (1994). *Wherever You Go, There You Are: Mindfulness Meditation for Everyday Life*. New York: Hyperion Press.

Kennedy, J. (2002). 'Developing Intuition in Marginal Trainees on Teaching Practice'. *ELTED – English Language Teacher Education and Development* 7. http://www.elted.net/issues/volume-7/index.html (accessed 2 October 2015).

Law, L. (1997). 'Dancing on the Bar – Sex, Money and the Uneasy Politics of Third Space'. In S. Piles and M. Keith (eds), *Geographies of Resistance*. London: Routledge.

Lister, R. (2004). *Poverty*. Cambridge: Polity Press.

Lloyd-Smith (1999). 'Arlie Hochschild: soft spoken conversationalist of Emotions' Special Edition on Emotional Labour, Soundings: a journal of politics and culture. Issue 11 Spring 1999, pp. 120–7

McLaren, P. (2008). 'Critical Pedagogy: A look at the Major Concepts'. In A. Darder, M. Baltodano and R. Torres, *The Critical Pedagogy Reader*. 2nd edn. London: Routledge.

Mda, Z. (1993). *When People Play People – Development Communication Through Theatre*. London: Zed Press.

Mouffe, C. (2001). 'Politics and Passions: The Stakes of Democracy'. Centre for the Study of Democracy, University of Westminster, London. http://www.westminster.ac.uk/__data/assets/pdf_file/0003/6456/Politics-and-Passions.pdf (accessed 2 October 2015).

Mouffe, C. (2005). *On the Political*. London: Routledge.

Neelands, J (2015). *Structuring Drama Work: 100 Key Conventions for Theatre & Drama*. UK. Cambridge University Press.

Newbold (2002) *Therapeutic Nursing, Emotional Labour, Economic Exchange: is there a link?* Themed edition: Regimes of Emotion Soundings: a journal of politics and culture. Issue 20 Summer 2002, pp. 163–71

Newman, J. and Clarke, J. (2009). *Publics, Politics, Power – Remaking the Public in Public Services*. London: Sage.

Prentki, T. (2015). *Applied Theatre: Development*. London: Bloomsbury Methuen Drama.

Prentki, T. and Selman, J. (2000). *Popular Theatre in Political Culture*, UK, Bristol, Intellect.

Preston, S. (2000). *Theatre for Development in Context*. PhD. Held in British Library.

Preston, S. (2011). 'Back on whose Track? Reframing Ideologies of Inclusion and Misrecognition in a Participatory Theatre Project with Young People in London'. *Research in Drama Education: The Journal of Applied Theatre and Performance* 16:2 (May): 251–64.

Preston, S. (2013). 'Managed Hearts? Emotional Labour and the Applied Theatre Facilitator in Urban Settings'. *Research in Drama Education: The Journal of Applied Theatre and Performance* 18:3 (August): 230–45.

Rattue, R. and Cornelius, N. (2002). 'The Emotional Practice of Police Work', pp. 190–201

Rogers, C. (1994). *The Freedom to Learn*. Upper Saddle River, NJ: Prentice Hall.

Schechner, R. (1988). *Performance Theory*. London: Routledge.

Schön, D. (1984). *The Reflective Practitioner: How Professionals Think in Action*. New York: Basic Books.

Schön, D. (1987). *Educating the Reflective Practitioner*. San Francisco: Jossey Bass.

Schwarz, T. (2002). *The Skilled Facilitator: A Comprehensive Resource for Consultants, Facilitators, Trainers and Coaches*. San Francisco: Jossey-Bass.

Thomas, G. (2007). 'A Study of the Theories and Practices of Facilitator Educators'. PhD thesis, La Trobe University, Victoria, Australia.

Thomas, G. (2008). 'The Theories and Practices of Facilitator Educators: Conclusions from a Naturalistic Inquiry'. *Group Facilitation: A Research and Applications Journal* 9: 4–13.

Van Manen, M. (1991). *The Tact of Teaching: The Meaning of Pedagogical Thoughtfulness*. New York: State University of New York Press.

Willett, J. (1964). *Brecht on Theatre: The Development of an Aesthetic*. London: Methuen.

Williams, M. and Penman, D. (2011). *Mindfulness: A Practical Guide to Finding Peace in a Frantic World*. London: Piatkus Press.

Chapter 4

Bentley, E. (2008). *Bentley on Brecht*. Evanston, IL: Northwestern University Press.

Foucault, M. (1976). *Mental Illness and Psychology*. Berkeley: University of California Press.

Huizinga, J. (1950). *Homo ludens*. London: Routledge and Kegan Paul.

Laing, R. D. (1959). *The Divided Self*. London: Penguin.

Mason, B. (1992). *Street Theatre*. London: Routledge.

Chapter 5

Aston, H. (2010). 'UN Slams Treatment of Aborigines'. *Sydney Morning Herald*, 29 August. http://www.smh.com.au/national/un-slams-treatment-of-aborigines-20100828-13wvo.html (accessed 11 February 2015).

Australian Bureau of Statistics (2012). *Census of Population and Housing –
Counts of Aboriginal & Torres Strait Islander Australians, 2011*. http://
www.abs.gov.au/ausstats/abs@.nsf/Latestproducts/2075.0Main%20Feature
s12011?opendocument&tabname=Summary&prodno=2075.0&issue=201
1&num=&view= (accessed 10 September 2014).

Australian Bureau of Statistics (2014). *Prisoners in Australia, 2013*. http://
www.abs.gov.au/ausstats/abs@.nsf/Lookup/4517.0main+features62013
(accessed 10 September 2014).

Baim, C., Brookes, S. and Mountford, A. (2002). *The Geese Theatre
Handbook: Drama with Offenders and People at Risk*. Winchester:
Waterside Press.

Balfour, M. (2004). *Theatre in Prison: Theory & Practice*. Bristol: Intellect.

Balfour, M. (2009). 'The Politics of Intention: Looking for a Theatre of Little
Changes'. *Research in Drama Education: The Journal of Applied Theatre
and Performance* 14:3: 347–59.

Bhabha, H. K. (1994). *The Location of Culture*. London: Routledge.

Big hART (2014). 'The Yijala-Yala Project'. Online, http://bighart.org/project/
yijala-yala/ (accessed 10 October 2014).

Boal, A. (2002). *Games for Actors and Non-actors*. 2nd edn. Trans. A. Jackson.
New York: Routledge.

Browne, A. J., Smye, V. L. and Varcoe, C. (2005). 'The Relevance of
Postcolonial Theoretical Perspectives to Research in Aboriginal Health'.
CJNR (Canadian Journal of Nursing Research) 37:4 (2005): 16–37.

Chinyowa, K. C. (2013). 'Interrogating Spaces of Otherness: Towards a
Postcritical Pedagogy for Applied Drama and Theatre'. *Applied Theatre
Research* 1:1: 7–16.

Daboo, J. (2007). 'Unveiled: Interrogating the Use of Applied Drama in
Multiple and Specific Sites'. *Research in Drama Education: The Journal of
Applied Theatre and Performance* 12:1: 55–64.

Eades, D. (2013). *Aboriginal Ways of Using English*. Canberra: Aboriginal
Studies Press.

Greenwood, J. (2001). 'Within a Third Space'. *Research in Drama
Education: The Journal of Applied Theatre and Performance* 6:2: 193–205.

Harkins, J. (1990). 'Shame and Shyness in the Aboriginal Classroom: A Case
for "Practical Semantics"'. *Australian Journal of Linguistics* 10:2: 293–306.

Hunter, M. (2008). 'Cultivating the Art of Safe Space'. *Research in Drama
Education: The Journal of Applied Theatre and Performance* 13:1: 5–21.

Johnston, E. (1991). *Final Report of the Royal Commission into Aboriginal Deaths in Custody.* http://www.austlii.edu.au/au/other/IndigLRes/rciadic/national/vol1/9.html (accessed 11 February 2015).

Kidd, J. (2014). 'Over-representation of Indigenous Australians in Prison a Catastrophe'. *News ABC,* 5 May 2014. http://www.abc.net.au/news/2014-12-04/number-of-indigenous-australians-in-prison-a-catastrophe/5945504 (accessed 11 February 2015).

McGuire, J. (2005). 'The Think First Programme'. In M. McMurran and J. McGuire (eds), *Social Problem Solving and Offending: Evidence, Evaluation and Evolution,* 183–206. Chichester: John Wiley & Sons Ltd.

Nicholson, H. (2005). *Applied Drama: The Gift of Theatre.* Basingstoke: Palgrave Macmillan.

Prentki, T. and Preston, S. (2009). *The Applied Theatre Reader.* London: Routledge.

Robinson, S. (2008). *Something Like Slavery? Queensland's Aboriginal Child Workers, 1842–1945.* Melbourne: Australian Scholarly Publishing.

Sharifian, F. (2005). 'Cultural Conceptualisations in English Words: A Study of Aboriginal Children in Perth'. *Language and Education* 19:1: 74–88.

Sharp, A. and Arup, T. (2009). 'UN Says Aboriginal Health Conditions Worse than Third World'. *Sydney Morning Herald,* 5 September. http://www.smh.com.au/national/un-says-aboriginal-health-conditions-worse-than-third-world-20091204-kay8.html (accessed 11 February 2015).

Wilkinson, S. and Kitzinger, C. (2009). 'Representing the Other'. In T. Prentki and S. Preston (eds), *The Applied Theatre Reader,* 86–93. Abingdon: Routledge.

Woodland, S. (2009). 'Memoirs of the Forgotten Ones: Theatre & Drama with Adult Survivors of Childhood Trauma and Abuse'. *UNESCO Observatory Refereed E-Journal* 1:4. http://education.unimelb.edu.au/about_us/specialist_areas/arts_education/melbourne_unesco_observatory_of_arts_education/the_e-journal (accessed 11 February 2015).

Chapter 6

Denzin, N. K. (2003). *Performance Ethnography: Critical Pedagogy and the Politics of Culture.* London: Sage.

Hargrave, M. (2015). *Theatres of Learning Disability: Good, Bad, or Plain Ugly?* Basington: Palgrave Macmillan.

Heathcote, D. and Herbert, P. (1985). 'A Drama of Learning: Mantle of the Expert'. *Theory into Practice* 24:3 (Summer): 173–80.

Kafer, A. (2013). *Feminist, Queer, Crip.* Bloomington: Indiana University Press.

Mackey, S. and Terret, L. (2015). 'Move Over, There's Room Enough: Performance Making Diploma: Training for Learning Disabled Adults'. *RiDE: The Journal of Applied Theatre and Performance* 20:4: 1–5.

McRuer, R. (2006). *Crip Theory: Cultural Signs of Queerness and Disability.* New York: New York University Press.

Morris, J. (1991). *Pride Against Prejudice: Transforming Attitudes to Disability.* London: Women's Press Ltd.

Oliver, M. (1992). 'Emancipatory Research: Realistic Goal or Impossible Dream?' In C. Barnes and G. Mercer (eds), *Doing Disability Research*, 15–31. Leeds: Disability Press.

Schweik, S. (2009). *The Ugly Laws: Disability in Public.* New York: New York University Press.

Sheldon, A., Traustadóttir, R., Beresford, P., Boxall, K. and Oliver, M., (2007) 'Disability Right & Wrongs?', in *Disability & Society*, 22:2, 209–34.

Siebers, T. (2008). *Disability Theory.* Corporealities: Discourses of Disability. Ann Arbor: University of Michigan Press.

Siebers, T. (2011). *Disability Aesthetics.* Corporealities: Discourses of Disability. Ann Arbor: University of Michigan Press.

Walmsley, J. and Johnson, K. (2003). *Inclusive Research with People with Learning Disabilities – Past, Present and Future.* London: Jessica Kingsley.

Chapter 7

Cohen, C. E., Varea, R. G. and Walker, P. O. (eds) (2011). *Acting Together: Performance and the Creative Transformation of Violence: Volume 1: Resistance and Reconciliation in Regions of Violence.* New York: New Village Press.

Duffy, P. (ed.) (2015). *A Reflective Practitioner's Guide to (mis)Adventures in Drama Education – or – What was I thinking?* Bristol: Intellect.

Emunah, R. (1985). 'Drama Therapy and Adolescent Resistance'. *The Arts in Psychotherapy* 12:2: 71–9.

Hochschild, A. R. (2003). *The Managed Heart: Commercialization of Human Feeling*. Berkeley and Los Angeles: University of California Press.

Hogan, C. (2005). *Understanding Facilitation: Theory & Principles*. London: Kogan Page.

Johnson, D. W. and Johnson, F. P. (2009). *Joining Together: Group Theory and Group Skills*. Upper Saddle River, NJ: Pearson Education.

Kolb, D. A. (1984). *Experiential Learning: Experience as the Source of Learning and Development*. Englewood Cliffs, NJ: Prentice-Hall.

Toivanen, T., Pyykkö, A. and Ruismäki, H. (2011). 'Challenge of the Empty Space: Group Factors as a Part of Drama Education'. *Procedia – Social and Behavioral Sciences* 29: 402–11.

Tuckman, B. (1965). 'Development Sequences in Small Groups'. *Psychological Bulletin* 63:6: 384–99.

Westwood, M. J. and Wilensky, P. (2005). *Therapeutic Enactment: Restoring Vitality Through Trauma Repair in Groups*. Vancouver: Group Action Press.

White, G. (2015). *Applied Theatre: Aesthetics*. London: Bloomsbury Methuen Drama.

Chapter 8

Arroyas, F. (2013). 'Improvisation's Ebb and Flow'. *Critical Studies in Improvisation / Études critiques en improvisation* 9:2: 1.

Hepplewhite, K. (2013). 'Here's One I Made Earlier: The Construction of an Applied Theatre Practitioner'. *Theatre, Dance and Performance Training Journal* 4:1: 52–72.

Hepplewhite, K. (2014). 'Here's Another Nice Mess: Using Video in Reflective Dialogue Research Method'. *Research in Drama Education: The Journal of Applied Theatre and Performance* 19:3: 326–35.

Johnston, C. (2005). *House of Games*. London: Nick Hern Books.

Nicholson, H. (2005). *Applied Drama: The Gift of Theatre*. London: Palgrave Macmillan.

Nicholson, H. (2010). 'The Promises of History: Pedagogic Principles and Processes of Change'. *RiDE: The Journal of Applied Theatre and Performance* 15:2: 147–54.

Prendergast, M. and Saxton, J. (2013). *Applied Drama: A Facilitator's Handbook for Working in Community*. Bristol and Chicago: Intellect.

Prentki, T. and Preston, S. (2009). 'Applied Theatre: An Introduction'. In T. Prentki, T. Preston and S. Preston (eds), *The Applied Theatre Reader*, 9–15. London and New York: Routledge.

White, G. (2015). *Applied Theatre: Aesthetics*. London: Bloomsbury Methuen Drama.

Chapter 9

Boal, A. (1992). *Games for Actors and Non-Actors*. New York: Routledge.

Casey, E. S. (1996). 'How to Get from Space to Place in a Fairly Short Stretch of Time'. In Steven Feld and Keith H. Basso (eds), *Senses of Place*. Santa Fe: School of Amercian Research Press.

Chen, C. (2003). *Coaching Training*. Alexandria, VA: American Society for Training & Development (ASTD) Press.

Crum, T. (1988). *The Magic of Conflict: Turning a Life of Work into a Work of Life*. New York: Touchstone.

Geertz, C. (1980). *Negra: The Theatre State in Nineteenth-Century Bali*. Princeton, NJ: Princeton University Press.

Jones, J. and Pfeiffer, (1973). *A Handbook of Structured Experiences for Human Relations Training*. San Diego: Pfeiffer & Co.

Lerman, L. and Borstel, J. (2003). *Liz Lerman's Critical Response Process: A Method for Getting Useful Feedback on Anything You Make, from Dance to Dessert*. Takoma Park, MD: Liz Lerman Dance Exchange.

Rogers, A. (1996). *Teaching Adults*. Buckingham: Open University Press.

Salas, J. (1993). *Improvising Real Life: Personal Story in Playback Theatre*. New Paltz: Tusitala Publishing.

Turner, V. (1969). *The Ritual Process: Structure and Anti-Structure (Foundations of Human Behaviour)*. Chicago: Aldine Publishing Co.

Turner, V. (1990), 'Are there Universals of Performance in Myth, Ritual, and Drama?' In *By Means of Performance: Intercultural Studies of Theatre and Ritual*. Cambridge: Cambridge University Press.

Afterword

Argyris, C. and Schön, D. A. (1972, 1992). *Theory in Practice: Increasing Professional Effectiveness*. San Francisco: Jossey-Bass.

O'Connor, P. and Anderson, M. (2015). *Applied Theatre: Research – Radical Departures*. London: Bloomsbury Methuen Drama.

Index

Milton Keynes UK
Ingram Content Group UK Ltd.
UKHW020957180823
427082UK00011B/249